Praise for *Wake Up and Reclaim Your Humanity*

What a wonderful book. *Wake Up and Reclaim Your Humanity* is an account of extraordinary courage. As a Jew, Richard Forer exposes the "crime against humanity" of willful blindness that fuels too many fires of hatred, fear, and violence. His decision to engage in a careful search for historical facts that might question his own unwavering acceptance of the Jewish/Zionist narrative enabled him to write about the Israeli occupation of Palestine with honesty, separating fact from fiction in an effort to save Israel from itself. This is a powerful book about Israel and Palestine and an inspiring example of integrity and assiduous pursuit of painful truth.

> – Marie Dennis, Senior Advisor to the Secretary General, Co-President (2007-2019) Pax Christi International

Wow. Wow. Wow. This is powerful. A brave and bold eleventh-hour clarion call for the world to wake up before it is too late. For those who are blindly loving Israel to death, this meticulously documented journey of enlightenment is meant to open minds and hearts. Invoking words from the horses' mouths and recounting his visits to the region, the most feebleminded will be shocked; older Palestinian readers will relive open wounds from the past and present; the younger ones will have a new appreciation for how much we have endured. This book rings the bell of our universal humanity if only we are willing to hear it. A word of advice before you start reading, you will not want to put this down.

> – Sam Bahour, Palestinian-American businessman, writer, and activist, Occupied Palestine.

Rich Forer is living an "examined" and thus a more meaningful life and his new and remarkable book on transformation and renewal is poignant and timely in our uncertain world. Read this fact-filled and captivating book and give it as a gift to others because the truths beautifully and gently articulated show us how to become more caring and thoughtful human beings. Simply brilliant!

— Mazin Qumsiyeh, Professor and Author,
Bethlehem University, Palestine.

Richard Forer's new book, like his earlier one, is a portal into a different future for Israelis, Palestinians, and those who love or hate them around the world. Thoroughly documented and exceptionally well written, this is a great read for the Coronavirus era: a vivid expose of humanity's failures and a loving guide toward the turning point we are all so desperately seeking.

— Deb Reich, author, *No More Enemies*

In his new book, Richard Forer, continues and expands his journey toward a Jewishness that seeks to erase the barriers that separate us from a deeper and more expansive sense of self and from others, especially the Palestinian people. For those who are stuck in the seemingly intractable division between Jews and Palestinians, Forer's ideas, which at first might seem foreign, hit home in a special way.

— Marc H. Ellis, Retired University Professor of Jewish Studies, past Director of the Center for Jewish Studies at Baylor University, and author of I AM WHO LOVES THE PROPHETS: *An Exile Devotional* (2020), *Finding Our Voice: On Embodying the Prophetic and Other Misadventures* (2018), and *Future of the Prophetic: Israel's Ancient Wisdom Re-presented* (2014).

I loved reading *Wake Up and Reclaim Your Humanity*. Forer challenges us to look at the biases and carefully constructed identities that keep us from feeling compassion for others. As he says, *"My new understanding is neither pro-Palestinian nor anti-Israeli. It is pro-humanity and anti-oppression. I advocate for the oppressed because I oppose oppression, not because I favor one people over any other people."* For those of us engaged in Israel-Palestine on any level, Forer's work uncovers a pathway toward peace.

– Suzann Mollner, Founder of Beirut and
Beyond, a Refugee Relief Organization.

Wake Up and Reclaim Your Humanity is a highly original contribution to the literature on the Israeli-Palestinian question: part conversion narrative, part psychospiritual guide to liberating the self from unexamined prejudices and conditioning, part thorough investigation of Israel's founding ideology and the violence it continues to perpetrate. Forer accomplishes the rare feat of showing readers *how* he came to renounce beliefs that had not only blinded him to Palestinians' humanity but that stifled his own humanity. Coaxing readers to follow the path that led him toward spiritual wholeness, Forer provides them at every step with facts that can help them discern the elements of a just resolution to a conflict dating back more than a century.

– Carolyn L. Karcher, editor of *Reclaiming Judaism
from Zionism: Stories of Personal Transformation.*

Richard Forer's book is a must read. His meticulous research and personal awakening offer the gift of understanding through transformative ways of self-discovery that embrace the common humanity of each and every one of us.

– Mary Neznek, child trauma educator and
former executive director of Peace Links,
a bipartisan coalition of community
leaders and congressional spouses

Also by Richard Forer

Breakthrough: Transforming Fear into Compassion—A New Perspective on the Israel-Palestine Conflict

Wake Up and Reclaim Your Humanity
Essays on the Tragedy of Israel-Palestine

Richard Forer

MINDSTIR MEDIA

Published by Mindstir Media, LLC
45 Lafayette Rd | Suite 181| North Hampton, NH 03862 | USA
1.800.767.0531 | www.mindstirmedia.com

Printed in the United States of America
ISBN-13: 978-1-7355880-4-9

Contents

Now here is my secret. It is very simple. It is only with one's heart that one can see clearly. What is essential is invisible to the eye. – Antoine de Saint-Exupéry[1]

To The Children. The Hope Of The World

Acknowledgments

Special thanks to Nancy Harmon, Anand Upahar, Mary Neznek, and Chris Boys, whose contributions have enhanced the quality of this book; to Sam Bahour for his help in choosing a title, and to Libby and Len Traubman for bringing Yehuda Amichai's poem, "The Place Where We Are Right," to my attention; to Kathy Felgran for referring me to information about Rabbis Dushinsky, Blau, and Katzenellenbogen; and to Rana Alshami and Tamer Ajrami for sharing details about life in the Gaza Strip.

Preface

Know yourself. – Delphic Maxim
No. 8 (often attributed to Socrates)

*An unquestioned mind is the world
of suffering.* – Byron Katie

Have you ever noticed how right most of us think we are even when we are wrong? I never thought this phenomenon applied to me until one day in 2006 when what I had taken for the truth of Israel-Palestine was exposed as fiction and what I had taken for fiction exposed as truth. Over many years I had maneuvered myself into this position by rejecting evidence that didn't conform to my worldview and clinging to evidence that did. Although I didn't know it, personal prejudice was the instrument that drove my judgments. I had believed only what I wanted to believe. My rigidity did not make me an outlier. On issues they identify with, many people think as I did. In 2005 and 2006, researchers at the University of Michigan found that few of us change our minds when presented with evidence that refutes strongly held beliefs. Instead, we become more rigid in our misconceptions.[2] Stanford University researchers arrived at similar conclusions: "[B]eliefs can survive the complete subtraction of the critical formative evidence on which they were initially based. In a complementary fashion …strongly entrenched beliefs can also survive the addition of nonsupportive evidence."[3]

A dramatic example of this rigidity is President Donald Trump and the Republican Party's resolve to disregard decades of scientific research on industrial society's impact on global warming, the gravest threat to life on Earth. Despite warnings from an overwhelming majority of scientists that rising sea levels, drought, wildfires, floods, hotter oceans, dwindling water supplies, and the probable extinction of one million plant and animal species threaten our existence, Trump and his base insist that global warming is a hoax. Their adherence to irrational and untested beliefs risks catastrophe on a scale never seen in human history.

Global warming's long-term consequences may be too gradual and abstract for many of us to incorporate into our worldviews, but the pull of belief systems is so inexorable few of us foresee the bleak future we are passing on to our children. Take the case of Libby, a remote northwest Montana town with a population of 2,600. From 1919 to 1990, 70 percent of the vermiculite sold in the United States came from a local mine that employed 200 workers.[4] Vermiculite is a shiny silicate mineral composed of small flakes that resemble mica. When heated, it can expand up to thirty times its original size. Sold as insulation under the trademarked name Zonolite, it is odorless and flame retardant. Chemical conglomerate W.R. Grace owned the mine, which also held deposits of asbestos, another silicate mineral. Most of the vermiculite insulation sold in the US in the 1900s was contaminated with asbestos.[5] Grace disposed of leftover vermiculite in playgrounds, roads, gardens, and other locations throughout Libby.[6] Miners returning home from a day's work carried asbestos dust on their clothes, which family members breathed into their lungs. The Environmental Protection Agency (EPA) determined that the mine discharged five thousand pounds of asbestos into the air each day it was in operation.[7] When inhaled or swallowed these needle-like fibers pierce the tissue layers that line the lungs and digestive tract. The mine closed in 1990, but between 1979 and 1998 Libby's death rate from asbestosis, a chronic lung disease, was forty to eighty times higher than average, while respiratory deaths were 20 to 40 percent higher.[8] Mesothelioma, a deadly and incurable cancer of the tissue that surrounds and protects the body's internal organs, is one hundred times more prevalent in Libby than the national average.[9] Its primary risk factor is exposure to asbestos. Asbestos exposure has a latency period of up to forty years before it manifests in symptoms which is why, thirty years after Grace shuttered its mine, Lincoln County, which includes Libby, still has the highest asbestos mortality rate in the United States.[10] The US government calls this calamity, "the worst case of industrial poisoning of a whole community in American history."[11] The Mesothelioma Center estimates that at least 400 Libby residents have died of an asbestos-related disease.[12]

Now in her mid-seventies, Gayla Benefield has lived in Libby her entire life. Her father, who worked in the mine for most of his adult life, was sixty four years old when he died of asbestosis in 1974. Her mother died of the same disease in 1985, and her husband died of lung cancer in 2015. She and four of her five adult children also have lung cancer. Thirty members of her extended family, including children, have died.[13] In the 1980s, suspicious there was a link between W.R. Grace's mine and the unusual number of health problems in her town, Gayla decided to investigate the company. She asked questions and shared her suspicions about the vermiculite operation with everyone she talked to, but nobody wanted to listen, not even people on oxygen tanks or people whose children had lung disease. Irritated by her search for the source of her town's affliction, residents affixed bumper stickers on their vehicles that said, "Yes, I'm from Libby, MT and No, I don't have asbestosis."[14] In conversations, they made comments such as, "Well, if it were really dangerous, someone would have told us," and, "If that's really why everyone was dying, the doctors would have told us."[15] Still, Gayla persisted until she met a reporter who wrote a story that got national attention and brought the EPA to town.

Convinced they could trust authority figures like doctors and mine supervisors, proud of Libby's legacy as a mining town, and identified with that legacy, most of Libby's residents were blind to the calamity unfolding before their eyes. That the source of their family's suffering was in their backyard did not fit into their frame of reference.

The findings of researchers, the delusions of the Republican Party, and Libby residents' inability to acknowledge the dangers they faced show how our attachments to ingrained beliefs affect relationships and communities and, on a larger scale, the entire globe. These attachments are building blocks our minds use to fortify core identities.

Like Libby, Israel-Palestine is infected with denial and replete with ingrained beliefs. I consider it an archetype for how we create a world of suffering for self and other. The gap between each side's narrative is so wide that proponents cannot help but ignore or ridicule evidence that does not comport with their beliefs. More than any topic I can think of, this one evokes intense feeling and passionate debate, making common ground almost impossible to find. Before I had read a single book on the topic, I judged and condemned others whenever their opinions contradicted mine. Until my confrontation in 2006 with the circumstances that obliged me to begin an intensive study of Israel-Palestine, I had never even bothered to research the history. My view of the Middle East had been shaped by my attendance in Sunday School in the 1950s, where my impressionable mind soaked up stories of my people's sometimes triumphant and often harrowing past and of the heroic establishment of Israel, the one sanctuary from the monstrosity of anti-Semitism.* History was not in doubt. We had maintained a presence in the Holy Land since time immemorial and, in spite of great hardships, had persevered to establish a Jewish state. With bravery and grit, we had repelled Arab forces that resented our presence and were too uncivilized to appreciate that after thousands of years of longing and prayer we had returned home. At the mercy of blind loyalty, I rejected any consideration my beliefs might be erroneous. Loyalty is an admirable quality, but when it masks fear,

---

* Although *Semite* refers to members of groups that speak a Semitic language (e.g.: Arabic, Aramaic, Hebrew, etc.), I strictly use "anti-Semitism" to refer to a hatred of or prejudice against Jewish people.

confusion, or prejudice, it makes a rational understanding of Israel-Palestine impossible.

With my journey as a guide, this book asserts that blind loyalty, false beliefs, and enemy images do not have to dictate our destiny. Through hard work and a commitment to the truth, we can undo their influence and achieve a just resolution to this tragedy. Because Israel-Palestine is an archetype, a just resolution could give birth to a global transformation in consciousness and a new destiny for humankind wherein Israel can be a "light unto the nations."

1

Willful Blindness is a Crime Against Humanity

There are two ways to be fooled.
One is to believe what isn't true;
the other is to refuse to believe what
is true.[16] – Soren Kierkegaard

I'm only lost until I see
I'm lost because I want to be.
– W.H. Auden, "The Labyrinth"

F OR MOST OF MY LIFE, I believed the cause of the Israel-Palestine problem was the Arab world's non-acceptance of a Jewish state in its midst; and I was sure this attitude resulted from thousands of years of hatred of Jewish people, their religion, and culture. I also saw elements within the Christian world as still harboring the anti-Semitic beliefs that had produced centuries of pogroms in Eastern Europe and the cruelest abomination in recorded history: the extermination of millions of Jews and others because they were judged to be less than human.

On July 12, 2006, Hezbollah militants killed three Israeli soldiers and abducted two in a cross-border raid into northern Israel. A mere three weeks after Hamas's capture of Israeli soldier Gilad Shalit on the Israel-Gaza border, this hostility reinforced my lifelong fear that the Arab world would not rest until it had wiped Israel from the face of the earth. Images of Arabs as Jew-haters and threats to my life convinced me I was as much a target as Shalit and the other innocent soldiers.

The day after Hezbollah's raid, Israel invaded Lebanon.* I supported the invasion, but was concerned for my Israeli brothers and sisters, so I arranged separate meetings with two of my wisest friends, neither of whom was Jewish. I wanted to persuade them that my concerns were justified. Although they had been critical of Israel in the past, this time I was confident they would agree with me. But to my amazement, neither friend sympathized with my viewpoint. Both blamed Israel for its disproportionate use of force against the people of Lebanon. Their reactions demoralized me. Afterwards, I dissected each conversation, trying to find something I had missed, something I'd misunderstood. Unable to find anything, I solemnly concluded that only we Jews can understand the suffering of our people. My friends' reactions confirmed that anti-Semitism was so embedded in the collective psyche of humankind that the Jewish state was in an epic battle for its life. Their inability or unwillingness to acknowledge the existential threat confronting all Jews only hardened my stance toward Israel's neighbors.

A week passed, during which I attended a rally at the Albuquerque Jewish Community Center where I donated money to AIPAC (The American Israel Public Affairs Committee), America's most influential pro-Israel lobby. I also spoke with Jewish friends whose comparable views helped to mollify my anxiety. Then I received an unexpected phone call from an old Jewish friend. Sam was calling from New Jersey to tell me he was coming out west and planned to visit me. After agreeing to the visit I launched into a two-hour diatribe against Israel's enemies. Sam just listened, never arguing, and barely saying a word. Unlike me, he had studied the history of Israel-Palestine for years, but he was very low-key about it. Toward the end of the diatribe, he suggested I look into the writings of two Jewish Israeli professors I'd never heard of: Baruch Kimmerling and

---

* The Second Lebanon War began on July 12, 2006 and ended when a UN-brokered ceasefire went into effect on August 14, 2006.

Tanya Reinhart.* Because Sam didn't judge me or resist my point of view, he gave me the space to snap out of a belief system I'd taken for granted my entire life. Until that moment in 2006, I had never allowed myself to consider the possibility that there was more to the Israel-Palestine story than what I already knew. There had been moments of doubt, but my reluctance to question my beliefs and investigate Israel's actions had always prevailed. It was safer to believe what I wanted to believe. Now, however, I was open to conducting at least a cursory investigation of this troubling subject.

After Sam and I hung up, I went online to Amazon to look for books by Kimmerling and Reinhart. I also compiled a list of other books on Israel-Palestine with the stipulation that I would consider Jewish authors only, knowing that otherwise I would suspect bias. What I could not have foretold was that I was about to uncover a lifetime of bias within myself.

I drove over to the library where I found two books from my list: *The Palestinian People: A History* by Baruch Kimmerling and Joel Migdal and *Beyond Chutzpah: On the Misuse of Anti-Semitism and the Abuse of History* by Norman Finkelstein. Unsure if I wanted to borrow *Beyond Chutzpah*, I began scanning the book jacket when, to my surprise, the name "Joan Peters" appeared along with the words, "exposed as an academic hoax." This unforeseen development startled me. Peters's book, *From Time Immemorial: The Origins of the Arab-Israel Conflict over Palestine*, was my Bible, the treasured resource I had used for over a decade to rebut criticism of Israel, and the only book I had ever read on the subject. The truth is I had not read it out of an impulse to understand the Palestinian perspective, nor had I read it to learn the history of the conflict. I had read it because my relatives told me it would erase any doubt I had about Israel's innocence and its eagerness to make peace with the Palestinians.

---

* Kimmerling (1939–2007) was professor of sociology at the Hebrew University of Jerusalem. Reinhart (1943–2007) was professor of linguistics at Tel Aviv University and at MIT, Duke University, Columbia University, and the University of Paris.

As I leafed through the pages of Finkelstein's book, an old memory surfaced. Years earlier, after hearing me praise Peters's scholarship, Sam had made a point of telling me that a New York Jewish professor, whose name he could not remember, had debunked her research. I recalled telling myself the professor must not have known what he was talking about. That excuse was all I had needed to dismiss Sam's warning from my mind.

Peters claimed there was no such thing as a Palestinian people. So-called Palestinians were actually Arab migrants who had come to Palestine from all corners of the Middle East because Jewish landowners were offering higher wages than they could earn in their home countries. Once settled, these imposters claimed Palestinian heritage. Now, both my belief system and my reverence for Peters were at risk of being discredited by a professor who concluded that "Cited sources were mangled, key numbers in the demographic study falsified, and large swaths plagiarized from Zionist propaganda tracts."[17]

Almost as unsettling, *Beyond Chutzpah's* book jacket said Finkelstein had exposed Alan Dershowitz's misrepresentation of Israel's human rights record. Although I was not aware that Dershowitz, a noted attorney, had written a book on Israel-Palestine, *The Case for Israel*, I had always admired his legal analyses because the positions he took usually reflected my view of the world. I had a difficult time envisioning Alan Dershowitz writing a book that was not diligently researched and intelligently reasoned. As I pondered this new information, I began to question my decision to educate myself. Although I wanted to reconcile my doubt and confusion, I sensed that researching an issue that kindled such strong emotions might backfire and leave me with even more doubt and confusion. I needed to either forgo or pursue my agenda. With the fragments of information I had just sampled only deepening my dilemma, I did what I had to do: I called my bluff and checked the books out.

Back home, mindful I was about to test my relationships with myself and with Israel, I set the books aside. I wanted to wait a day before diving into this project, but one nagging thought would not go away, so I googled "Norman Finkelstein." I found out he had taught at Brooklyn College, Hunter College, and New York University and that he had refuted Peters's findings in his doctoral thesis at Princeton University. Finkelstein was the New York Jewish professor whose name Sam had forgotten.

The next morning I woke up to a warm and bright day. After breakfast I sat down in my recliner and picked up *Beyond Chutzpah*. With hardly an idea of what I was getting myself into, I began reading. Thus began a conscientious study of the history of Israel-Palestine. My singular allegiance was to the truth, and I knew that if I wanted to separate fact from fiction I had to give equal attention to both sides of the debate. I was not about to allow preconceived notions to influence my research. As I took in the book's opening paragraphs, I couldn't help but take note of the author's brilliance. That I had assessed his mental acuity so quickly, however, seemed odd and I remember wondering how I could arrive at such a judgment. As Finkelstein's exposé became more and more challenging, this first impression restrained me from abandoning my project. Even now, I think my readiness to overcome the confusion that had affected me for so long must have made me receptive to an intuition that would guide me beyond the plethora of myths that has constantly shrouded the history of Israel-Palestine.

After a solid hour of reading I became preoccupied with the idea that Finkelstein's scholarship was uneven. While he criticized the Israeli side, he left the Palestinian side untouched. I kept expecting him to bring up acts of violence and other Palestinian transgressions, but each turn of the page introduced me to further disappointment. Although my internal logic at the time accommodated the idea that only a Jew-hater would question the integrity of the Jewish state, I held off on reaching that conclusion out of my pledge to unearth the truth. Given that Finkelstein's thesis concerned the misuse of anti-Semitism, the book became a riddle I hoped would resolve itself. I kept asking, "Who is misusing anti-Semitism, Finkelstein or me?" If I wanted an answer, I had to persist in my inquiry. From my standpoint, since Israel's policies for dealing with Palestinians were necessary for the security of its citizens and in line with what other countries would do in the same situation, any criticism was anti-Semitic. From Finkelstein's standpoint, Israel's policies had little to do with security and were unnecessary and illegal under international law.

Finkelstein's sources included Human Rights Watch, Amnesty International, and B'Tselem, the Israeli Information Center for Human Rights in the Occupied Territories. Consistent with each other, their findings castigated Israeli policy and behavior. Documented charges included deadly force by Israeli soldiers against unarmed men, women, and children; the bulldozing of houses, sometimes with inhabitants still inside; collective punishment of large numbers of civilians based on alleged crimes by lone individuals; using Palestinians as human shields; the theft of water from Palestinian villages; Israel's commonplace use of torture and its reliance on political assassinations.

Many of the reports Finkelstein cited were posted online, so I spent hours going over passages he had quoted. I wanted to catch him taking information out of context or changing a word here or there to present Israel in a negative light, but after reviewing numerous passages I had to concede that in every instance his documentation was beyond reproach.

At the same time I was engrossed in Finkelstein's exposé, I was experiencing a range of emotions. As I learned about the abuse and humiliation Palestinians were routinely subjected to, I felt shocked that a country in which I had invested a lifetime of loyalty would treat people this way. My shock turned to anger that Israel was perpetrating these abuses in my name as a Jew. For a moment, I saw myself in uniform holding a rifle and on the lookout for Palestinians. I was no less responsible for the abuses than an Israeli soldier on the battlefield. These human beings were suffering profoundly from my ignorance. If not for my moral support, Israel would not be oppressing Palestinians, and both peoples could be living together in peace. Information on Israel-Palestine, among the most documented subjects in human history, is available to anyone interested in educating themselves. So it is discouraging when people refuse, as I once did, to test their beliefs. Willful blindness enables this travesty of justice, which is why I refer to it as a crime against humanity.

My anger turned inward, rebuking me for the years I had assumed that Israel was an innocent victim of a society that taught its children to hate us. I could not accept anymore what my society had taught me to believe. That would have felt like hypocrisy. Then came shame and embarrassment which, as I contemplated my new understanding, turned into sorrow for the cries of the Palestinian people. I was in the initial stages of learning that every argument I had ever made in defense of Israel was either inaccurate or taken out of context to blame the Palestinians and exonerate the Israelis.

Two things became clear: first, just as throughout Eastern Europe my people had been guilty of the crime of *being* Jewish, under Israeli domination every Palestinian is guilty of the crime of *not being* Jewish. And second, much of the anger my brethren direct toward Palestinians stems from a seething frustration at the latter's refusal to collaborate in their own dispossession. My unquestioned acceptance of the Jewish/Zionist narrative had distorted my ability to empathize with another people. Under the spell of false beliefs, I had assumed that the anger Palestinians felt for Jews was so obsessive it surpassed their desire for peace. By latching onto false beliefs and by taking information out of context, I had duped myself into believing a self-righteous historical narrative that preserved an idealized image of my people.

It occurred to me that our elders had lied to my generation to enlist us into their state of mind, but I could not hold on to that idea. After the trauma of World War II, we felt an urgency to find a home where we could live without fear of persecution. Anti-Semitism had not gone away and the United States and western

Europe's slow response during the war to the genocide of my people was disturbing. Unless we took matters into our own hands and fought for a Jewish homeland, we would always be on the brink of another Holocaust.

2

We Are All Palestinians and Israelis, Muslims, Christians and Jews

Truth is by nature self-evident. As soon as you remove the cobwebs of ignorance that surround it, it shines clear. – Mohandas K. Gandhi[18]

The distinction between past, present and future is only a stubbornly persistent illusion. – Albert Einstein[19]

OVERWHELMED AND NEEDING A BREAK from this life-altering re-evaluation of a cherished part of my being, I put *Beyond Chutzpah* down and shut my eyes. I have no idea how long my eyes were shut, but when I opened them I felt cleansed and free. The difficult emotions I had been suffering were gone. Their absence was so startling, I began searching for them as if they were solid objects that could hide in physical locations. I scoured my bookcase and the corners of the room: "Where's the shock, the anger, the shame?" But I could not find a single sign of the emotions. Once it became obvious I was not going to find them, I sat back in my recliner and relaxed into my newfound state of wonderment and freedom. I had nowhere to go and nothing to do. Not looking for one experience nor avoiding another, I was perfectly neutral. I had

WAKE UP AND RECLAIM YOUR HUMANITY

no interest in the past, nor was I attracted to the future. The *Present* was all there *is*.

My attention was drawn to my face, which felt as if a soft veil was covering both eyes, its gentle weight so soothing I sank more deeply into the chair. A short interval passed, then the veil began to unravel in a spiral motion from left to right. When the unraveling ended, the world was brighter, and I understood that we give meaning to the world by projecting onto it our beliefs and images, fear and confusion. Indian Vedic philosophy refers to this as the deluding power of *Maya*, a shared illusion that tricks us into mistaking our perception of the world for reality.* Our emotions, our attitudes toward others, how we evaluate events, what we notice, and what we don't notice mirror our worldview. In a never-ending cycle of unconsciousness, we persist in creating the same worldview over and over again.

A profound inner peace permeated my being. It was everything I had ever wanted. It was the heart's desire. As I looked out, the world reflected my inner peace and I saw that my relationship with it is more than physical. It is interactive, or psychophysical. If we are going to find peace outside us, we first must find it within us. To transform the world, we have to transform ourselves.

Next, I couldn't detect any fear of Arab extremists. My enemy images seemed to have vanished. Given the terror I experienced whenever I heard of atrocities in the Middle East, I decided to test myself to see if the images were really gone. I imagined myself in the place of Nick Berg, the young man whom Iraqi extremists beheaded in 2004. Because Berg was a Jew, I could see myself in his place, but as I tried to resuscitate the enemy images, instead of experiencing fear or distress, a blissful sensation filled the interior of my body, from the tips of my toes all the way up through my torso, and somehow I recognized the sensation as equanimity. I could see without judging, and I knew that beneath their hatred even the most bloodthirsty of extremists crave the same right to self-determination

---

* Maya (*that which does not exist*) refers to illusion or deceit.

as do I. I had judged them as monsters because of their monstrous deeds, but they were still human, and in denying their humanity I had robbed myself of mine.

When I realized that culturally-determined enemy images had deceived me into dehumanizing the other, I marveled at the boundless relief I felt discovering this flaw in my character, and I forgave myself for my past insensitivities. My new self-awareness endowed me with the freedom that comes when we reclaim valuable parts of ourselves. At our core, we all want to be free, so revelations that penetrate our defenses and bring us closer to our deeper selves are a great relief. As I contrasted the difference between my old way of looking at the world and the new, I realized that my beliefs and judgments about Arabs had been warnings that I was not in touch with my heart, and so I suffered. Suffering had to end for me to know, by comparing the new condition with the old, how much I had suffered. All of us suffer in distinct ways, some more than others, but most suffering is unconscious. It is alienation from our true selves.

Sensing something was missing, I tried to inquire into my Jewish identity, but could find neither a Jewish identity nor any other limited identity. I hadn't noticed my Jewish identity falling away, nor had I pondered the possibility that I could let go of *who I am*, but there was no doubt my Jewish identity was gone. The letting go was choiceless, with a momentum of its own. In hindsight, I prefer saying my identity let go of me rather than I let go of it, but even that statement is imprecise because what I had taken for my identity was an illusion, an idea, a mental construct made of a lifetime of presumptions whose existence I had never questioned.

An image of a balloon materialized, its elastic boundaries representing the limit on understanding enforced by a limited identity. The balloon burst and the air inside the balloon equalized with the air outside the balloon and *Truth* revealed itself: we are all Palestinians and Israelis, Christians, Muslims, and Jews. All of us, from the most depraved to the most enlightened, share a common humanity.

How many of us have investigated this question of identity? I am asking an urgent question. As my anxiety compelled me to search for the facts of Israel-Palestine, I was forced to reflect upon myself and upon conflicts inside me I had never examined. This shift in emphasis became more an investigation into me than into Israel-Palestine. At a certain point, the entire edifice of me began to buckle under the weight of my inquiry and everything I was suffering collapsed. From a search for the facts of Israel-Palestine, I had become involved in something greater, a physics that would not settle for just factual truth. Once the physics reached a critical mass, it became about Truth with a capital T, and through a remarkable purification my sense of duality and separation was nowhere to be found; and the "I" I presumed myself to be was transformed.*

Compassion replaced existential fear and clarity replaced confusion. Compassion is the ability to step into the shoes of others and empathize with their need to build safe and gratifying lives for themselves and their families. It is to recognize our common reality. Therefore, along with compassion, clarity arises. Compassion and clarity, seeking to understand our fellow man, ask why others behave as they do. What motivates their behavior? Have I provoked their behavior? Compassion and clarity recognize that no behavior occurs in a vacuum, that we are all responsible for the suffering in the world, and that each one of us contributes to the collective heart of humankind. Compassion + Clarity = Peace.

Without a solid identity and its complementary beliefs and images to hold onto, I could see from all perspectives, effortlessly and without bias. How could I be biased if the beliefs and images that fed the bias were gone? My worldview had not been, as I

---

* Since I never noticed a segment of time during which my sense of duality was in the process of disappearing, dissolving, or dying, I feel more comfortable saying my sense of duality "was nowhere to be found" than "it disappeared, dissolved, or died."

once presumed, essential to my being. It had been a product of indoctrination into the illusion of identity. What is essential is the absence of indoctrination—compassion and clarity, purity and innocence—and the absence of a world of "us" against "them." Free of enemy images, I had lost the motivation to defend any position as superior to any other or to assign or withhold value regarding one people versus another.

I felt like I had awakened from a dream and was no longer burdened with the emotional pain I had misidentified as a part of my being. Within the dream the pain had lasted for a lifetime, and, because I had not been aware that I was dreaming, I had bought into the story the dream had woven, but in this awakened state it was all merely a faint memory. My new relationship with the world was so natural, and so free of a need to make meaning of it that I wondered why I hadn't always lived like this. Struck by this simplicity, I pinched myself to make sure I wasn't still asleep.

My awakening happened spontaneously, like an unexpected inheritance. It expressed itself as identification or connection with all beings. This sense of non-separateness had always been present, but it was buried beneath layers of attachment to beliefs and images that conjured a limited identity. When fear ceased to enliven the beliefs and images, non-separateness emerged.

My new sensitivity came from the heart, beyond the duality of the mind, and it manifested with no conscious effort on my part. The relief it brought was not indicative of a talent that set me apart from anyone else. My mind could never have conceived this dawning of clarity and freedom. The psychological and spiritual insights I awakened to did not result from the engagement of conventional thought to solve a problem, seek a resolution, or gain a reprieve from suffering. Although my mind registered the insights, the insights were the fruits of a transformation that took place when it let go of a belief system that had captivated it for most of a lifetime. That relinquishment allowed the natural intelligence of the heart to take its rightful place as sovereign over the mind. The insights, then, were not fruits of the mind's activity. They were fruits of the mind's inactivity, of awakening to the non-conceptual mind, to *no-mind* or *not knowing*. These fruits are accessible to everyone, but as long as we live in the past and future they remain obscured.

My use of *no-mind* and *not knowing* parallels Zen Buddhism's understanding of these terms, which are not meant to imply stupidity. Nor are they meant to imply we know nothing. The terms apply to a condition in which we are not limited by what we know, or think we know. Enlightened beings who live in a state of no-mind or not knowing can still use their minds to fulfill life's responsibilities, but they do not *have to know*. Their minds are not addicted to thinking and analysis and do not dwell on expectations, which project a future. Relaxed and fully present, empty of concepts, and accepting what *is*, they are beyond duality.

A good analogy to awakening is the instant before the Big Bang. The world-to-be was a self-existing, infinitesimal speck that, mysterious unto itself, contained time and space, but was itself not within time and space. Then its creative potential was unleashed, giving birth to the universe. In my awakening, it was as if I had reversed the historical order and returned to the zero point of non-differentiation, before the one becomes many and before the presumption of separateness (and in my case, identification as a Jew).

My understanding is that the non-separate state is the only state. It is beyond all relative phenomena and yet contains all relative phenomena as itself without separation. All things are impermanent and arise out of and decay back into this always existing state. From this perspective, my beliefs were an illusion that never truly existed or had any substance in the first place. They too decayed and were absorbed back into their original state. Although my narrative implies that a transformation occurred from non-awakening to awakening, in fact, when the awakening occurred, there was the intuition that the awakened state is always already the case, that it is primary, that there is no other state, nor could there be another state, because there is only this: the Eternal Present.[*]

———————

Describing my awakening has been and remains a challenge. One discussion that requires less effort is an explication of the factors that pushed me to a place from where I could fall more easily into the timeless moment. Here I can explain the events that culminated in awakening. To begin with, I can point to my friends' repudiation of my portrayal of Israel's rivalry with its neighbors. Even though I knew where they normally stood on the issue, I was sure they would side with me over the egregiousness of Hezbollah's cross-border raid and the fact it came only weeks after Hamas's capture of Gilad Shalit. If the aggression of one terrorist group was unable to persuade them Israel was an innocent victim of hatred, I figured the aggression of two groups would. But my reaction to the start of the Second Lebanon War led me to misjudge my friends, and their lack of understanding for my point of view stoked the fires of frustration and hopelessness.

When Sam phoned, I was near the peak of this anguish. By letting me speak without judging or arguing with me, he helped me let go of some of my pain. Then, in a relaxed manner, he offered me a chance to learn about the roots of this latest belligerence. From that time on I resolved to carry out my own exploration and establish, once and for all, whether my beliefs were grounded in fact. That resolution led me to Norman Finkelstein. While reading his book, the compassion I acquired for the Palestinians broadened my vision to include all people, without a preference for one group versus any other. That serendipitous expansion showed me that my attachment to a limited identity had left me incapable of real compassion and clarity. The outcome was a breakthrough in consciousness.

My need for justice was also fertile soil for a breakthrough.

———————

[*] I am indebted to the late Spiritual Master Adi Da Samraj (1939–2008) for his words, "always already the case," which apply to my understanding.

To profit from false evidence would have felt unprincipled, and I was unwilling to avoid genuine evidence that might undermine my position simply to maintain my stubborn convictions. In that light, and given the potency of Finkelstein's discourse, I had no alternative but to undergo a crisis that aligned my integrity with the persuasiveness of the material I was reading.

I am certain I will never know how the awakening came about. From the positionless position of the Eternal Present awakenings are acausal, meaning there can be no explanation for their emergence. From the thinking mind's position, the most honest statement I can make is that if there was a cause, my mind was and is unable to fathom what that cause may have been. However, neither knowing the cause nor undergoing an awakening as dramatic as mine is a necessary precondition for developing clarity about disagreements between individuals or groups of people. All that is required is a readiness to assess one's beliefs with honesty and to follow the facts wherever they may go.

———————

A few years ago, I read an interview with an American rabbi who had just returned from the West Bank. At the start of his trip he believed Israel treated its subjects with decency and respect and he was skeptical of reports that detailed Israel's abuse of Palestinians. In occupied Palestinian territory he saw modern roads for Jewish drivers and dirt roads for non-Jewish drivers, Jewish settlements with green lawns and swimming pools next to Palestinian villages with scarcely enough water to survive, and ordinary people on their way to work or school waiting in line for hours before passing through cage-like, metal turnstiles at checkpoints. He met many Palestinians and learned about life under Israeli rule. By the time he came home, he was a critic of the occupation and an advocate for Palestinian rights.

During the interview, the rabbi explained that his change of heart had put him more in touch with his Jewishness. If my experience tells me that Jewishness and other limited identities are illusions, ideas, and mental constructs, I have to suspect that the rabbi is conflating Jewishness with humanity. It seems to me that what he experienced was an easing of attachment to his *concept* of Jewishness. That easing allowed him to get in touch with his common humanity. His mind then mediated an explanation that avoided challenging core elements of his presumed identity and its belief system, while not hindering him from acknowledging Palestinian suffering.

When white Christian nationalists or Islamophobes recognize the evils of bigotry, it is not because they have gotten more in touch with the religion or ideology they once used to justify their bigotry. It is because their attachments to their identities eased enough so as not to block their humanity from emerging. Though misunderstood and routinely hijacked by the ego, the value of authentic religion lies in teachings and revelations that help us connect with our heart, our essence, not in dogma that puts prescribed behavior and futuristic fantasies ahead of love and compassion, or that separates people according to identity and then categorizes them as saved or damned, us or them.

If I define myself as a Jew, Christian, Muslim, American, Israeli, or Palestinian first and a human being second, I will presume that the worldview dreamed up by my identity eclipses other worldviews. But if I define myself as a human being first, my relationship with my identity is less likely to be cultic. Then I will think for myself and appreciate the similarities and inquire into the differences between various religions and ideologies. I will have the leeway to discard the less enlightened teachings of one religion or ideology for the more enlightened teachings of another. Not beholden to a limited identity, I will be a human being with the free will to investigate any religion, ideology, or spiritual practice I believe can guide me toward wisdom, insight, and greater self-understanding. Belief systems function within the dimension of mind, whereas our common humanity is prior to mind and arises in Being.

3

The Illusion of Identity

The evil that is in the world almost
always comes of ignorance, and good
intentions may do as much harm as
malevolence, if they lack understanding.
– Albert Camus, *The Plague*

A PRINCIPAL REASON ISRAEL-PALESTINE HAS BEEN so difficult to solve is that we have never explored its roots. We think we are dealing with a political, territorial, religious, ideological, cultural, or humanitarian problem, but those are all secondary to suffering, which is a psycho-spiritual problem that affects everyone, regardless of background. The psycho-spiritual dimension operates primarily in the unconscious and has a profound influence on how we relate to the world. When I got in touch with my psyche, or deeper mind, and my identification with a presumed, limited, and mortal identity became clear, I was able to understand how suffering takes shape.* The following principle describes my discovery: *the root of suffering and conflict is the attachment to a presumed, limited, and mortal identity and to the beliefs and images that emanate from and reinforce that presumption.*

---

* Although my insights into the psycho-spiritual dimension focus predominantly on Israeli loyalists, I do not mean to imply that they are any more susceptible to its influence than other groups. I define an Israeli loyalist as someone whose identification with Israel's innocence and its struggle for security makes them unwilling to question either Israeli policy or the Zionist narrative.

The presumption of a separate *self* also presumes an *other*. When seen as a threat, the dynamic of a self in relation to an other exacerbates our fears, marshals our defense mechanisms—denial, projection, blame, and rationalization—and sows the seeds for a world of *us against them*. That this mental-emotional process is unconscious does not diminish its potential to foment suffering on both personal and collective levels. Rather, it magnifies that potential because neither self-awareness nor conscience impedes its influence.

The various ego-identities and self-images that contribute to self may have unique expressions or idiosyncrasies, but their principal function is survival and self-validation. Therefore, contemplating their non-existence arouses mortal fear, which confuses us and makes the mind incapable of processing information it perceives as threats to the continued existence of the self and its core beliefs. In our confusion, we form enemy images and project them onto the groups and individuals we have branded as threats. They then become personifications of that which we deny within ourselves.

Core beliefs and images operate in visceral ways and are so deep-seated that to question them seems unimaginable. This explains why, rather than inquiring into their religious, nationalistic, or ideological identities, so many are ready to send their children to war to kill or be killed. From the perspective of identity, being right comes before the fate of our children and the entire world. Being right trumps peace.

Our attachment to core beliefs and images also explains why the I in my dream would lash out when confronted with facts that threatened the images of Israel it had incorporated into its identity. If Israel was not what he thought it was, then neither was he. To survive such threats and remain inside the dream, he relied on whatever tools were available to subvert the truth of that potential discovery.

Armed with myriad strategies to carry out its deceptions, the ego will try to mediate awakenings in ways that keep attention absorbed in the mind, so it never drops into the heart. One mediation is the use of intellectual knowledge about awakening to limit awakening.

The separate self's compulsion to be right alienates us from our true selves. It is an addiction, and its dominant symptom of withdrawal is mortal fear. The paradox is that the undoing of identities gives rise to a consciousness free of existential fear and confusion and the compulsion to be right. Limited identities manifest as emotional recoil from our common humanity. If the beliefs and images they embody disappear, we will still be here, but more connected to ourselves and our humanity. The self in the dichotomy, *self* and *other*, is not our true and unlimited Self.

When I began my research into Israel-Palestine, I was confident I would reach a point where the density of historical evidence would reveal which side's arguments were secured by fact and which were not. I never conceived that along the way I would run into my indoctrination into a lifetime of beliefs about myself and my people. I had never thought of myself as indoctrinated. I was a rational person who looked at the "facts" and drew rational conclusions. This collision between objective and subjective evidence taught me that when divorced from self-understanding, history can never produce clarity. By itself, it cannot compete with the thought processes at the root of core identities. How we see and interpret the world, what historical evidence we incorporate into our worldviews, and what historical evidence we reject are functions of identity.

The collision left a wound, but the wound was necessary because it was the doorway to the end of existential fear and confusion. Identities, which bind themselves emotionally to seemingly relevant beliefs and images, are veils through which we perceive the world. They are the root of fear and confusion. Having observed the world through a Jewish veil, I had assumed that a significant part of the world's population held anti-Semitic views. This assumption led me to interpret the ideas and behavior of the other as predisposed to incite or ignore my people's suffering. While we are all receptive to ideas and behavior that fit within the boundaries of our identity, ideas and behavior that fall outside these boundaries, that originate from the other, are less welcome and often interpreted as existential threats. Desperate to restore a sense of security to our lives, we hide from, disable, dehumanize, or destroy the other. This unconscious process is the underpinning for all kinds of prejudice and bigotry. And, because it is unconscious, it is automatic and reactive and never inspected with intelligence and discrimination.

Separative identities impel us to defend policies that trample upon the rights of the other. Beliefs that do not conform to our expectations about how the world should be give rise to fearful reactions, making a consideration of facts not aligned with our worldviews impossible. For example, many are certain the Torah is the word of God and that He promised the Holy Land to the Jewish people. This belief is so sacred it is a part of our individual and collective identities, of how we interpret the world. It blinds us to Israel's inhumanity toward the Palestinians and fools us into believing that Palestinians are obstacles to God's will, unworthy of His grace. The longing to enjoy the gifts of what we insist is God's promise activates self-righteousness and willful ignorance. Behind these states of mind sits the ego-identity's deepest fear, the transformation of our presumed and limited selves into our unlimited selves, where the illusion of identity or separateness fades and our humanity shines. That transformation is the ultimate destination of all the great religions, a destination few have reached.

We may have all the gifts we think the Torah promises, including the fulfillment of what we believe is God's covenant, but what if, in the process of acquiring these gifts, we sacrifice our humanity at the altar of dogma and greed? Are we free or are we enslaved to identity? I am not saying we have to give up our limited identities to create a better world. I am saying we need to become more conscious of how our attachment to these identities can mislead us into losing our humanity. Our attachment to some identities is tenuous, and losing them is not problematic. But as the state of the world attests, our attachment to core identities can be problematic. To use a common identity, or self-image, if we take on the role of the victim, we will need to prove to ourselves that we are indeed victims. Our minds will attract or interpret circumstances in ways that confirm that we are victims traumatized by the actions of the other. This pattern will repeat itself until its consequences become so insufferable we commit to resolving it.

The conviction that my people were more righteous and entitled than Palestinians sheltered me from knowing myself and from recognizing the inhumanity of my perspective. When Palestinians stood firm against my people's assaults on their dignity, I complained their stance posed an existential threat to my people. Then I supported even more repressive policies, which brought the world's anger down upon Israel and confirmed and perpetuated my victim mentality.

The healing energy of inquiry can help us recognize that our inborn humanity precedes exclusive identification with any nationality, religion, or ideology; and it can bring to light our chief concern, which is to cleave to a presumed and mortal identity and its fundamental demand that we be right. It also gives us the freedom to acknowledge that the other is as entitled to self-determination as are we. We do not have to like the other, but without this acknowledgment peace has no chance and the people we claim to care about will continue to suffer and die—in Israel, in Palestine, and throughout the world. Without inquiring within, our concern for those we identify with is less the language of humanity than it is the aggrandizement of a false self.

4
The Internal Logic of Oppression

[Fear] makes people think in abstractions about the enemy, the terrorists, the insurgents who threaten us, who thus must be destroyed. Once we begin thinking of people as a class of entities, as abstractions, they meld into "faces of the enemy," and primitive impulses to kill and torture them surface even among ordinarily peaceful people. – Dr. Philip Zimbardo[20]*

What we do not understand, we fear. What we fear, we judge as evil. What we judge as evil, we attempt to control. What we cannot control ... we attack. – Author unknown.

THE STRATEGY I ONCE USED to defend Israel from criticism was to accuse advocates for Palestinian rights of being willfully blind to Palestinian violence. Then I would react to the activities of a violent minority by generalizing a hatred of Jews upon an entire people. From numerous conversations, I learned that many

---

* A psychologist and professor emeritus at Stanford, Zimbardo created the landmark Stanford Prison experiment.

of my fellow Jews are obedient to the same internal logic. When informed that Israeli soldiers had killed children, we would react with disbelief, if not outright denial. Then we would argue that since Arabs embedded their soldiers within civilian populations, nobody could make Israel responsible for the deaths and maiming of children. Those crimes were the sole responsibility of the Arabs, who knowingly sacrifice their people so they can make it appear that Israeli soldiers defending themselves in the heat of battle are child killers. None of us had evidence to justify our insistence on Israeli innocence and Arab provocation, but those characteristics seemed so obvious and logical they had to be true. Therefore, there was no point in wasting time doing research that would only confirm what we already knew.

Later, after realizing the necessity of researching the entire Israel-Palestine history, I found a small number of cases where Hamas and other militants used their people as human shields, but nowhere near the extent to which Israel would like the public to believe. I also realized that the state of Israel uses the same logic I and my fellow Jews used. Having spent decades demonizing Palestinians and Muslims as having an affinity for terror, it was easy to make the case that they would do anything to demonize us. In fact, it is the Jewish state that has a history of using civilians as human shields. In 2017, B'Tselem wrote about Israel's "official policy":[21]

> Since the beginning of the occupation in 1967, Is-raeli security forces have repeatedly used Palestinians in the West Bank and in the Gaza Strip as human shields, ordering them to perform military tasks that risked their lives. As part of this policy, soldiers have ordered Palestinians to remove suspicious objects from roads, to tell people to come out of their homes so the military can arrest them, to stand in front of soldiers while the latter shoot from behind them, and more. The Palestinian civilians were chosen at

random for these tasks and could not refuse the demands placed on them by armed soldiers.[22]

In 2002, Human Rights Watch documented an Israeli Defense Forces "practice" it deemed a "serious violation of international humanitarian law":

> The IDF *routinely* [emphasis added] coerced civilians to perform life-endangering acts that assisted IDF military operations... friends, neighbors, and relatives of "wanted" Palestinians were taken at gunpoint to knock on doors, open strange packages, and search houses in which the IDF suspected armed Palestinians were present.[23]

In 2013, the UN Committee on the Rights of the Child expressed its "deep concern about the continuous use of Palestinian children as human shields."[24]

―――――――――――

We can begin to take responsibility for this nightmare of fear and confusion through self-inquiry, which questions every belief and presumption of who we are, coaxes elements of the unconscious into consciousness, and generates deep insight and self-understanding. With self-understanding, compassion replaces fear and clarity replaces confusion. True understanding sets free the natural intelligence of the heart and enables us to evaluate problems without the bias of social or cultural conditioning. As we get more in touch with our humanity and recognize the humanity of everyone else, prejudices we are unaware of will rise to the surface and be resolved. If, as a society, we choose not to inquire within, our moral decay is inevitable.

A fruit of self-inquiry is the insight that the real enemy is not someone or something outside us. The real enemy is the unexamined mind that unconsciously projects its suffering onto the other and then blames or scapegoats the other for its suffering. Whenever the object of our blame reacts to our judgments, much as we would if we were in their shoes, we take their reaction as validation for our logic. If we look upon Palestinians as terrorists, we will judge their reaction to our behavior as further proof they are terrorists, and we will fear them and be in conflict with ourselves. To achieve a more balanced perspective, wherein we become responsible for our projections, we need to develop a curiosity into the causes of suffering. Then we will investigate the beliefs and assumptions we have treated as inviolable and become interested in the circumstances that motivate the behavior of the other.

In my case, when I broke through my resistance to educating myself about Israel-Palestine I was able to apprehend the astonishing reality that criticism of Israel had not distressed me. I had *never* defended the real Israel. What I had always defended were idealistic images that I had projected onto the real Israel. This projection allowed me to deny the actual source of my distress, which were painful observations about myself and the real Israel that I would have noticed if only I had looked without the influence of an unexamined mind. As previously stated, Israel was a part of my identity as a Jew. When someone criticized Israel, I heard them criticizing me, and I refused to consider information that would have darkened my image of Israel. That reaction was motivated more by the fear of taking on the challenge the criticism posed to my identity than by genuine disagreement with the criticism or concern for Israel. The challenge was a threat because, for a split second, it made me aware of the prejudices that wanted me to turn my back on the Palestinian people. But I suppressed this awareness and remained willfully blind to the destruction of their society and the dehumanization of their people. My blindness preserved an image of me and my people as fair and humane. It goaded me into joining the chorus of fear-mongers who rationalize Israel's actions as necessary for security and who interpret a people's resistance to their own destruction as an existential threat to Israel. And it induced me to judge Palestinian violence as a pathological expression of hatred, not the tormented cry of an oppressed people, a small minority of whom resort to violence as the only way they know to retain a measure of self-respect amid generations of violence inflicted upon them.

Denial and projection work together. What I denied about Israel and myself, I projected onto the other, who I made into my enemy. While it is easy to have an enemy, it is much harder to research a subject and acknowledge that the other is a human being too. The real threat is our ignorance. Clinging to false beliefs when the facts are right in front of us cripples an essential part of ourselves: our ability to feel the humanity of the other.

If defenders of Israel want to distinguish the source of conflict and find peace as much as they want to be right, they must inquire within. If they do, they will find that just as the real enemy is not someone or something outside us, the real conflict is not Israel versus the Palestinian people or Israel versus a hostile world. The real conflict is the fear of integrating the hard-to-believe but unmistakable reality of Israel's treatment of Palestinians with unquestioned loyalty to the Jewish state. One consideration recognizes Israel's dark side. The other denies it exists.

———————

My new understanding is neither pro-Palestinian nor anti-Israeli. It is pro-humanity and anti-oppression. I advocate for the oppressed because I oppose oppression, not because I favor one people over any other people. Freed from tribalism and exclusivity, I embrace universality and inclusivity.

There seems no end in sight to the tragedy of Israel-Palestine, but hopelessness is not an option. The only practical option is to separate fact from fiction and recognize that the collective pain of the Jewish people that lies at the heart of this tragedy can only be healed when the collective pain of the Palestinian people is healed. This recognition can help us transform into compassion and clarity the fear and confusion that has informed this and so many other tragedies throughout time. The truth is that the truth *will* set us free and awaken us to our common humanity with all people.

5

A Mitzvah to Kill

WAR IS PEACE
FREEDOM IS SLAVERY
IGNORANCE IS STRENGTH

— George Orwell[25]

IN A 1951 CABINET MEETING, David Ben-Gurion, Israel's first prime minister, said: "[Some Israelis] think Jews are people but Arabs aren't, so you can do anything to them. And some think it's a mitzvah to kill Arabs …because there will be fewer Arabs here."[26]*

Foreign minister and future prime minister Moshe Sharett concurred, adding, "[Some Jews think] every Arab is a dog, a wild dog that it's a mitzvah to kill."[27]

Ben-Gurion: "Soon we won't be able to show our faces to the world. Jews meet an Arab and murder him."[28]

Israeli leaders have habituated their citizens to see Palestinians as anything but human. They are donkeys, crocodiles, cockroaches, snakes, psychopaths and serial killers, animals …not human …not entitled to live, shrapnel in the buttocks; they deserve to have their heads chopped off; the Israeli government should turn "the army of searchers to an army of avengers, an army that will not stop at 300 Philistine foreskins."[29]

---

* A mitzvah is a commandment or a praiseworthy deed. The plural of mitzvah is mitzvoth.

Current Israeli Prime Minister Benjamin Netanyahu said, "beat them up, not once but repeatedly, beat them up so it hurts so badly, until it's unbearable."[30]

In 1971, Joseph Sisco, US assistant secretary of state for Near Eastern and South Asian Affairs, said that Prime Minister Golda Meir's inability to negotiate with the Arabs was due to a Masada complex. Israeli academic Daniel Bar-Tal defines that complex as a "state in which members of a group hold a central belief that the rest of the world has highly negative behavioral intentions towards the group."[31] In her reply to Sisco, Meir touched upon historical Jewish suffering: "It is true. We do have a Masada complex. We have a pogrom complex. We have a Hitler complex."[32]

Political analyst Jaacov Reuel agreed: "[The Masada] complex... is not so much a personal affliction of Mrs. Meir but a national neurosis."[33]

Meir also talked about "the spirit of Israel, a spirit that would prefer death rather than surrender to the dark terrors of the Jewish past."[34]

American Secretary of State William Rogers believed Meir's psychology was the principal obstacle to peace in the Middle East.[35]

In A.D. 72, toward the end of the First Jewish-Roman war, and two years after destroying the second temple in Jerusalem, Roman troops laid siege to Masada, a fortress atop a rocky plateau in southern Israel's Judean desert where the Sicarii had been living since A.D. 66. Named for their use of *sicae*, or small daggers, these Jewish extremists fought against Rome's occupation of Judea. They were infamous for blending into crowds, then pulling out their daggers and murdering not only Romans, but Jews they suspected of being Roman sympathizers. They also plundered Jewish villages. Flavius Josephus, a Jewish historian of the era, recorded that during a raid on the village of En Gedi, the Sicarii murdered 700 Jewish women and children. Driven from Jerusalem by other Jews, they fled to Masada. By A.D. 73, knowing that defeat was imminent, their leader, Elazar Ben-Yair, swore that death as free men was preferable to living under the yoke of tyranny. One thousand perished in one of humankind's most memorialized mass suicides. The only survivors were two women and five children who hid in a nearby cave. An integral part of Jewish lore and identity, the last stand of the Sicarii symbolizes the trauma of a people whose only choices, Meir believed, were death or surrender.

When she swore her people would prefer death to "the dark terrors of the Jewish past" and when she brought up Masada and Hitler complexes, uppermost in Meir's mind must have been the Nazi Holocaust, the greatest catastrophe in Jewish history. When I was growing up in the United States in the 1950s and 1960s, memories of the Holocaust permeated Jewish society and its relationships with the non-Jewish world. Decades later, Israeli legislators regularly invoke the potential of a future Holocaust as justification for their nation's control over the lives of millions of Palestinians; and they perpetuate the beliefs behind this justification by sending thousands of Israeli schoolchildren on annual pilgrimages to concentration camps in Poland, where they are exposed to the kinds of atrocities that await Jews if they put their trust in non-Jews.

There is no denying that exposing students to tragic chapters from their people's past can help us understand the motivations of those who came before us. The problem is that when we infuse into the conversation dehumanizing language and reactionary and categorical beliefs such as, "the world hates Jews," "the world is against us," "Arabs are the new Nazis" or, "all Arabs want to kill all Jews," we set ourselves up for further tragedy. Notice the projection. When we fear all Arabs want to kill all Jews, wouldn't we feel safer if our leaders incapacitated or killed all Arabs? "All Arabs want to kill all Jews" becomes, "We need to kill all Arabs." I have heard several normally good-hearted Jews vocalize this exact sentiment. Thus, we rationalize policies that oppress Arabs day in and day out. And, if "the world hates Jews," criticism of these policies is likely to be equated with anti-Semitism.

Preoccupied with his people's history of persecution and suffering, the Holocaust was the lens through which Menachem Begin saw the world. Egypt's president, Colonel Gamal Abdel Nasser, was the

"Arab Hitler," Palestinian leader Yasser Arafat was "Hitler in his bunker," the Palestinian Liberation Organization (PLO) the "Arab SS," and the Palestinian national covenant the equivalent of Hitler's *Mein Kampf.* In 1981, afraid another Holocaust was looming, Prime Minister Begin ordered the bombing of an Iraqi nuclear reactor.[36]

On June 6, 1982, alarmed that PLO forces in Lebanon were too close to its border, Israel invaded its northern neighbor. The stated purpose of "Operation Peace for Galilee" was to drive PLO forces twenty-five miles further north of the border. Begin explained to his cabinet ministers that "the alternative to the operation is Treblinka, and we agreed that it would never happen again."[37*]

More ambitious than Begin, Defense Minister Ariel Sharon's stated goals were to destroy the PLO as a political and military organization, to expel Syrian forces from the country, and to install a pro-Israel Lebanese government headed by Christian Maronite Bashir Gemayel. Sharon believed that Gemayel, who headed the right-wing Lebanese Phalange Party, shared his aspirations, and would sign a peace treaty with Israel.[38] Named after Spain's Falange Party and founded in 1936 as a Maronite Catholic paramilitary force, the Phalange party's ideology was similar to the fascism of Generalissimo Francisco Franco.

Another, less publicized, motive Sharon had for invading Lebanon was to turn Jordan into a Palestinian state. If he could drive the Palestinians into Syria, the Syrians could drive them into Jordan, where they would overthrow the Hashemite kingdom.[39]

On June 14, 1982, the Israel Defense Forces began a siege of Beirut, bombarding the Lebanese capital from the sea, air, and land and killing thousands. A few weeks later, Begin told the Knesset, "No one, anywhere in the world, can preach morality to our people."[40]

To put an end to the hostilities, the US brokered a ceasefire that took effect on August 18. Under its terms, the Multinational Force in Lebanon, an international peacekeeping team, supervised the evacuation of the PLO leadership and its thirteen thousand

---

* With the exception of Auschwitz, more Jews were exterminated at Treblinka concentration camp in Poland than at any other concentration camp.

combatants. Most went to Tunisia with the rest spread out among other Arab countries. On August 23, Lebanese voters elected Gemayel to the presidency. On September 10, its mission accomplished, the MNF left Lebanon. Four days later, before he could take office, Gemayel was assassinated when a bomb exploded in the Phalangist's East Beirut headquarters. The president-elect had many enemies, including Muslims, Palestinian guerrillas, and other leftists who had opposed him during the first two years of Lebanon's civil war, which began in 1975 and ended in 1989. Phalangists and the PLO had fought and killed each other and Gemayel had led a brutal massacre that wiped out most of the denizens of a Palestinian refugee camp.[41]

News of Gemayel's death sparked a cry for revenge as his followers jumped to the conclusion that the assassins were PLO militants. American and Israeli intelligence would later determine that Syrian nationalists opposed to Gemayel's cooperation with Israel had carried out the plot. The day after the assassination, the IDF violated the ceasefire by invading and re-occupying Beirut. Another day later, on Thursday, September 16, Sharon and Chief-of-Staff Rafael Eitan, both of whom also believed Palestinians were Gemayel's assassins, sent the Phalangists, whom they had armed and trained, into the Lebanese Palestinian refugee camps of Sabra and Shatila. For four days, until Sunday, September 19, 1982, Israeli troops surrounded the camps and sealed all exits. At night they illuminated the skies with flares. With no PLO combatants to stop them, Phalangists dismembered, raped, and massacred residents in a bloodbath the UN General Assembly denounced as "an act of genocide."[42] Israeli soldiers did nothing to stop the carnage. Estimates of fatalities ran as high as 3,500. Sharon called the dead, who were mostly children and older men and women, "terrorists [who needed] mopping up."[43]

On September 17, while the slaughter was taking place, the Israelis and Americans convened a meeting at which US Middle East envoy Morris Draper demanded that Sharon withdraw the Phalangist soldiers from the camps. The Israeli replied: "Nothing will happen. Maybe some more terrorists will be killed. That will be to the benefit of all of us."[44] Sharon's comment was consistent with his view that there was no distinction between Palestinian militants and ordinary citizens of any age or gender.

Sharon continued: "If you don't want the Lebanese to kill them, we will kill them."[45]

Draper reacted: "You should be ashamed. The situation is absolutely appalling. They're killing children! You have the field completely under your control and are therefore responsible for that area."[46]

Briefed about the details of the meeting, Assistant Secretary of State for Near Eastern Affairs Nicholas A. Veliotes replied, "Vintage Sharon, it is his way or the highway."[47]

The United States had guaranteed that it would protect Palestinian refugees. In a series of memos that were a part of the PLO-Israeli ceasefire, Presidential Special Envoy Philip Habib had written:

> Law-abiding Palestinian non-combatants remaining in Beirut, including the families of those who have departed, will be authorized to live in peace and security. The Lebanese and US governments will provide appropriate security guarantees ... on the basis of assurances received from the government of Israel and from the leaders of certain Lebanese groups with which it has been in contact.[48]

On Saturday, September 18, Begin responded to widespread criticism by lecturing the *New York Times*: "Goyim kill goyim, and they immediately come to hang the Jews."[49]

After the *London Times* reported on the IDF's role in the massacres, Begin scolded: "A newspaper that supported the treachery of the Munich agreement [to dismember Czechoslovakia in the 1930s] should be very careful in preaching morality to a small nation fighting for its life."[50]

In February 1983, the Kahan Commission of Inquiry issued its "Report into the Events at the Refugee Camps in Beirut." Accusing the Israeli government of "indirect responsibility for what occurred in the refugee camps," it found that Sharon had disregarded the likelihood the Phalangists "were liable to commit atrocities," and that "From the Defense Minister himself we know that this consideration did not concern him in the least."[51] The commission reprimanded Begin "for not exercising greater involvement and awareness in the matter" and criticized other officials, some—Sharon included—with the recommendation they be removed from their posts, but it recommended no indictments.[52] Aside from Kahan, no other deliberative body charged a single Phalangist or Israeli soldier for crimes related to Sabra and Shatila. The message from the international community was that Israel could get away with murder. Had the Kahan Commission demanded a punishment commensurate with the crimes it investigated, Israel might have thought twice before initiating its later assaults against the people of Gaza.

Begin was not above abandoning his standards for self-serving reasons. A few months before Israel invaded Lebanon in 1982, and just before the start of the April–June Falklands War between England and Argentina, his government sold fighter jets, artillery, and air-to-air and anti-tank missiles to the South American country's military dictatorship, which used them to bomb British warships. Dozens of British soldiers and naval personnel died in the attacks.[53] Begin's thirst for revenge against England for its past crackdown on the Irgun (The National Military Organization in the Land of Israel), the terrorist group he led from 1944 until 1948, overruled any apprehension he might have had about the dictatorship's use of Nazi ideology or its history of attacks against its political opponents. During its "Dirty War" in the late 1970s and early 1980s, the dictatorship "disappeared" between ten and thirty thousand it suspected of left-wing activities. Its methods included torture, executions, and the use of airplanes to dump the "Desaparecidos," pregnant women among them, into the Atlantic Ocean. Military families loyal to the regime adopted stolen babies. Although they represented less than 1 percent of Argentina's population, over 12 percent of the victims were Jewish.[54] The dictatorship incarcerated Jews in prisons where walls were adorned with giant swastikas, and at detention centers decorated with portraits of Hitler, where guards forcibly daubed swastikas on their backs.[55] Recordings of Hitler's speeches played in the background of torture sessions.[56] Parallels to Treblinka could not have escaped Begin's notice.

In its report on this period of Argentine history, the Commission of Solidarity with Relatives of the Disappeared concluded that the military had enacted "a specific anti-Semitic genocidal plan."[57]

Upset that "anti-Semites who themselves identify with Hitler and Mussolini serve in high educational and cultural posts in the government," the US Congress accused Argentina of "hundreds of anti-Semitic acts against Jews," and of delinquency for failing to arrest a single perpetrator.[58]

6

Ariel Sharon: The Deluding Power of Dualistic Thinking

Jew hatred is a platonic hatred, a hereditary mental disease which two thousand years' duration has so aggravated as to render it incurable. As the Jewish problem is international, it can be solved only by nationalism. – Dr. Leo Pinsker[59]*

That which is hateful to you, do not do to your fellow. That is the whole Torah. – Hillel†

ARIEL SHARON OPERATED UNDER THE maxim that "Israel may have the right to put others on trial, but certainly no one has the right to put the Jewish people and the State of Israel on trial."[60]

He also shared Meir's Masada-like perspective: "Today we are in the arena opposite the entire world. It is the people of Israel, a small and isolated people, against the entire world."[61]

---

* Leo Pinsker (1821–1891), a Russian Jew, was the founder of Hovevei Zion (Founders of Zion) and author of the influential pamphlet, *Auto-Emancipation* (1882), which called for a Jewish national consciousness and self-rule.

† A religious leader and scholar, Hillel (also known as Hillel the Elder) was born in Babylon in 110 BCE and died in 10 CE. The 120 years he is reputed to have lived equals the lifetime of Moses.

The lesson Sharon took from the Holocaust was that "no one cared that Jews were being murdered."[62]

There was some truth to Sharon's beliefs, but the doctrine of Jewish racial superiority he subscribed to was grounds for rationalizing the ethnic cleansing of the Palestinians as essential for a Jewish haven.

Like Meir and Begin, Sharon equated an indigenous people's defense against a foreign invader with terrorism, and terrorism against an indigenous people with self-defense. As minister of defense, he pushed for Israel's invasion of Lebanon, which took the lives of thousands of civilians. In his role as a politician, he insisted that "Jordan is Palestine." As a conqueror, he devoted himself to the systematic destruction of Palestinian villages. Born in what is now Israel, throughout his long career he rejected compromise in favor of violence and settlement expansion. A father of the illegal settler movement, his strategy for redeeming the land was to initiate campaigns of brute force and terror against its inhabitants. Palestinians feared him for his wanton disregard for human life. His legacy consisting of countless tragedies, this self-described warrior's nicknames, "butcher of Sabra and Shatila" and "bulldozer," were well-earned.

While serving as an officer under Yitzhak Rabin in 1948, Sharon helped drive thousands of Palestinians from their homes. In 1952, he was appointed the head of special commando Unit 101, which was formed to handle reprisal actions against "infiltrators." A misleading term, "infiltrators" were actually fellaheen (native peasants) who had been expelled by the Israeli army. Poor and hungry, most of them risked the dangers of returning to their homes to recover possessions, harvest crops, graze their sheep, or visit relatives. Israeli historian Benny Morris reports that "only a very small proportion, certainly far less than 10 percent, of the infiltrators came with the express purpose of attacking people or sabotaging Israeli targets."[63] From 1949 to 1956, Israel killed between 2,700 and 5,000 of these natives.[64]

With his authority, Sharon instigated skirmishes between Arabs and Jews. The excessive number of casualties on both sides was emblematic of his military strategy. On August 28, 1953, during a search for infiltrators in Bureij refugee camp in Gaza, his troops killed forty-three men, women, and children and injured twenty-two. The Mixed Armistice Commission (MAC), which the UN formed after the 1948 war to supervise the truce between Israel and its Arab neighbors, determined that Unit 101's action was "an appalling case of deliberate mass murder."[65]

One of Sharon's missions was to end "terrorism" in Gaza. His strategy was simple: kill every armed Arab. When Uri Avnery, former soldier, past member of the Irgun, and founder of the Gush Shalom peace movement, asked him about "killing prisoners," he replied, "I did not kill prisoners. I did not take prisoners!"[66]

Sharon seized another opportunity to terrorize civilians after a grenade explosion killed a woman and two children in the Jewish settlement of Yehuda, near Tel Aviv. Quick to condemn the murders, the Jordanian government offered to open the border to the West Bank so Israeli police could track down the killers.* Prime Minister Ben-Gurion declined, but on October 14, 1953, two days after the murders, Unit 101 unilaterally crossed the armistice line into the West Bank and snuck into the Palestinian village of Qibya, nineteen miles northwest of Ramallah. As residents slept, soldiers booby-trapped forty-five homes with dynamite, then moved from house to house, firing their weapons and throwing grenades. When the shooting stopped, sixty-seven people, again mostly women and children, were dead. The Israeli side suffered no casualties.[67]

Arriving at the scene within hours of the killings, UN observers found that "Bullet-riddled bodies near the doorways and multiple bullet hits on the doors of the demolished houses indicated that the inhabitants had been forced to remain inside until their homes were blown up over them."[68]

In the subsequent investigation, Sharon claimed he had given his soldiers orders to go to each house and warn the occupants to leave.

---

* Jordan held control over the West Bank until 1967.

41

The soldiers denied receiving the orders. Jordanian pathologists ascertained that most of the dead had been killed by bullets and shrapnel.[69] Israeli archives later disclosed that "operational orders …had explicitly ordered 'destruction and maximum killing.'"[70] A month after the raid, the United Nations passed Security Council Resolution 101, which "expresses the strongest censure of that action."

Also in 1953, Sharon led a raid on the al-Burg refugee camp, an alleged base for infiltrators. When he first described the operation to his soldiers, one of them protested its objective seemed to be to kill as many civilians as possible. Sharon replied that the women of the camp were whores who served the infiltrators. His unit killed fifteen people, almost all women and children.[71]

In his book, *Sharon: An Israeli Caesar*, Uzi Benzamin chronicled incidents away from the battlefield that exposed the depths of Sharon's inhumanity. In one, Sharon laughed "as he watched a junior officer torment an old Palestinian man and then murder him at close range."[72]

In another, Sharon was "amused by inventive ploys to murder civilians, such as trapping a peaceful Bedouin boy as he shepherded his flock."[73]

Sharon would have regarded as preposterous the idea that targeting civilians made him a terrorist. Convinced he was fighting for his people's survival, he saw his mission as necessary and noble.

––––––––––

Fear of the other distorts reality. Trapped in duality and anxious to rid itself of painful images, the unexamined and self-righteous mind transforms the apparent other into a repository for its prejudice and hatred.

The other is a mirror that reflects our dark side. The unacceptable qualities we see in them are often qualities we have not faced within ourselves. The greater the resistance to inquiring into these qualities, the greater the force with which we project them onto others. The dependence on denial and projection to insulate our presumed selves only strengthens illusion and causes more suffering.

Dualistic thinking induces so many who profess peace to support war. It is why so many normally decent people, who ordinarily believe in justice, rationalize indecency and injustice; why so many who extol morality and democracy defend immorality and sabotage democracy; and why so many who avow that *Never Again* should the world turn its back on the persecution of an entire people do exactly that.

My friends and relatives who defend Israel are, as I once was, unaware of their prejudices against Arabs. They think their ideas about Arabs reflect what is happening in the world. The opposite is true. What is happening in the world largely reflects their ideas and the enemy images that occupy deeper layers of their minds. Like Sharon and Begin, they project images of Nazis onto Arabs and then justify Israeli violence as necessary to prevent another Holocaust.

Imagine the confusion that exists within a mind that justifies oppression yet claims it wants peace. This mind is so afraid of inquiring into its thought patterns, it cannot comprehend that when we oppress people and deny them basic rights, they have legitimate reasons to resist. Instead, it labels the resistance terrorism and acts accordingly.

A mind that doesn't inquire within can never find peace. If we want peace, we have to go beyond duality and take responsibility for our beliefs and images, judgments and prejudices. Where do they come from, what are they trying to tell us, what urges do they appear to satisfy, what terror lies beneath them? Without asking and answering these questions, we will be mired in ideology, delusion, disagreement, and a compulsive need to be right.

We see the world through the prism of identity. If we identify with the role of the persecuted, the scapegoat, or the victim, we will interpret the behavior of those we fear as intending to persecute, scapegoat, or victimize us. Except to the degree to which they have been taught to see themselves in these roles, the Jews of the modern State of Israel are none of those things, yet they act as if they are.

Revered figures in Israel's history, Sharon and Begin are models of how the unexamined mind projects its pain and suffering onto the world. That they were never held accountable for their crimes reflects upon a society whose members are prone to surrender their native intelligence and self-respect to charismatic authority figures and know-it-alls. Through an inscrutable alchemy, they deceive themselves into thinking they too can escape the burden of accountability that requires all of us to contemplate issues we do not yet understand and to find answers to questions we are afraid to ask.

7

"True" Friends of Israel

When Zionism first appeared on the world scene most Jews opposed it and scoffed at it. – Nahum Goldmann[74]*

It's a trick. We always use it. When, from Europe, somebody is criticizing Israel, we bring up the Holocaust. When, in [the United States], people are criticizing Israel, then they are anti-Semitic. – Shulamit Aloni[75]†

FROM ITS INCEPTION, ISRAEL'S LOYALISTS have associated criticism of Israel, its Zionist ideology, and the measures it has taken to establish a Jewish state with anti-Semitism. The association seemed valid because I could not understand why anyone would criticize a movement that made the world safer for my people unless they disliked us or resented our accomplishments. My vision used to be so narrow, my worldview so one-sided, there was no room in

---

* Goldmann was both founder and former president of the World Jewish Congress and the World Zionist Organization.

† Aloni (1927–2014) was an Israeli politician, Knesset member. and co-founder and leader of the Meretz (Hebrew: "Vigor") party. From 1992 to 1993 she served as Minister of Education. In 2000, she was awarded the Israel Prize "for her struggle to right injustices and for raising the standard of equality." (Jodi Rudoren, "Shulamit Aloni, Outspoken Israeli Lawmaker, Dies at 86," *New York Times*, January 24, 2014).

me to empathize with Palestinian suffering, and without empathy the notion we were committing injustices against Palestinians was incomprehensible. I could never bring myself to compare the Palestinian struggle for equality to that of the South African or African-American peoples. Both were victims of bigotry and discrimination, but Palestinians were not. How could they be when my people were eager to share the land and live in peace with them? Despite our kindnesses, they wanted to push us into the sea. They were the bigots, and any inequality they suffered was their fault. With my dualistic thinking equating compassion for Palestinians with hatred toward Jews, it was easy to besmirch Palestinian society as an aggregation of anti-Semites.

Criticism of Israel stimulated anger and righteous indignation which, I eventually discovered, were symptoms of existential or mortal fear. Fear was the primal emotion out of which the anger and indignation were born, but the immediacy of the anger and indignation prevented the fear from rising to conscious awareness. Fear incapacitated and confused me, making it inconceivable to look beyond my need for security and question my core beliefs and images. To a rational person, my attitude toward Palestinian suffering must have seemed callous. It was, but my survival was at stake and I didn't know what to do to mollify my painful feelings except to denounce what I perceived as ignorance and insensitivity on the part of the fools who were gullible enough to fall for Palestinian propaganda. That was pure projection. Had I been more open-minded, I would have discerned that I had options for dealing with my fear and confusion, but the nucleus of my presumed self, my ego-identity, was unwilling to entertain threats to its worldview. Devotion to ignorance consoled me and shielded me from knowing myself.

In due course, I discovered the remedy for my suffering, which is always at hand: inquire into the beliefs and images and unexamined prejudices that feed the negative emotions, and study the history to discriminate between fact and fiction. For over a decade I have offered this remedy to Israeli loyalists, some of whom are friends, but not one has shown interest. All have ignored my assurances that the Palestinian narrative holds important truths and that reading a book could reward them with a fresher and more inclusive way of relating to the world. I have stressed that they can test this remedy in the comfort of their home; nobody has to know what they are reading; they can put the book down anytime they want; and they are under no obligation to believe a word they read. I remind them that whatever they discover does not have to affect their loyalty to Israel and that taking this simple and clarifying step will anchor that loyalty in the self-esteem that comes from the courage to question a lifetime of assumptions and beliefs. I explain that freedom from my prior ignorance allows me to commiserate with Palestinian suffering without it weakening or prejudicing the affection and kinship I feel for my people and our tradition. That is why I support reparations for the suffering our people have caused, just as I have always supported reparations for the suffering others have caused us.

Loyalists' refusal to educate themselves is not just self-destructive, it is selfish, for it falls upon all of us to sow the seeds of peace by overcoming our prejudices, deconstructing our false beliefs, and helping our brethren do likewise. Instead, the mind's fear of self-discovery has no aim except self-preservation. This is why religion is such a battlefield of egos and ideologies and it is why we interpret religious teachings in ways that justify our egoic tendencies rather than surrendering our egoic tendencies to the teachings. It is a rare individual who takes on challenges to his or her beliefs. With Israel, the threat to one's identity seems too much to bear. As I mentioned before, while it is easy to have an enemy, absent self-inquiry, aversion to research that threatens core identities can be too powerful to overcome. Fear overshadows appeals to educate oneself or to see the humanity in all people.

———————

Israel's loyalists contend that the force behind unfavorable characterizations of Israel is anti-Semitic bigotry. Dutch Holocaust survivor Hajo Meyer said, "Once an anti-Semite was a man who hates Jews. Today an anti-Semite is a man whom Jews hate."[76] Israeli prime ministers, David Ben-Gurion, Moshe Sharett, and Yitzhak Rabin would likely be accused of anti-Semitism for their words:

> If I was an Arab leader I would never make terms with Israel. That is natural: We have stolen their country.[77]

> There is no Arab who is not harmed by the Jews' entry into the country.[78]

> Ruling over another people has corrupted us.[79]

The *Merriam-Webster Dictionary* defines anti-Semitism as "hostility toward or discrimination against Jews as a religious, ethnic, or racial group." Known for his dovish views, Abba Eban was one of the foremost political philosophers of the twentieth century and a founding father of Israel. He served as deputy prime minister, foreign minister to the United States, and ambassador to the UN. It was he who coined the familiar phrase that Yasser Arafat "never missed an opportunity to miss an opportunity." He also expanded the definition of anti-Semitism: "One of the chief tasks of any dialogue with the Gentile world is to prove that the distinction between anti-Semitism and anti-Zionism [generally understood as criticism of policies of the Israeli state] is not a distinction at all."[80]

David Ben-Gurion and Theodore Herzl were of like mind, with Ben-Gurion declaring, "henceforth to be anti-Zionist was to be anti-Semitic."[81] Herzl, the founder of political Zionism, said, "No true Jew can be an anti-Zionist."[82]

These men knew that religious Jews rejected Zionism as heresy because it reneges on the promise made to God not to acquire the Holy Land through human effort.[83] Their rejection of a central tenet of Judaism, combined with the disparaging way they spoke and thought about Judaism, was classic anti-Semitism.

The Torah teaches that only God, through the Moshiach (Messiah from the House of David), can establish the Jewish nation.

Herzl was so disaffected with his heritage, he offered to convert Jews to Roman Catholicism if the Pope would back his plan for a Jewish state.[84] His disaffection may explain a prediction he made, one that has come to pass: "The anti-Semites will become our most dependable friends, the anti-Semitic countries our allies."[85] In Herzl, who did not circumcise his son, religious Jews saw an *Am Ha'aret* (ignoramus).[86] In religious Jews, Herzl saw *kikes*.[87] This founder of a movement so influential it supplanted "God" with "Israel" and transformed a religion into a nationalistic movement gave validation to Jew-haters everywhere when he said:

> Yid is anti-Zionist. We have known him for a long time, and just merely to look at him, let alone approach or, heaven forbid, touch him was enough to make us feel sick… The Yid …is a hideous distortion of the human character, something unspeakably low and repulsive… The Yid is the curse of the Jews… The Yid is anti-Zionist!… We'll breathe more easily, having got rid once and for all of these people whom, with furtive shame, we were obliged to treat as our fellow tribesmen… Watch out, Yid.[88]

In word and deed, a "true Jew" is true to Israel's government, not to the Torah, which the Zionist movement deserted long ago. Justifying their tribalism under the rubric of security, "true Jews" advocate criminalizing racism directed against Jews, as they define it, and legalizing racism directed against Palestinians.

In contrast, Jews who value self-determination for all people, who honor the humanistic values they learned at synagogue, or who identify with the Torah's commandment to care for the stranger— which the Torah mentions more than any other commandment, including the commandment to love God—can no longer be a part

49

of the tribe.* They have been excommunicated by an ideology that rejects the universality of our humanity for tribal exceptionalism, or ethno-nationalism. *Haaretz's* editorial board diagnosed this propensity, consistent with Herzl's prediction, within Israeli society:

> The more nationalistic Israel becomes, the more the hatred of those carrying the banner of moral values and a universalist identity will grow, and they will be perceived as enemies even if they are Jews. At the same time, Israel's affection will grow for those who promote nationalism and xenophobia, even if they are anti-Semites.[89]

To paraphrase, critics of the Israeli occupation, even if they are Israeli Jews, are anti-Semites, but not all anti-Semites are critics of the Israeli occupation. Therefore, their bigotry is acceptable. Benjamin Netanyahu, who cries "anti-Semitism" whenever someone criticizes Israel for its violations of international humanitarian law, turned a blind eye when Donald Trump referred to white supremacists, Ku Klux Klan members, and neo-Nazis as "very fine people." For the prime minister, the president's anti-Muslim immigration policies outweigh his white supremacist and anti-Semitic proclivities.

In June 2018, angry at the European Union for approving the Iran nuclear deal, Netanyahu spurned a meeting with EU Foreign Affairs chief Federica Mogherini, who had scheduled a visit to Israel.† Mogherini canceled her trip. A month later, Netanyahu welcomed Hungarian Prime Minister Viktor Orban, whose animosity toward minority rights, asylum seekers, and refugees resembles that of the Israeli. Like Netanyahu, who champions a Jewish "democracy" that

---

* E.G.: Exodus 23:09: "And a stranger shalt thou not oppress; for ye know the heart of a stranger, seeing ye were strangers in the land of Egypt." And Exodus 22:20: "And a stranger shalt thou not wrong, neither shalt thou oppress him; for ye were strangers in the land of Egypt."

† The Iran nuclear deal, known as the Joint Comprehensive Plan of Action (JCPOA), was signed on July 14, 2015 by Iran and the P5+1 countries. The P5+1 are the permanent members of the UN Security Council—China, Russia, United Kingdom, France, US—plus Germany.

is anti-immigrant, Orban champions a Christian "democracy" that is anti-immigrant. His attitude toward Jews is another example of classic anti-Semitism:

> [Jews] do not fight directly but by stealth; they are not honourable, but unprincipled …they do not believe in work, but speculate with money; they have no homeland but feel the whole world is theirs. They are not generous, but vengeful, and always attack the heart.[90]

In December 2018, Netanyahu announced that the two leaders were in talks over how the House of Fates, the new Holocaust museum set to open in Budapest, would portray Hungary's role in the Holocaust. They were working on an acceptable "consensus narrative" that would allow Orban to minimize his country's past treatment of Jews, 565,000 of whom, nearly seventy percent of Hungary's Jewish population, died in the Holocaust.[91;92] To Netanyahu, Orban is "a true friend of Israel."[93]

When the Israeli Foreign Ministry advised that any new Holocaust museum should respect "the historical record" as depicted by Yad Vashem, the Jewish state's official memorial to the victims of the genocide, Netanyahu banned the Ministry's representatives from the talks.[94]

Yair Lapid, leader of Israeli centrist political party Yesh Atid (There Is a Future) and the son of a Holocaust survivor, said Netanyahu's "only response" to Orban must be "that the museum should reflect the truth and nothing else. No negotiations, no consensus, just the truth."[95]

The director of Yad Vashem's library reacted to Netanyahu's dereliction of his moral authority:

> [Hungary's] museum concept clearly avoids addressing the role and responsibility of … Hungarian leaders of that era for the plight of the nation's Jews, and their eventual abandonment to the hands of Nazi

Germany. ... It is implied that Hungary was actually a nation of rescuers. This is a grave falsification of history.[96]

In July 2018, Netanyahu and Polish Prime Minister Mateusz Morawiecki signed a joint statement endorsing a bill Morawiecki's government passed earlier in the year that criminalizes accusations of Polish complicity in the Holocaust as well as language that refers to Nazi concentration camps as "Polish" camps. The statement equated anti-Polonism with anti-Semitism and praised Poland's wartime government-in-exile for having raised "awareness among Western allies of the systematic murder" of Polish Jews.[97] Of 3.35 million Polish Jews, three million died in the Holocaust.[98] Nazi death camps, Majdanek, Chelmno, Auschwitz, Belzec, Sobibor, and Treblinka were in Poland.

Yad Vashem countered:

A thorough review by Yad Vashem historians shows that the historical assertions, presented as unchallenged facts, in the joint statement contain grave errors and deceptions ...Much of the Polish resistance ...not only failed to help Jews, but was also not infrequently actively involved in persecuting them... Poles' assistance to Jews during the Holocaust was relatively rare, and attacks against and even the murder of Jews were widespread phenomena.[99]

Devised to rehabilitate Poland's image at the expense of the truth, both the new law and the joint statement are examples of Holocaust denial. Yad Vashem continued:

The attempt to amplify the relief that was extended to the Jews and portray it as a widespread phenomenon, and to minimize the role of Poles in persecuting the Jews, constitutes an offense not only to the historical truth, but also to the memory of the heroism of the Righteous Among the Nations.[100]*

Yair Lapid called the joint statement, "a scandalous debasement of the memory of those who perished," while Education Minister Naftali Bennett called it a "lie-ridden disgrace."[101]

The Centre of Organisation of Holocaust Survivors in Israel also reacted to the Netanyahu-Morawiecki statement:

Signing this agreement is a public betrayal of the memory of the Holocaust, akin to dancing on the graves of the deceased. The state of Israel has no authority to change the course of history for political needs devoid of values and content.[102]

In another display of hypocrisy, in September 2018, Israel rolled out the red carpet for Philippine President Rodrigo Duterte, who has murdered thousands of his citizens and compares himself to Adolf Hitler. None of that matters because Duterte's government granted an oil exploration license to Israel's Ratio Petroleum Energy and has often abstained from or voted in Israel's favor on UN resolutions. During his time in Jerusalem, the Philippine president visited Yad Vashem where it is likely he identified more closely with the Nazi perpetrators featured there than the victims of their crimes.

On October 28, 2018, voters elected Jair Bolsonaro to the Brazilian presidency. Netanyahu was quick to congratulate the former army captain and invite him to visit the Jewish state. Branded "the most misogynistic, hateful, elected official in the democratic world," Bolsonaro supports sterilizing the poor, defends the use of

* The honorific, *Righteous Among the Nations*, refers to Gentiles who risked their lives during the Holocaust to protect Jews.

torture, and has heaped praise upon Brazil's military dictatorship, which killed or "disappeared" 434 dissidents between 1964 and 1985.[103;104;105] As a congressman in 1999, he said the dictatorship "should have killed 30,000 more."[106] Along with his favorite motto, "A good criminal is a dead criminal," he believes "a policeman who doesn't kill isn't a policeman," refugees are "scum of the earth," and black activists are "animals."[107;108;109;110] Ilona Szabó, director of the Igarapé Institute, a Rio de Janeiro think tank, warns that under Bolsonaro's presidency, "There will be more extrajudicial killings, especially of people in the slums and of blacks."[111] In 1998, while defending students who selected Adolf Hitler as an admirable historical figure, Bolsonaro said, "They have to choose those who knew, in one way or another, how to impose order and discipline."[112] Ernesto Geisel, head of the military dictatorship from 1974 to 1979, says Brazil's new president is "completely beyond the pale" and "a military evil."[113] None of this kept Netanyahu away from Bolsonaro's January 1, 2019 inauguration. After the ceremony, the two ideological allies shared a warm embrace.[114]

Bolsonaro may be beyond the pale, but killing and torture is nothing new to Israel's security establishment, and the contempt right-wing Israelis feel for people of color, many of whom are refugees, comports with Bolsonaro's feelings. As a senior Israeli diplomat explained, what is vital to the Netanyahu government is that "Brazil will now be colored in blue and white [the colors of the Israeli flag]."[115] Bolsonaro has vowed to close the Palestinian embassy in Brasilia and move Brazil's embassy from Tel Aviv to Jerusalem.[116] To date, only the US and Guatemala have made that move.

Past Israeli governments would have had enough self-respect to keep their distance from the leaders cited above. In contrast, today's government, which insists that Jews who believe in equal rights for all people are anti-Semites, allows real anti-Semites to debase Jewish history and engage in Holocaust revisionism. So long as these racists refrain from criticizing the occupation their anti-Semitism is kosher and Israel will treat them as friends.

Knesset member (MK) Ksenia Svetlova of the Zionist Union Party submitted a bill that would have prohibited Holocaust deniers and those who have uttered anti-Semitic slurs from entering Israel. Not a single MK on the right supported her.[117]

8

The Territorial Answer to the Jewish Fear

Land is the most necessary thing for
our establishing roots in Palestine.
Since there are hardly any more arable
unsettled lands in Palestine, we are
bound in each case of the purchase
of land and its settlements to remove
the peasants who cultivated the land
so far, both owners of the land and
tenants. – Arthur Ruppin, 1930[118]*

THE POLITICS OF EBAN, BEN-GURION, Herzl, and the Likud Party have never been theoretical.† Before Israel became a state, Jewish paramilitary organizations, the Haganah (Hebrew: Defense), Irgun, and Stern Gang hijacked British military vehicles, lynched, kidnapped, and murdered soldiers and officials, terrorized the public with drive-by-shootings and car and truck bombs, and placed bombs in bus stations and marketplaces.[119] Besides targeting Brits and Arabs, these organizations had no compunctions about murdering Jews who worked for the British or who were friends

---

* Known as "the father of Zionist settlement" and "the father of Jewish sociology," Arthur Ruppin (1876–1943) was a founder of the city of Tel Aviv.

† Founded in 1973 by Menachem Begin and Ariel Sharon, Likud (the Consolidation) was a merger of Herut (Freedom) and other parties. Begin founded Herut in 1948 as successor to the Irgun. In 1977, he became the first member of a right-wing party to be elected prime minister of Israel.

with or did business with Arabs. There is strong evidence they killed more Jews than members of any other group.[120]

Until 1894, Herzl, an Austro-Hungarian journalist, dreamed of Jewish emancipation and assimilation within European society, but in December of that year a sensational event altered his views. The *New Free Press*, a Viennese newspaper, had sent him to Paris to cover the trial of Alfred Dreyfus, a French Jewish army officer who would be convicted of treason and exiled to Devil's Island to serve a life sentence. After years of fighting in the courts, Dreyfus was exonerated in 1906. The Dreyfus affair was among the most politically charged dramas in modern French history. Driven by a rise in nationalism and clericalism, anti-Semitism exploded throughout society, with riots breaking out in twenty cities across the country. In Paris, Herzl witnessed crowds screaming, "A mort les Juifs" (Death to the Jews). Coming from the birthplace of the *Declaration of the Rights of Man and of the Citizen*, this hysteria shattered his dream.* The gentile world would never give up its contempt for Jews. The only alternative was for Jews to leave the Diaspora and establish a nation of their own. Herzl reasoned that Jews "naturally move to those places where we are not persecuted, and there our presence produces persecution." He concluded that anti-Semitism is an "absolute condition in all nation-states wherein Jews constituted a minority."[121;122] His transformation in thinking was to be the root of political Zionism. For Herzl, "the Jewish question [was] no more a social than a religious one …It is a national question."[123] With anti-Semitism the justification for the birth of a Jewish nation, the master plan had to be massive colonization combined with the ethnic cleansing of the region's non-Jewish inhabitants.

Former Israeli Minister of both Foreign Affairs and Internal Security, Shlomo Ben-Ami has described Zionism as "the territorial answer to the Jewish fear."[124] I agree with Ben-Ami, but I must

---

* A manifesto of the French Revolution, the *Declaration of the Rights of Man and of the Citizen* was passed by the Constituent Assembly on September 27, 1791. It was the first formal expression of universal equality issued by a European Christian nation and was perceived by Jews as a statement of social and political emancipation.

digress. In 1913, only eight thousand of three hundred thousand British Jews and twelve thousand of three million American Jews were members of Zionist organizations.[125;126] Before the First World War, of the 2.5 million Jews who emigrated from Europe, most went to the United States.[127] Between 1900 and 1914, 1.5 million Russian Jews entered the United States, including a signficant number who re-emigrated from Palestine.[128] More Jews left Palestine for the US than left the Russian Empire, home to a plurality of the world's Jews, for Palestine.[129] Israeli historian Tom Segev found that at the height of Jewish immigration, only 4 percent of the world's Jews came to Palestine.[130] Of the three-quarters of a million Jews who left Europe in the 1920s, at least half came to America even though the Johnson-Reed Immigration Act of 1924 effectively put an end to immigration by restricting it to 2 percent of the total of each nationality on the basis of the 1890 census.[131*] Under Johnson-Reed, the annual quotas from Poland and Russia for all immigrants regardless of religion were 5,982 and 2,248, while quotas from Hungary and Lithuania were 473 and 344.[132] By the 1920s, Poland's Jewish population had grown to nearly three million, while Russia's topped five million. Congress's xenophobia doomed millions of European Jews to the Nazi death chambers.

In 1944, President Franklin Roosevelt proposed suspending America's closed-door immigration policy. The US and its European allies agreed to resettle all Jewish Holocaust survivors, who numbered about five hundred thousand. To elicit the approval of American Jewish organizations, the president dispatched his friend and adviser Morris Ernst. A prominent attorney, co-founder of the American Civil Liberties Union (ACLU), and a Jew, Ernst encountered fierce opposition, which he described as arising out of "a deep, genuine, often fanatical emotional vested interest in putting over the Palestinian movement [Zionism]."[133] The Zionists'

---

*   Johnson-Reed, which remained in effect until 1965, contained an exception that excluded 100 percent of Asians from immigrating to the US. In 1890, the Jewish population in the US was between 400,000 and 475,000. In 1920, it was about 3.5 million (jewishvirtuallibrary.org/jewish-population-in-the-united-states-nationally).

"pet thesis [that for displaced Jews] Palestine or detestable Nazi Germany seemed to be [their] only choices [was] endangered by the generosity and humanity of the F.D.R. program."[134] Troubled that some men "are little concerned about human blood if it is not their own," Ernst recounted that "active Jewish leaders decried, sneered, and then attacked me as if I were a traitor... I was openly accused of furthering this plan of freer immigration in order to undermine political Zionism."[135]

Forced to withdraw his plan, Roosevelt regretted that "The dominant vocal Jewish [Zionist] leadership of America won't stand for it."[136] Jewish refugees, many of whom were afraid to go back to the eastern European cities and towns they had been driven from, were left with little choice but to emigrate to Palestine. A May 1945 survey of 2,190 Jewish survivors of Dachau concentration camp found that only 15 percent had any interest in relocating to Palestine.[137]

Because coming to the aid of Holocaust survivors was, as Ernst understood, the generous and humane thing to do, he may have misjudged the uphill battle he faced. Ernst thought Zionism's main goal was to save the Jews of Europe, but it was to steer as many Jews to Palestine as it could. Both he and FDR were probably unaware of Moshe Sharett's vow that "under no circumstances" would the Jewish Agency allow Jews to leave Palestine or emigrate to anywhere but Palestine.[138] The Jewish Agency was so fixated on Jewish immigration that as early as 1938 David Ben-Gurion had proclaimed his readiness to abandon thousands of Jewish children in exchange for a Jewish state:*

> If I knew that it was possible to save all the [Jewish] children of Germany by their transfer to England and only half of them by transferring them to Eretz Israel, I would choose the latter – because we are faced not

---

* The Jewish Agency was founded in 1929 to bring Jews to Palestine. Its mission today is to bring Jews to Israel. David Ben-Gurion chaired the Agency from 1935 to 1948. Moshe Sharett was chairman from 1961–1965.

only with the accounting of these children but also with the historical accounting of the Jewish people.[139]

In February 1943, Yitzhak Greenbaum, the chairperson of the Jewish Agency's Rescue Committee and a future Israeli interior minister affirmed the Agency's preference for land over life:

> For the rescue of the Jews of the Diaspora, we should consolidate our excess strength and the surplus of powers that we have. When they come to us with two plans – – the rescue of the masses of Jews in Europe or the redemption of the land – – I vote, without a second thought, for the redemption of the land[140]

Rabbi Moshe Shonfeld criticized the Agency: "The rescue committee of the Jewish Agency falsely bore the name 'rescue.' It would be more appropriate to name it the 'Committee for Covering up, Ignoring and Silencing.'"[141]

Later in 1943, the New Zionist Organization of America appealed to anti-Semitic biases with an ad in the *New York Times* which claimed that without a Jewish state in Palestine, "America will face increasing pressure to open her doors [to displaced Jews]. It will be difficult for her to refuse."[142] A half-century later, during a period of mass immigration of Russian Jews to Israel, journalist Bo'az Evron of *Yediot Ahronot* chastised his government for putting its colonial ambitions ahead of immigrants' well-being:

> Israeli and Zionist emissaries have left no stone un-turned in prodding the nations of the world to deny entry to Jewish refugees, so as to force them to settle in Israel…
>
> If they were guided by the best interests of these Jews, the [Israeli] government and the Jewish Agency would seek to open all the doors in the world to everyone wishing to leave the USSR… But who cares about the best interests of these Jews? They concern Shamir and

Sharon only insofar as they can populate the settlements, or serve as a pretext for grabbing more land in the West Bank, or become soldiers in future wars…

Here the great secret of Zionism in the past few generations stands revealed. Long ago, Zionism ceased its concern for what is good for the Jews. Quite the contrary, Zionism is interested in seeing to it that the Jews suffer, so that they will leave their homes and come to Israel. This is why each glimmer of anti-Semitism fills the hearts of Zionists with relief. Zionism needs Jews in order to boost the Jewish population and military strength of Israel, not for their own sake …As human beings, they are of no concern to either the State of Israel or the Zionist Movement.[143]

Although millions of Jews have never set foot in Israel, many still identify with the Jewish state as a haven where, if ever again they become scapegoats for the world's frustrations, they can exercise their right of return. That same right is *verboten* to millions of Palestinians, many of them condemned to live in overcrowded refugee camps in Gaza, the West Bank, Syria, Lebanon, and Jordan. Israeli analysts know that in its zeal to, as Ariel Sharon urged, "grab as many hilltops as [it] can to enlarge the settlements because everything we take now will stay ours," the Israeli government has made the rest of the world less safe for Jews.[144] While Israel's land grab continues unabated, instead of holding itself accountable, the Israeli government complains that the Jewish people are the innocent victims of anti-Semitism. Meanwhile, the real victims of racism continue to suffer.

9
A People Who Shall Dwell Alone

For from the top of the rocks I see him,
and from the hills I behold him: lo,
it is a people that shall dwell alone,
and shall not be reckoned among
the nations. – Numbers 23:9

In reality, the concept of "people who
*dwell alone" is the **natural** condition of*
the Jewish people.[145] – Ya'acov Herzog[*]

AN ATTACHMENT TO ZIONIST MYTHS makes it next to impossible for Israeli loyalists to reflect upon the narcissism inherent in denying Palestinians the same rights and quality of life they demand for themselves. Consumed with their people's history of persecution, they interpret criticism of Israel as propaganda and regard the proposition that it is immoral to withhold equal rights from Palestinians to be yet another permutation of anti-Semitism. While repeating the mantra, "Israel is the only democracy in the Middle East," they equate the application of anti-democratic principles with the Jewish state's preservation and the application of democratic principles with its destruction. In their minds, bowing to pressure and respecting international law threatens the Jewish

---

[*] Herzog was Director-General of the Prime Minister's Office under Menachem Begin.

people with another Holocaust. They cannot comprehend that accountability, which applies to other nations, might also apply to Israel. Two former heads of Mossad, Tamir Pardo and Efraim Halevy, the latter also a former national security adviser, dispute the view that the world wants to destroy Israel.* Pardo: "Israel has only one existential threat, [the occupation and the underlying conflict with the Palestinian people]."[146] Halevy: "I do not believe there is an existential threat to Israel."[147]

From the start of its membership in the UN, Israeli leaders have argued that resolutions criticizing the Jewish state betray a hostile predisposition toward Jews. Not as certain as they pretend to be, they know these resolutions do not criticize Israel because of its Jewish character. They criticize Israel, as they would any country, for its illegal policies. The irony is that Israel exploits the reactions its policies provoke as validation for its collective identity as "a people who shall dwell alone." Jewish or not, any nation under the illusion that inhumane policies are justifiable would become a pariah to the global community. Instead of cooperating and resolving disputes according to laws that treat people equally, Israel thwarts Palestinian rights by slandering the global community as anti-Semitic. *Haaretz's* Gideon Levy explains this mindset:

> [T]o speak for consciousness, to speak for morality, to speak for maintaining the international law, is perceived in Israel as treason. Not less than this... This atmosphere, violent, aggressive, and lacking any kind of tolerance, is above all dangerous for the future of Israel.[148]

For decades, European countries have given considerable latitude to Israeli behavior, often out of sensitivity to the profound effect the Holocaust has had on Jewish society. Rather than appreciating this thoughtfulness, Israel demands it as an exclusive right.

---

* The Mossad is Israel's national intelligence agency.

Israel defines itself as the nation-state of the Jewish people, but it would be more accurate if it defined itself as the nation-state of the *right-wing* Jewish people. In March 2017, the Knesset passed the Entry Law, which prohibits active members of organizations supporting BDS (Boycott, Divestment, and Sanctions) from entering Israel or Palestinian territory. The law suppresses speech critical of Israel and is meant to keep its citizens in line with their government's anti-democratic tendencies. It is part of a campaign to associate the BDS movement with anti-Semitism, precisely because it espouses a democratic solution to the Israel-Palestine problem consistent with international law.

Driven by fear of the other, a conspicuous number of those who attack BDS as racist support racist behavior toward Palestinians. Their unwarranted judgments about the BDS movement are projections. The Statement of the Palestinian BDS National Committee begins with, "The global Boycott, Divestment and Sanctions (BDS) movement for freedom, justice and equality of the Palestinian people is an inclusive, nonviolent human rights movement that rejects all forms of racism and racial discrimination."[149]

Inspired by South Africa's anti-apartheid movement, BDS's goals are: 1) An end to Israel's occupation and colonization of Arab lands, and the dismantling of the separation wall; 2) Recognition of the right to equality for Arab-Palestinian citizens of Israel proper; 3) Palestinian refugees' right to return to their homes and properties as stipulated in UN Resolution 194.

While many loyalists agree with Israel's critics that sanctions on North Korea and Russia for their contraventions of international law are necessary, when critics recommend sanctions on Israel for its contraventions, loyalists fantasize that Jews are, once again, being singled out for criticism. Their expectation is that among the nations of the world, the Jewish state continue to be exempt from normative standards of behavior. Israel enjoys such extraordinary treatment because it is a "beacon of democracy," and, "the US and

Israel have a special relationship." Anxious to dilute the efficacy of reports that bring attention to Israel's crimes, loyalists demand these platitudes be in the foreground of any discussion of Israel-Palestine.

Most loyalists supported or would have supported the international boycott against South Africa's apartheid regime, but their unquestioning loyalty blinds them to the devastating effects of the Israeli government's apartheid-like policies. No wonder Jews who champion social justice refuse to accept that Israel represents all Jews. Disheartened by its lack of humanity, many call for boycott, divestment, and sanctions because they care about Israel and want it to live up to a standard of behavior more virtuous than the behavior of countries that once scapegoated and dehumanized Jews. It is because they are *not* racist that they support BDS. Their fight is to rescue the integrity of their religious tradition from those who make excuses for Israel's unlawful behavior and who shield it from its obligations under international law. Organizations like Jewish Voice for Peace (JVP), which has over two hundred thousand members, work tirelessly to encourage Israel to come to its senses and end the decades of enmity that have taken the lives of Palestinians and Jews.

In January 2018, Israel published the names of the twenty organizations blacklisted by the Entry Law. Along with JVP, the list includes the American Friends Service Committee, a Quaker organization. In 1947, the Norwegian Nobel Committee awarded AFSC its Peace Prize for the wartime aid it provided to Jewish and Christian victims of the Holocaust and for helping twelve thousand Jewish children escape to safety.[150] For its humanitarian service to Palestinians, the Israeli government has tarnished AFSC as anti-Semitic. In 2011, AFSC published its *Principles for a Just and Lasting Peace Between Palestinians and Israelis*, which promotes a peace that "will be not merely the absence of war, but the presence of justice – justice between nations, and within nations as well."[151]

10

The Religion of Zionism

Zionism was always seen, rightly, as the new Jewish "religion." – Israel Harel[152]*

> *Neither Jewish ethics nor Jewish tradition can disqualify terrorism as a means of combat. We are very far from having any moral qualms as far as our national war goes. We have before us the command of the Torah, whose morality surpasses that of any other body of laws in the world: "Ye shall blot them out to the last man."* – Yitzhak Shamir, 1943[153]

To be fair to the memory of the millions killed or traumatized by authentic anti-Semitism, I can attest that virtually every Jew of my parents and grandparents' generation believed Zionism was a movement whose purpose was to protect us from the centuries of Jew-hatred that reached its climax with the Holocaust. In the 1950s, Israel was only a few years old and the atrocities perpetrated by the Nazis were fresh in the minds of my elders, most of whom lost relatives to the death camps. My friends and I learned from our

---

* A regular columnist for *Haaretz*, Harel is the founder of both the Institute for Religious Zionism at the Shalom Hartman Institute and the Council of Jewish Communities in Judea, Samaria, and Gaza.

families, Sunday school teachers, and rabbis that the establishment of a Jewish state was a reaction to a virulent form of European Christian racism. Although much of our learning was taught to us directly, many of the ideas and biases we incorporated into our collective worldview were taught to us indirectly. Just as we adopted the speech and physical patterns of our caregivers and mentors, the unresolved traumas our ancestors lived through and the horror that human beings are capable of such cruelty were transmitted to us through feeling.

In Sunday school, the classroom walls were decorated with photographs of David Ben-Gurion and Israel's first president, Chaim Weizmann. Grateful that for the first time in our history we had a haven, when I looked at the faces of those benevolent men who had worked so tirelessly on our behalf, I saw leaders who wanted to preserve life, not squander it.

Along with this way of interpreting the information available to me, there arose the view that Jews would never do to others the shocking things Adolf Hitler and others had done to Jews. After all, it had never occurred to me to do such things, and the Jews I knew were caring people, so it must never have occurred to them. They were incapable of such crimes. What they were capable of was planting millions of trees and turning a barren desert into a land of milk and honey. With a childlike faith in the goodness of my people, it was a natural progression in thinking to deduce that the non-Jewish world, much of which was silent while Jews were being persecuted and murdered, differed from the Jewish world. For some inexplicable reason, maybe because we were special or "chosen," Jews were more humane than non-Jews. Our soldiers were defending our land from the irrational hatred of those who, like Hitler, wanted us dead. The conditioning of my youth became the prism through which I perceived the world.

Every human being is born into a particular society, is given a name, and told who he or she is. This is how we assume the matrix of an identity. In my case, I was told I was a Jew and an American, this is my story. These labels demarcated the boundaries of my worldview.

My thinking developed along a spectrum from idealism—Jews are good and their leaders honorable—to cynicism—others are neither good nor honorable. I had created a gulf between myself and others, and I was reluctant to question my worldview. My unquestioning acceptance of my conditioning became the limit on my ability to see clearly.

When I was twelve years of age, *Exodus*, Leon Uris's historical novel about the founding of the Jewish state, was popular within the Jewish community. One day, I was with my friend at his house down the street when I noticed the book lying on a table. I picked it up and began to leaf through it. Eddie's parents happened to notice and prodded me to take the book home with me. They told me that no Jew should ever forget the injustices our people had suffered. I knew my friend's parents were from Lithuania and had been prisoners in concentration camps, but they had always seemed normal, so their past didn't make much of an impression on me. This time, however, they showed me the numbers Nazi guards had burned into their forearms. Their scars were damning evidence of the dehumanizing treatment we had gone through and it was enough for me to want to understand what motivated the Nazis to sink to such depravity. Sixty years later, it is why I cannot stay silent while my people perpetuate their cycle of depravity upon another people.

Unaware that Herzl, Ben-Gurion, and their fellow ideologues insisted on the removal of Palestinians from Eretz Israel, my friends and I would have found incomprehensible the charge that Zionism was racism. How could a need for survival be racist? This charge was insensitive to the thousands of years of heartache we had suffered. In our way of thinking, anyone labeling us as racist had to be racist themselves. We believed the Zionist aphorism that through hard work and cultivation of "a land without a people for a people without a land" Israel would be redeemed, and we hoped that over time that redemption would motivate its neighbors to leave behind their grievances and see the wisdom of living with us in peace. We were not mature enough to discern that what we had inferred as insensitivity to Jewish suffering was, in truth, a reaction to policies Israel had enacted on behalf of the Jewish people. Nor did we comprehend that Zionism is the ideological foundation that justifies the dispossession of an entire people; and that in the hands of Israel's leaders it is racism. Israeli policy that favors one people over another affects millions every day, and the resulting dehumanization is a product of Zionism. We also would have been shocked had we known that Ben-Gurion slurred Jews from Arab countries as "avak adam," subhuman, or that future prime minister Levi Eshkol called those same people "human rubbish."[154]

––––––––––––

In his book, *Ideas and Opinions*, Albert Einstein wrote:

> I am afraid of the inner damage Judaism will sustain–
> especially from the development of a narrow nation-
> alism within our ranks, against which we have already
> had to fight strongly, even without a Jewish state. We
> are no longer Jews of the Maccabee period. A return
> to a nation in the political sense of the word would be
> equivalent to turning away from the spiritualization
> of our community which we owe to the genius of our
> prophets.[155]

Einstein recognized that a movement based on nationalism would drive his people away from the Torah, whereas Judaism's spiritual dimension undertakes to bring them closer. In 1929, Orthodox Rabbi Aaron Samuel Tamarat explained: "Judaism is Torah, ethics and exaltation of spirit. If Judaism is truly Torah, then it cannot be reduced to the confines of any particular territory. For as Scripture said of Torah, 'Its measure is greater than the earth.'"[156]

In 1885, the American Reform Movement in Judaism drafted the Pittsburgh Platform, a set of principles that offered a modern and progressive approach to the Jewish faith:

> We consider ourselves no longer a nation, but a re-

ligious community, and therefore expect neither a return to Palestine, nor a sacrificial worship under the sons of Aaron, nor the restoration of any of the laws concerning the Jewish state.[157]

Neturei Karta (Aramaic for Guardians of the City, i.e. Jerusalem), an Orthodox sect of Judaism, has acknowledged that Jews and Arabs lived in peace for centuries until the emergence of Jewish nationalism and the racism it spawned. Its rabbis teach that the Moshiach will come when Israel ends its oppression of the Palestinian people. I agree with the rabbis, but I do not consider the Moshiach, or Messiah, to be a unique individual endowed with mystical powers. For me, the Moshiach is a consciousness that is *Here* and *Now*, always already *Present*, and beyond duality and ideologies that divide the world into tribes of us and them. The Moshiach consciousness silently waits for a critical mass of human beings to awaken to its Reality. To that end, we must uproot the ideologies and their beliefs and images that separate us from our humanity, especially beliefs and images that incite fear and anger and justify hatred. Authentic religion, not the religion of the ego, aspires to link us to the broader principles at the heart of all genuinely human endeavors. Principles like purity and innocence, love and compassion, tolerance and justice are reminders of our true nature, of who we are once we recognize that our beliefs and images, and the prejudices, presumptions, and expectations they give birth to, are unnecessary and counterproductive.

On July 16, 1947, four months before the passage of the Partition Plan, UN Resolution 181, Yosef Zvi Dushinsky and Zelig Ruven Bengis, the Chief Rabbis of the Ashkenazi Jewish community in Jerusalem, gave written testimony to the United Nations Special Committee on Palestine (UNSCOP) announcing their community's "definite opposition to a Jewish state in any part of Palestine." They demanded that Jerusalem be an international zone where "there should be implemented the unity of international brotherhood towards all Mankind…"[158]

Later in the year, Dushinsky and two other rabbis from

Jerusalem, Amrom Blau, the founder of Neturei Karta, and Aron Katzenellenbogen, implored the UN that if it recognize a Zionist state, it proclaim Jerusalem "an international city and its citizens under the protection of the United Nations."[159] The rabbis accused "the Zionist state [of usurping] without any justification, the holy name of Israel," and they added, "Torah true Jews wish to live in peace and harmony with their neighbors and with the community of nations and …do not want to impinge upon the rest of the inhabitants of the Holy Land…" [160]

Queens, NY rabbi David Shapiro criticized Zionism's insistence that Jerusalem is the eternal capital of the Jewish people. In December 2017, he said:

> The Jewish people don't have a capital. We have never had a capital. Countries have capitals…. *The Jewish people are not a country or a region*, the Jewish people are a religious community. We pray towards Jerusalem, but we relate to Jerusalem only as a holy city not as a political capital city of the Jewish people.
>
> And all of those overtures that we make to Jerusalem, and the yearning we have for Jerusalem is only as a holy city, not as a capital city. And because it's a holy city, it doesn't matter who has sovereignty over it. Jerusalem is just as holy and just as much Jerusalem whether it's under the auspices of the Turks or the Romans or the British or whoever.
>
> It's important to know that the Zionists are the ones that started this business of the capital of the Jewish people, and it's an idea that directly conflicts with the teachings of Judaism.[161]

An appreciation for knowledge as a key to solving problems has always been a hallmark of Jewish culture, but the refusal to investigate Israel's treatment of the Palestinians for fear it might jeopardize our images of Israel and, especially, of ourselves turns knowledge into ignorance and ignorance into knowledge. In this Orwellian universe, we regard indisputable evidence, even if drawn from the Israeli state archives, as anti-Semitic libel, and self-serving fantasy as the unqualified truth of Israel's character. As an example, look no further than the prime minister of Israel. With a straight face, on September 9, 2016, Benjamin Netanyahu alleged that Palestinians' "demand [for] ethnic cleansing [was] outrageous." He also voiced incredulity that anyone could claim that "[Jewish] communities in Judea and Samaria, the West Bank, are an obstacle to peace."[162*]

Anyone, Mr. Netanyahu? What about virtually the entire membership of the UN, most of which respect international law and expect Israel to do the same? And, did you forget how Israel acquired those communities?

"Would you accept ethnic cleansing in your state," he asked. "Since when is bigotry a foundation for peace?"[163]

Ethnic cleansing shouldn't be acceptable to anyone, prime minister, which is why the hypocrisy of your comments horrifies so many. Ethnic cleansing and theft of Palestinian land flaunts bigotry and makes peace impossible.

"I think," said Netanyahu, "what makes peace impossible is intolerance of others. Societies that respect all peoples are the ones that pursue peace. Societies that demand ethnic cleansing don't pursue peace."[164]

I agree. Look in the mirror.

Former Shin Bet (Internal Security Agency) directors, the late Avraham Shalom and Carmi Gillon, differ with Netanyahu over Israel's role in the West Bank. Shalom admitted that Israel acts as "a brutal occupation force." Gillon reflected: "We are making the lives of millions unbearable."[165]

---

* Israel refers to the West Bank, excluding East Jerusalem, with the ancient names of Judea and Samaria. Judea corresponds to the Southern Kingdom, also known as the Kingdom of Judah, while Samaria represents the northern kingdom, which was also known as the Kingdom of Israel.

11

Tribal Thinking

Two roads diverged in a wood, and
I – I took the one less traveled by, And
that has made all the difference.

— Robert Frost "The
Road Not Taken"

WHEN OUT OF CONTROL, TRIBALISM begets conformity, even at the expense of humanity. Conformity to my tribe was the reason the death of a single Jew at the hands of a Palestinian aroused greater distress than the deaths of hundreds of Palestinians at the hands of Jews. Convinced that under the right circumstances, I could have been a victim of a hate crime, it was a logical step to rationalize Israel's persecution of Palestinians as necessary for my people's security, and to interpret Palestinian resistance as evidence of anti-Semitism. Now that I am free of the need to conform to the irrational thinking of my tribe, or of any tribe, I recognize that accusations of anti-Semitism are often misplaced. Afraid to ask why someone is critical of Israel, and indifferent to the humiliations Palestinians suffer every day, accusers vilify anyone who questions their narrative. Abdicating responsibility for their fear, confusion, and anger, they project those feelings onto critics, then attempt to blackmail them into silence by accusing them of anti-Semitism. Their dastardly scheme is to convince themselves that neither they nor Israel are guilty of crimes against the Palestinian people.

On May 4, 2016, Holocaust Remembrance Day, Major General Yair Golan warned against a future he feared his nation was moving toward:

> The Holocaust, in my view, must lead us to deep soul-searching about the nature of man. It must bring us to conduct some soul searching as to the responsibility of leadership and the quality of our society. It must lead us to fundamentally rethink how we, here and now, behave towards the other.
>
> There is nothing easier and simpler than fear-mongering and threatening. There is nothing easier and simpler than in behaving like beasts, becoming morally corrupt, and sanctimoniousness.
>
> On Holocaust Remembrance Day it is worthwhile to ponder our capacity to uproot the first signs of intolerance, violence, and self-destruction that arise on the path to moral degradation.[166]

The Holocaust will continue to influence Jewish identity and behavior for generations, just as the Nakba will continue to influence Palestinian identity and behavior.* This does not mean we have to remain stuck in tribal thinking and a predetermined future where we continually repeat our self-destructive behavior, as when we categorize the other as the enemy and misinterpret their motives. Instead, by being open to and recognizing the pain of the other and by suspending our attachments to identities, we can step into their shoes, empathize with their fears, and find resolutions that respect the needs of both peoples.

Deep soul-searching about the nature of man is the key to peace.

---

* Nakba is Arabic for catastrophe. Although the Nakba generally refers to the expulsion of Palestinians in 1948, it is an ongoing tragedy for Palestinians, who Israel continues to uproot from their homes and villages to make way for Jewish settlements.

I call this contemplation self-inquiry. With patience, it reveals that our common humanity is part of our true nature and that the primary obstacle to that revelation is the attachment to presumed, limited, and mortal identities.

12

The Disinherited

It doesn't matter if justice is on your
side. You have to depict your position
as just. – Benjamin Netanyahu[167]

ETWEEN 2006 AND 2012, TENS of thousands of African asylum
seekers crossed the Sinai desert into Israel. To Netanyahu, they
are "[a threat to] our existence as a Jewish and democratic state …[that]
threatens the social fabric of society, our national security, our national
identity."[168] To prevent a further influx, Israel constructed a five-meter-
high, 242 kilometer-long electronic fence along its southern border
with Egypt. Completed in 2014, the fence extends from the Gaza
Strip to Eilat on the Red Sea. By 2015, crossings into Israel fell to
213, a massive reduction, but not enough to placate policymakers.
In 2016, after Israel increased the fence's height to eight meters along
a busy seventeen kilometer stretch, breaches declined to eleven.[169]
Not content with keeping out migrants from the south, Netanyahu
proposed surrounding his nation with a security barrier to "defend
ourselves against the wild beasts."[170]

A large number of refugees are survivors of torture and violence.
Twenty percent are Sudanese who fled their country's conflict with
South Sudan, and 72 percent are Eritrean. The rest are Congolese or
South Sudanese. Eritreans face a future limited to war, mandatory
military service that can last for decades, arbitrary imprisonment,
slavery, and torture. Desperate to escape their government's barbarous

policies, 12 percent of the population has fled the country, with a majority heading north to Europe. On the way, they have to navigate the world's most deadly migration trail, which takes them through the Sahara and across the Mediterranean.[171] Migrants who flee to Israel risk interception by Egyptian forces, who torture, murder, or kidnap them for ransom.[172] Most who make it to Israel work for low wages in jobs other citizens shun, but their hopes for asylum have been dashed. Between 2013 and 2017, Israel granted that status to twelve out of 15,200 petitioners.[173] In 2016, the European Union approved 92.5 percent of Eritrean asylum requests.[174]

In November 2017, the Netanyahu government released a plan to deport thirty-eight thousand Africans. Like its attitude toward the fellaheen, the country's right-wing has stigmatized these asylum seekers as "infiltrators," with Culture Minister Miri Regev deriding them as "a cancer in our body."[175] In early 2018, the first batch of twenty thousand deportation notices went out to single men.[176] Along with written assurances that work permits and visas were awaiting them, the deportation plan provided each deportee with $3,500 and a plane ticket to Rwanda, Uganda, or the country they fled from, despite the fact that Israel is better equipped than those countries to offer asylum. Its gross domestic product is fifty-five times Uganda's and fifty times Rwanda's, while its refugee population is one-twentieth of Uganda's and a third of Rwanda's.[177] Africans who rejected Israel's offer were subject to imprisonment for an indefinite length of time, then forced deportation, which is illegal under international law. To expedite its plan, Israel placed a freeze on refugee bank accounts and offered a $9,000 bounty for each African migrant its citizens hunted down.[178;179]

Netanyahu's plan exempted most women and children, but not members of the LGBT community. Israeli authorities know that many African countries persecute individuals because of sexual orientation and gender identity and that Uganda has a history of brutality toward the LGBT community. That knowledge was not enough to convince the Population and Immigration Authority to grant refugee status to gay and transgendered men and women.[180]

Africans who accepted the $3,500 and left Israel never received the promised work permits or visas. Israel paid their new countries $5,000 per deportee, but when deportees arrived police confiscated their travel documents and left them out on the streets, vulnerable to exploitation and crime.[181] One deportee, who hasn't been able to find a job, said: "I didn't want to go to the [Israeli] prison. I thought maybe it would be better for me in Rwanda than in prison, but it has become like a prison for me here."[182]

Another deportee, who learned to speak Hebrew during his seven and a half years in Israel, regrets choosing Uganda over the Holot detention center in the Negev desert. The Ugandan government has done nothing for him, he is about to spend the last of his money, and he has had no success finding a job.[183] Holot, at least, feeds its detainees.

Anwar Suleiman Arbab, who fled Sudan for Israel in 2008, said, "If it's between going back to Africa or to jail in Israel, I'll go to jail."[184]

The UN Refugee Agency (UNHCR) in Rwanda knows of only nine deportees who have remained in that country.[185] The rest have undertaken frightful journeys through conflict zones in Libya, Sudan, and South Sudan.

Israel's deportation plan touched a nerve among Holocaust survivors, rabbis, pilots, retired diplomats, Jewish human rights groups, and ordinary citizens. On February 24, 2018, a crowd of twenty thousand rallied in Tel Aviv, where most of the Africans live. Demonstrators held signs affirming, "We're all humans" and, "Refugees and residents refuse to be enemies."[186] Appeals rang out for Israelis to hide migrants in their attics and cellars, much like Europeans hid Jews from Nazis. These Israeli Jews recognize the resemblance between stateless Africans and once stateless Jews who fled Europe to create Israel, a nation of refugees. Their concern for Africans is a genuine expression of the inborn capacity to connect with the humanity of the other. This begs the question: Why are Jews who fight to humanize Israeli policy toward Africans unwilling to fight to humanize Israeli policy toward Palestinians?

If Israel's expulsion of Africans touches a nerve, why hasn't its expulsion of Palestinians touched a similar nerve? The answer is that whatever prejudices liberal Jews might have about Africans, they are not convincing enough to inhibit either their empathy or their conscience. In contrast, the prejudices toward Palestinians they grow up with are so imprinted on their minds that they do inhibit empathy and conscience. The danger empathy for Palestinians poses is that it would open Jewish hearts to the realization that Israel, in the name of all Jews, has stolen a preponderance of the land and dispossessed its natives. Empathy would awaken them to the inhumanity of the Zionist project, relieve them of their personal and collective images of their people as singularly humane, and force them to confront the reality that Jews are as capable of crimes against humanity as the people who once committed crimes against them. For most, this truth is too hard to bear, so they conceive or find alternative "truths" that preserve their self-images. One such truth is that God's covenant with the Jewish people makes them, not the Palestinian people, the custodians of the Holy Land. Another is that their historical suffering entitles them to special treatment no one else is entitled to and greater leeway in how they treat other people.

On April 2, 2018, Netanyahu yielded to the demands of activists opposing deportation and announced he was canceling his plan and granting permanent status to at least 16,250 Africans. With the cooperation of the United Nations High Commissioner for Refugees, Israel would resettle the rest in western countries. Six hours later, reacting to a backlash from his right-wing base, the prime minister rescinded his announcement.[187] Fourteen hours after that he canceled the agreement with the UNHCR altogether and falsely accused the New Israel Fund, and sources in the European Union, of pressuring the Rwandan government not to accept "infiltrators" from Israel who were "forcibly deported."[188]

The NIF, a US based non-profit organization, was created over thirty years ago to actualize the promise made in Israel's Declaration of the Establishment of the State of Israel to "ensure complete equality of social and political rights to all its inhabitants irrespective of religion, race or sex."[189] Its leadership responded:

> Prime Minister Benjamin Netanyahu has once again resorted to lies about the New Israel Fund in order to score cheap political points. The New Israel Fund had nothing to do with Rwanda's decision to refuse to participate in the Prime Minister's cruel mass deportation plan. It is pathetic, shameful, and a stain on Israel in the global arena that the Prime Minister would blame Israel's human rights defenders for his ineptitude and his immoral policies.[190]

A few weeks after defaming the NIF, Netanyahu vowed to reopen the Holot and Saharonim prisons, which once held thousands of asylum seekers, but which Israel had closed earlier in 2018.[191]

13

Favoring One Side at the Expense of the Other

The greatest destabilizing element in the Middle East and the cause of all other problems in the region is Israel's policies toward the Palestinians and U.S. support for it.[192] – Saudi Foreign Minister Prince Saud, March 2, 1997

Left unresolved, the Palestine-Israel conflict will become a religious conflict of global dimension. – King Abdullah II of Jordan, at the Munich Security Conference, February 2016[193]

ON MAY 14, 2018, WHILE members of the Trump and Netanyahu administrations were sipping champagne at a ceremony celebrating the opening of the American embassy in Jerusalem, Israeli police were outside, beating and arresting Palestinian protesters. Jewish counter-protesters, chanting, "Burn them," "Shoot them," "Kill them," egged the police on.[194] President Donald Trump's December 6, 2017 decision to move the US embassy from Tel Aviv and to recognize Jerusalem as the capital of the Jewish state nullifies America's letter of assurance—sent during the 1991 Madrid peace conference—and provisions of the 1993

Oslo Accords that multilateral and final status negotiations would decide how Jerusalem would be apportioned. It reverses decades of American policy, gives legitimacy to an illegal occupation, emboldens the state's right-wing, and diminishes the prospects for peace. As if to prove the point, on December 31, a few weeks after Trump's decision, the Likud Central Committee voted unanimously in favor of a resolution calling for the formal annexation of the West Bank and an increase in settlements. Science, Technology and Space Minister Ofir Akunis explained the committee's vote:

> The first clause in the Likud constitution is that the right to Israel was given to the Jewish people. Two states for two peoples is a concept that has disappeared from the world. And to my joy, U.S. President [Donald] Trump is sitting in the White House and does not accept this mistaken concept.[195]

Following the committee's lead, the 120-seat Knesset passed an amendment that raised the number of MK votes required to turn over part of East Jerusalem to "a foreign party" from a simple majority of sixty-one to eighty. By making it more difficult to legislate recognition of East Jerusalem as the capital of a Palestinian state, the government reaffirmed its rejection of two states for two peoples. Public Security Minister Gilad Erdan left no doubt: "We are telling the world that it doesn't matter what the nations of the world say. The time has come to express our biblical right to the land."[196]

While Israeli police were preoccupied with the protesters outside the embassy walls, IDF soldiers fifty miles away were confronting thousands of demonstrators—men, women, and children—inside the Gaza Strip. Aside from their frustration over the US embassy's relocation, Gazans, over 70 percent of whom are refugees, were protesting Israel's stranglehold over their lives and the lives of their children. They were reaching out to a world they have no access to, declaring their right to live in dignity, and crying out to Israel to give them the freedom to return to the towns and villages it expelled their families from in 1948 and 1967. Their pleas were met with violence. That day alone, trained snipers, who were stationed behind earth mounds on the Israeli side of the fence and whose firing positions were well over one hundred meters from the demonstration, took the lives of fifty-eight unarmed Gazans, including children, and injured three thousand. The bullets they used were fabricated to leave survivors maimed for life. Every casualty was on the Gaza Strip side of the fence.

Israel depicted the demonstration as a Hamas-instigated event and a threat to its citizens, but it was part of a grassroots-organized Great March of Return that began on March 30 and ended on Nakba Day, May 15, one day after the embassy opening, though smaller demonstrations continue. Organizers included refugees, students, doctors, lawyers, and civil society associations.

On March 31, 2018, the IDF published a series of tweets on its official Twitter account. One encapsulated its strategy for dealing with the demonstrators: "Yesterday we saw 30,000 people; we arrived prepared and with precise reinforcements; Nothing was carried out uncontrolled; everything was accurate and measured, and we know where every bullet landed."[197] The IDF, which was referring to the fifteen Gazans it killed and the 1,416 it wounded that day, removed the tweet, but not before media sources archived a cached version of it.[198;199]

On April 2, Likud spokesman and Foreign Affairs Director Eli Hazan told Israeli television station i24NEWS that all thirty thousand demonstrators were "legitimate targets."[200] Less than a week later, Defense Minister Avigdor Lieberman explained, "You have to understand, there are no innocent people in the Gaza Strip."[201]

Sticking to the law, the High Commissioner for Human Rights argued that justifying lethal force against civilians requires an "imminent threat to life or deadly injury."[202]

For Israelis, worried that the scene at the Gaza border could become uncontrollable, former Shin Bet director and current Knesset member Avi Dichter went on TV to reassure them: "[The Israeli army] has enough bullets for everyone."[203]

Symptomatic of the sanctimoniousness and moral corruptness Major General Golan warned about, Israel's spokespersons were not above flaunting their indifference to the intolerable conditions and collective punishment their country has imposed on Gaza for years. Golan's is not a lone voice within Israel. In 2014, President Reuven Rivlin, a Likudnik, said, "It's time to admit honestly that Israeli society is sick [and that its Jewish citizens] have forgotten how to be decent human beings."[204]

From the end of March 2018 through March 2019, Israeli snipers killed 277 Palestinians, including fifty-two children, and injured twenty-eight thousand.[205] For perspective, between 1961 and 1989, police killed 140 defectors trying to scale the Berlin Wall that separated East from West Berlin.[206] Israeli soldiers sustained four injuries plus one death.[207]

Philip Luther, Amnesty International's Advocacy Director for the Middle East and North Africa, denounced Israel's response to the March of Return as "another horrific example of the Israeli military using excessive force and live ammunition in a totally deplorable way." He also accused Israel of "what appear to be willful killings constituting war crimes."[208]

With eyewitness accounts, photographs, and videos showing "a pattern of Israeli forces shooting people who posed no imminent threat to life," Human Rights Watch criticized Israel for its "blatant disregard for Palestinian lives" and for "greenlight[ing] the use of live ammunition against demonstrators."[209]

Citing "reasonable grounds to believe that …Israeli soldiers committed violations of international human rights and humanitarian law," the *UN Independent Commission of Inquiry on the 2018 Gaza protests* concurred with HRW, "Some of those violations may constitute war crimes or crimes against humanity…"[210]

In agreement with the IDF's admission that "Nothing was

carried out uncontrolled," the Human Rights Council, an intergovernmental body within the United Nations, found that "Israeli snipers intentionally shot health workers, despite seeing that they were clearly marked as such."[211] HRC added:

> 67. Israeli security forces used lethal force against children who did not pose an imminent threat of death or serious injury to its soldiers. Four of the children were shot as they walked or ran away from the fence. 68. Several children were recognizable as such when they were shot. The commission finds reasonable grounds to believe that Israeli snipers shot them intentionally, knowing that they were children.[212]

> 95. Victims who were hundreds of metres away from the Israeli forces and visibly engaged in civilian activities were shot, as shown by eyewitness accounts, video footage and medical records. Journalists and medical personnel who were clearly marked as such were shot, as were children, women and persons with disabilities.[213]

In the first nineteen days of April 2019, Medicins San Frontieres (Doctors Without Borders) cared for over 500 patients, a "huge majority [of which] have unusually severe wounds to the lower extremities [that will leave them with] serious long-term physical disabilities."[214]

Israel's eleven-year blockade prevents up-to-date medical equipment from entering Gaza, which forces hospitals to treat patients with outmoded procedures. The same mindset that strangles Gaza's health sector is equally stingy when it comes to the issuance of medical exit permits. As a result, surgeons had to amputate in excess of 120 limbs in a twelve month period.[215] In May 2019, Jamie McGoldrick, the UN Humanitarian Coordinator for occupied Palestinian territory, explained that another 1,700

Gazans are likely to lose their limbs in the next two years unless Israel relaxes its exit policy.[216]

Back in Jerusalem, an ebullient Netanyahu thanked President Trump "for having the courage to move the embassy."[217] He boasted, "We are here in Jerusalem, protected by the brave soldiers of the army of Israel."[218]

US Ambassador to Israel David Friedman praised, "the vision, the courage and the moral clarity of one person to whom we owe an enormous and eternal debt of gratitude, President Donald J. Trump."[219] Friedman, a longtime benefactor of the Jewish state's settlement enterprise—the primary obstacle to peace—has disparaged Jews who advocate peace through a two-state solution, which would end settlement expansion, as "worse than kapos."[220]*

Trump's son-in-law and senior adviser to the president Jared Kushner, another settlement patron, spoke of peace and laid the blame for the killings on the unarmed protesters and their children, not the armed snipers who were obeying their government's orders: "As we have seen from the protests of the last month and even today, those provoking violence are part of the problem and not part of the solution."[221] Kushner's sophomoric analysis was ill-conceived and infected with willful blindness. Whenever oppressors deny their fellow human beings hope for a positive future, they plant the seeds of resistance.

Kushner also fantasized that the US and Israel "both believe in human rights."[222] Neither Friedman nor Kushner took a moment to caution Netanyahu to order his "brave" snipers to exercise restraint and respect the human rights of unarmed protesters.

Another "dignitary" at the celebration was Sephardi Chief Rabbi of Israel Yitzhak Yosef, who has likened black people to monkeys and who reserves his "blessing" for a "person with a white father

---

* Kapos (blockheads) were Jewish collaborators in concentration camps who assisted the Nazis in controlling and sometimes murdering Jews.

and mother."[223] Kushner and his wife, Ivanka Trump, capitalized on their privileged racial status and the rabbi's largesse by asking for and receiving his blessing.[224]

Seated in the audience was casino magnate Sheldon Adelson, who has pressed for the US to drop a nuclear bomb on Iran.[225] The self-described "richest Jew in the world" paid for his seat with the eighty-two million dollars he donated in 2016 to the Republican Party and Trump's presidential campaign.[226] Disappointed that he served as a soldier in an American not an Israeli uniform, Adelson has expressed the hope that one of his sons will become an Israeli sniper. [227]

Contrary to Netanyahu and Friedman's assertions that it took courage for Trump to move the American embassy, the president was repaying both Adelson and his Christian evangelical base for helping him get elected.

Highlighting a frightening kinship between Israel, the United States, and that base, Robert Jeffress, pastor of the First Baptist megachurch in Dallas, Texas and a spiritual adviser to Trump, delivered an opening prayer in which he lauded the president's leadership and informed the Almighty: "[Trump] stands on the right side of You."[228]

When Trump first authorized the embassy move, Jeffress told CNN, "God gave Jerusalem–and the rest of the Holy Land–to the Jewish people."[229]

In a 2010 interview, Jeffress said, "You can't be saved being a Jew."[230] He has also theologized: "Not only do religions like Mormonism, Islam, Judaism, Hinduism …lead people away from God, they lead people to an eternity of separation from God in Hell."[231] Jeffress's imperviousness to the cries of Palestinians and his inability to recognize his common humanity with all peoples is the epitome of separation from God in Hell.

Former presidential candidate Mitt Romney tweeted, "Such a religious bigot should not be giving the prayer that opens the United States Embassy in Jerusalem."[232]

One can be sure that in the eyes of Israel's government, Jeffress's belief that Islam is "a heresy from the pit of Hell" mitigates his anti-Semitic views, but his inclusion at this long-prayed-for event must come as a shock to any Jew who recognizes that Israel came into being as a refuge from anti-Semitism.[233]

In the next chapter, I look further into Israel's exploitation of anti-Semitism when I compare the views of former president Jimmy Carter with those of Reverend John Hagee, founder of the seven million-strong Christians United for Israel (CUFI) and another guest at the celebration. Hagee offered the closing benediction in which he thanked God "for President Donald Trump's courage in acknowledging to the world a truth that was established 3,000 years ago—that Jerusalem is and always shall be the eternal capital of the Jewish people."[234] Against a backdrop of Palestinian demonstrators demanding the same rights the Israeli forces killing and wounding them take for granted, Hagee, who has praised American support for Israel as "God's foreign policy," assured the crowd that Trump's "courage" was a reminder to "the dictators of the world that America and Israel are forever united."[235;236]

14

"Our Most Dependable Friends"

How, indeed, is a mind to become
conscious of its own bias when
that bias springs from a communal
flight from understanding and is
supported by the whole texture of
civilization? – Bernard Lonergan[237]

I F SOMEONE YOU CARE ABOUT is behaving irrationally, do you make excuses for them or do you speak candidly and persuade them to take responsibility for the harm they are causing themselves and others? If you were the one misbehaving would you rather a friend tell you a hard truth that can help you take notice of and modify your behavior or would you rather your friend overlook your behavior so you can continue on your self-destructive course? Most of Israel's critics are friends who have elected to tell a hard truth. Their criticism is not meant to harm Israelis. It is meant to prevent Israelis from harming Palestinians. Their earnest view is that exempting a single people from its obligations under international law causes harm to all peoples. These critics agitate for equal rights for all because they know that equal rights lead to peace. In addition, by opposing policies that dehumanize Palestinians, Israel's Jewish critics also aspire to rescue the integrity of their religious tradition. How does their commitment to equality and human rights make them bigots of any kind? If criticizing deliberate violations of international law is bigotry, what is turning one's back on the suffering of millions? Consider these passages:

> The Arabs must acknowledge openly and specifically that Israel is a reality and has a right to live in peace, behind secure and recognized borders, and with a firm Arab pledge to terminate any further acts of violence against the legally constituted nation of Israel.[238]

> Israel's right to exist within recognized borders–and to live in peace–must be accepted by Palestinians and all other neighbors.[239]

The man who made these statements has been labeled an anti-Semite, a bigot, and a Nazi sympathizer, but from my perspective he is a true friend of Israel. His name is Jimmy Carter, and anyone who has read or listened to his accounts of his time in Israel knows he loves the land and its people. But what makes Carter the best friend Israel has ever had was his skill in crafting peace between the Jewish state and Egypt. In 1967, when Israel defeated the armies of Egypt, Syria, and Jordan, it captured the Sinai Peninsula and Gaza Strip from Egypt, the Golan Heights and Shebaa Farms from Syria, and the West Bank and East Jerusalem from Jordan. Upon Nasser's death in August 1970, Anwar Sadat succeeded to Egypt's presidency. With his most pressing national concern the return of the Sinai, Sadat began making peace overtures to his neighbor. Despite knowing an injudicious response could lead to war, Prime Minister Golda Meir rebuffed him.[240]

In December 1970, Defense Minister Moshe Dayan advised Meir that repositioning Israeli troops twenty miles further back from the Suez Canal would lessen Egypt's motivation to go to war. Meir rejected Dayan's advice, a decision she would later regret. Over two years passed until February 25–26, 1973, when National Security Advisers Hafez Ismail of Egypt and Henry Kissinger of the United States held talks in Armonk, New York. Ismail conveyed Egypt's readiness to make peace with Israel in exchange for its withdrawal from the Sinai Peninsula and the granting of self-determination to the Gaza Strip. Ismail accepted that negotiations regarding the West Bank, including East Jerusalem and the Golan Heights, would be left to Jordan and Syria, though he stressed, "the Arab part of Jerusalem is Arab."[241] Kissinger passed Ismail's offer on to Meir, but the prime minister was too fixated on establishing settlements in the Sinai to bother reviewing the offer with her cabinet. Kissinger said of her, "She considered Israel militarily impregnable; there was, strictly speaking, no need for change."[242]

Frustrated with Israel's occupation of the Sinai and impatient to restore the honor lost to Arab nations in 1967, Egypt and its allies attacked Israel on Yom Kippur, the holiest day of the Jewish calendar, October 6, 1973. During the next three weeks, nearly three thousand Israelis died, a loss that on a per capita basis was three times America's death toll during its decade-long entanglement in Vietnam. Estimated casualty numbers for Egypt and Syria were 15,000 and 3,500. Although the Egyptian military failed to reclaim the Sinai, it proved itself adept at inflicting significant damage.

In November 1973, one month after the war's end, Meir expressed remorse for her failure to take Dayan's advice and pull back from the Suez Canal. She left office eight months later. By 1978, its armed forces rebuilt, Sadat's urgency to reclaim the Sinai made another act of aggression inevitable. Desperate for peace, yet powerless to bring it about, Israel turned to the United States and to President Carter. Carter's dexterity in keeping two sworn enemies, Prime Minister Begin and President Sadat, at the negotiating table culminated in the 1978 Camp David Accords. Six months later, Begin and Sadat signed the Egypt-Israel Peace Treaty, which resembles Sadat's overtures of 1970–71 and the offer Ismail presented to Kissinger. Had Meir been less complacent about her country's impregnability, she could have avoided war, but her obsession with acquiring more territory took priority over the security of her citizens. In her 2011 article, "Israel's Leaders Sacrifice the People for Their Own Ego," Knesset member Merav Michaeli lamented:

> For 44 years, the regime in Israel has forced its citizens, the vast majority of whom want peace and do not want the settlements, to continue to die on the front and to be blown up on the home front, simply because it can.[243]

With Egypt removed from its ranks, no Arab force or combination of forces has since posed a credible threat to Israel. Neither has any other American president done as much to ensure Israel's security as Jimmy Carter. In speaking about the president's achievement, Shlomo Ben-Ami said: "That the dramatic encounter between two extraordinary political figures like Begin and Sadat should not have been allowed to decline into another failure had much to do with the leadership of President Carter."[244]

Compare Carter's statements above with the words of John Hagee, who has said the Holocaust happened, "because God said my top priority for the Jewish people is to get them to come back to the land of Israel."[245] The reverend preaches that Theodore Herzl "went to the Jews of Europe and said, 'come and join me in the land of Israel.' So few went, Herzl went into a depression. Those who came founded Israel; those who did not went through the hell of the Holocaust."[246]

Because only a small number heeded Herzl's call, the Nazis appeared on God's behalf to chase them from Europe and shepherd them to Palestine. Adolf Hitler, who was born from a lineage of "accursed, genocidally murderous half-breed Jews," was tasked with expediting God's will of having the Jews re-establish the State of Israel. [247;248]

For Hagee, "Hitler was a hunter. And the Bible says, 'they shall hunt [the Jews] from every mountain and from every hill and from out of the holes of the rocks.'"[249*]

---

*   The biblical passage Hagee refers to is Jeremiah 16:16.

In his mind, Jews "have everything but spiritual life," and, "spiritually blind and deaf" Jews brought the Holocaust down upon themselves: "It was the disobedience and rebellion of the Jews …that gave rise to the opposition and persecution that they experienced beginning in Canaan and continuing to this very day."[250;251]

Notwithstanding his anti-Semitic theology, Hagee, who raises millions yearly for Israeli settlements, is, to borrow Herzl's phrase, a "dependable friend" of Israel. Dispensationalists like Hagee do not believe in a Holy Land shared by Muslims and Jews, Christians and Jews, or all three together.[*] Peace is incompatible with their theology, which celebrates the tribal consciousness of "us" against "them" and is oblivious of or selective toward Jesus's teachings on love and compassion. They believe the ethnic cleansing of the Palestinian people to make way for the Jewish people will usher in the Rapture, during which believers will ascend to Heaven and be united with Jesus. Seven years of Tribulation will follow, ending in Armageddon, a battle between the forces of good and evil. In the midst of the battle, Jesus will return to defeat the Anti-Christ—described by Hagee as, "at least …partially Jewish, as was Hitler"—and establish the Second Coming, God's promised kingdom.[252†] Christians will then return from Heaven, while Jews will face a choice either to repent their "spiritual blindness," accept the once-spurned Jesus as their Messiah, and convert to Christianity, or be cast into the fires of Hell. Dispensationalists are also known as Christian Zionists, but inasmuch as the Second Coming, like the Final Solution, envisions

[*] Popular among evangelical Christians, dispensationalist theology "divides history into distinct ages or dispensations. According to this teaching, when first-century Jews rejected Jesus, a new 'church age' began in which Christians would act as 'God's chosen people.'" (Jonathan Merritt, "Understanding the Evangelical obsession with Israel," *America, The Jesuit Review*, December 11, 2017, americamagazine.org/politics-society/2017/12/11/understanding-evangelical-obsession-israel).

[†] A 2010 Pew Research Center survey found that 41% of the American public expects Jesus Christ to return by 2050. Among white evangelicals, 58% expect his return. ("Public Sees a Future Full of Promise and Peril," June 22, 2010, 4, people-press.org/2010/06/22/public-sees-a-future-full-of-promise-and-peril).

an end to world Jewry, categorizing them as either Christian or Zionist contradicts the original meaning of both ideologies.

The difference between Hagee and Carter illustrates how confused our thinking becomes when we have not dealt with irrational fears of extermination and unexamined enemy images. Supporters of Israel revere as a dependable friend a fundamentalist who blames the Jewish people for the Holocaust, assigns to Adolf Hitler the stature of Moses, and prays for the eventual demise of Israel, and revile as an anti-Semite a Nobel Peace Prize laureate who offers constructive criticism so that Israel can live in peace with its neighbors. This redefining of anti-Semitism leads to the conclusion that indifference to the lives of Palestinians, refusal to learn the documented history of the Israel-Palestine tragedy, acceptance of Israel's justifications for its daily human rights violations, and disregard for international law exempt a person from charges of anti-Semitism. A product of an unexamined and dualistic mind, this configuration of existential fear and confusion portrays the Jewish people as inhumane and perpetuates unconsciousness of the horrors made possible by blind loyalty to Israel.

15

Inciting Anti-Semitism Cannot Cure Anti-Semitism

*Ultimately considered, evil is done
not so much by evil people, but
by good people who do not know
themselves.* – Reinhold Niebuhr[253]

T**RUE LEADERS STRIVE TO RAISE** the consciousness of their
constituents, but in a political climate where money dictates
policy, a majority of lawmakers are afraid to stand up to interest
groups even when they represent a foreign country. Twenty-seven
state legislatures have adopted laws that strike at the heart of the
BDS movement by making it illegal to do business with or reward
contracts to companies and individuals that boycott, divest from,
or sanction Israel. Another fourteen are considering comparable
legislation. An investigation by the Center for Public Integrity found
that pro-Israel activists wrote these laws and that their language is
nearly identical from one state to the next.[254] Unaware of basic facts
about Israel-Palestine, and intimidated and manipulated by Israeli
loyalists, American lawmakers repeat the Jewish state's contention
that appeals by the BDS movement for Israel to comply with
international law are anti-Semitic hate speech, despite knowing that
a large number of Jews support the appeals.

On May 2, 2017, as he was signing anti-BDS legislation into
law at the Austin, Texas Jewish Community Center, Texas Governor

Greg Abbott said, "Anti-Israel policies are anti-Texas policies and we will not tolerate such actions against an important ally."[255] On the heels of judgments against Kansas and Arizona, federal courts ruled Texas's anti-BDS legislation unconstitutional because it infringes upon Americans' rights to freedom of expression. To circumvent these and probable future rulings, in January 2019 the US Senate advanced a motion to proceed with debate on the *Strengthening America's Security in the Middle East Act*. Title Four of the Act would shield states from lawsuits that contest their authority to punish sectors of the public for activities that "inflict economic harm on …Israel or Israeli-controlled territories…"[256] Jewish organizations J Street and T'ruah (the rabbinic call for human rights) countered by circulating a letter signed by over 300 rabbis and cantors asking federal and state legislators to oppose these unconstitutional measures.[257]

Not only do lawmakers vote on legislation that affects millions, they howl "anti-Semitism" whenever human rights organizations publish reports criticizing Israel's abuse of children. Their indignation is insincere because they know that criticizing Israel for denying Palestinians their civil rights is no more anti-Semitic than it is anti-American to criticize the United States for separating migrant children from their parents. One of many non-governmental organizations that attempt to shake Congress out of its willful blindness, Defense for Children International has noted: "Israel is the only country in the world that automatically and systematically prosecutes children in military courts that lack basic and fundamental fair trial rights and protections."[258]

While bills that shelter Israel from accountability for its behavior are routinely passed with huge majorities, only twenty-four members of the House of Representatives have stood up to sponsor H.R. 2407, the *Promoting Human Rights for Palestinian Children Living Under Israeli Military Occupation Act*. The Act "require[s] that United States funds do not support military detention, interrogation, abuse, or ill-treatment of Palestinian children…"

Members of Congress have the power to bring Israel to its

senses, but they have to prioritize the well-being of defenseless children over their re-election prospects, and they have to listen to their consciences. If they do, then they can pave the way toward an authentic peace process.

The Anti-Semitism Awareness Act of 2018, S. 2940/H.R. 5924A, is a pending bi-partisan congressional bill that directs the US Department of Education to add criticism of Israel to the definition of anti-Semitism drafted in 2010 by the State Department's Special Envoy to Monitor and Combat Anti-Semitism.* The Act would penalize criticism of the Israeli narrative, hasbara and all, but do nothing to curtail false accusations and criticism of the Palestinian narrative.† In combating alleged bigotry toward Jews, the Act implies that Palestinians are a nation of bigots. After all, what Palestinian would not be critical of the horrors that Israel has unleashed upon their families for generations?

The ACLU opposes the bill, warning that college administrators are likely to restrict constitutionally protected speech out of fear the government will investigate their institutions for tolerating criticism of Israel.[259] If the bill becomes law, it will put a damper on the public's access to information about the history of the two peoples, and it will lessen any incentive Israel might have to cease its draconian treatment of Palestinians and Judaization of Palestine. By immunizing Israel from transparency and accountability, the Anti-Semitism Awareness Act will anger people all over the world who believe in a level playing field. The inevitable result will be the

---

* US State Department definition: "Anti-Semitism is a certain perception of Jews, which may be expressed as hatred toward Jews. Rhetorical and physical manifestations of anti-Semitism are directed toward Jewish or non-Jewish individuals and/or their property, toward Jewish community institutions and religious facilities." (Fact Sheet, SPECIAL ENVOY TO MONITOR AND COMBAT ANTI-SEMITISM, Washington, DC, June 8, 2010, Capitol.tn.gov/Bills/110/Bill/SB2389.pdf).

† Hasbara is Hebrew for explanation. In this context, it refers to propaganda aimed at international audiences.

opposite of the Act's stated intention, with Jews once again coming under attack. In that case, it would behoove Congress to correct its linguistic blunder by renaming the bill the Anti-Semitism *Incitement* Act of 2018.

General Yehoshafat Harkabi was Israel's longest serving chief of military intelligence, its foremost expert on Arab relations, and an adviser to Menachem Begin. In *Israel's Fateful Hour*, he wrote:

> It would be a tragic irony if the Jewish state, which was intended to solve the problem of anti-Semitism, was to become a factor in the rise of anti-Semitism. Israelis must be aware that the price of their mis-conduct is paid not only by them but also by Jews throughout the world.[260]

―――――――――

In the summer of 2017, category 4 Hurricane Harvey battered Dickinson, Texas, which is thirty miles south of Houston and home to twenty thousand. With speeds reaching 130 miles per hour, Harvey carried out seven days of devastation. By the time it moved on, it had destroyed over seven thousand homes and eighty-eight businesses, most of which did not carry flood insurance. Federal, state, and local governments and the generosity of individuals, charitable organizations, and corporations provided millions in grants and donations, which the city earmarked for its distressed citizens and businesses. Hopeful the aid would prop up Dickinson's property values and sales tax revenue, the city council urged affected townspeople to apply for assistance. But there was a catch. The application included a clause titled, *Verification not to Boycott Israel*. It said: "By executing this Agreement below, the Applicant verifies that the Applicant: (1) does not boycott Israel; and (2) will not boycott Israel during the term of this Agreement."[261]

The ACLU slammed the verification as "an egregious violation of the First Amendment, reminiscent of McCarthy-era loyalty oaths."[262]

Faced with a legal challenge, the city removed the offending clause, but its effort to prevent citizens from articulating their heart-felt opposition to Israel's human rights violations, and the moral and financial support the city and churches in the area contribute to the dismantling of Palestine, are themselves violations of basic norms of decency and concern for one's fellow man.

Why would an American city require its residents, some of whom may be Palestinian or friends of Palestinians, to think a certain way regarding a foreign country? The population of Texas is 31 percent evangelical Christian and the Houston area is home to some of the largest evangelical megachurches in the US.[263] Given these conditions, it should come as no surprise that lawmakers would jump at an opportunity to eliminate obstacles to Israel's colonial mission and Jesus's Second Coming, even at the expense of the US Constitution's implied separation of church and state and the right to free speech.

16
Ilhan Omar

We have a mission as humans to love one another, to care for our neighbors, to raise compassionate children and to fully every single day show up and make sure that we are furthering justice. – Ilhan Omar[264]

Especially at a time when white supremacist violence is on the rise, we all need to condemn hate against any religious group – something the current President has shamefully failed to do. – Ilhan Omar[265]

IN THE NOVEMBER 2018 CONGRESSIONAL elections, Minnesota's Ilhan Omar, who spent four years of her childhood in a Kenyan refugee camp after her family fled Somalia's civil war, became the first naturalized citizen of African descent elected to the United States House of Representatives. She and first time representative Rashida Tlaib of Michigan, a Palestinian American whose grandmother lives in the West Bank, are the only Muslim women ever elected to Congress. Both are critical of the Israeli occupation and both applaud the BDS movement's core principle that "Palestinians are entitled to the same rights as the rest of humanity."[266]

In 2012, after tweeting that Israel had "hypnotized the world," Omar was accused of being a "proud Jew hater."[267] She answered: "Drawing attention to the apartheid Israeli regime is far from hating Jews."[268]

Omar had previously spoken out against human rights violations committed by Saudi Arabia and other Islamic governments, so allegations of anti-Semitism on her part were unfounded.

On February 8, 2019, a month after the 116th Congress convened its first session, House Minority Leader Kevin McCarthy (R-CA) swore that if the majority party did not take action against Omar and Tlaib for their outspokenness toward Israel, he would do so himself. Journalist Glenn Greenwald reacted to McCarthy's threat: "It's stunning how much time US political leaders spend defending a foreign nation even if it means attacking free speech rights of Americans."[269]

A few months earlier, McCarthy had used what many commentators consider an anti-Semitic trope when he accused Jewish billionaires George Soros, Tom Steyer, and Michael Bloomberg of trying to "BUY" the November 2018 mid-term elections.[270]

Omar answered McCarthy and Greenwald's tweets with a line from a Puff Daddy song that references Benjamin Franklin's face on the front of $100 bills: "It's all about the Benjamins baby."[271]

Her reply drew a prompt rejoinder from all corners of the political spectrum, with House Speaker Nancy Pelosi and the Democratic leadership reprimanding her for her use of "anti-Semitic tropes and prejudicial accusations about Israel's supporters."[272] Senate Minority Leader Chuck Schumer, among the top ten congressional recipients of campaign donations from pro-Israel organizations, called her words "reprehensible."[273]

American attorney and activist Ady Barkan of the Center for Popular Democracy took a different stance: "As a Jew, an Israeli citizen, and professional lobbyist …I speak from personal experience when I say that AIPAC is tremendously effective, and the lubricant that makes its operation hum is dollar, dollar bills."[274]

Omar apologized the next day: "Anti-Semitism is real and I am grateful for Jewish allies and colleagues who are educating me on the painful history of anti-Semitic tropes. My intention is never to offend my constituents or Jewish Americans as a whole."[275] She also apologized for her "hypnotized" tweet, explaining that she was unfamiliar with the "ugly sentiment" it holds for Jews, and she agreed with *New York Times* journalist Bari Weiss that she had been "sincerely befuddled."[276]

A day later, eager to sow division within the Democratic Party, President Trump, who has a history of Islamophobic and anti-Semitic pronouncements and who never apologizes for anything, dismissed Omar's apology as "lame" and joined McCarthy and Vice-President Mike Pence in demanding that she resign her seat on the Foreign Affairs Committee or leave Congress.[277]*

A congenital liar, who is congenitally incapable of admitting to his mistakes and misrepresentations, Trump uses denial and projection to prop up his false self. The endless accusations of bigotry, treason, and other manufactured evils that he makes against his critics are accurate, even precise, descriptions of himself. As corrupt as anyone in politics, during his presidential campaign he evoked age-old caricatures of Jews when he tweeted a picture of Hillary Clinton and a pile of cash next to the Star of David, inside of which was written, "Most Corrupt Candidate Ever!"[278]

Because Trump brooks no challenges to his ego, self-awareness and personal growth repel him. So does honesty, which is why his circle of advisers is dominated by sycophants. Tormented by an interminable childhood temper tantrum, Trump's raison d'être is to make the world pay for his suffering—his alienation from his humanity. This explains why he is infatuated with Kim Jong-un, Vladimir Putin, and Rodrigo Duterte. As leader of the world's "greatest democracy," his indifference to suffering makes the cruelty of his fellow despots acceptable. Israel has exploited his inattention

---

* For example, in March 2016, Trump said, "I think Islam hates us… There's an unbelievable hatred of us." (Jenna Johnson and Abigail Hauslohner, "'I think Islam hates us': A timeline of Trump's comments about Islam and Muslims," *The Washington Post*, March 20, 2017).

to human rights by exercising its most severe expulsion policies in decades. The Trump administration's zero-tolerance policy, which rips migrant children away from their parents and puts them in cages, is an admission of the president's indifference to the suffering of anyone besides himself.

Mike Pence, Trump's most devoted sycophant, tweeted:

> @Ilhan MN tweets were a disgrace & her apology was inadequate. Anti-Semitism has no place in the United States Congress, much less the Foreign Affairs Committee. Those who engage in anti-Semitic tropes should not just be denounced, they should face consequences for their words.[279]

Like his friend John Hagee, Pence sees himself as a devout Christian, yet the policies he defends are a far cry from the tolerance, compassion, and love that are essential to Jesus's teachings. When the president rails against his detractors, inspires racists, or puts his infantile demands above the welfare of the country, Pence reacts by justifying his superior's acting out. Undeterred by Trump's antagonism toward women, immigrants, Muslims, the nation's intelligence services, or his attempts to divide the country into white nationalists and everyone else, Pence has been his superior's most reliable ally. Neither Trump's comment that right-wing demonstrators in Charlottesville, VA inveighing against Jews ("Jews will not replace us!"), immigrants, and people of color "were some very fine people," nor the anti-Semitic trope he used to attack Hillary Clinton could elicit righteous indignation from Pence. If the vice-president's devotion to Christianity is sincere, he ought to inquire within and contemplate the teachings of Jesus. Otherwise, the self-righteousness he displays toward his political opponents is hypocrisy. And if, as he says, there are consequences to face, then he, for one, ought to face them.

At a town hall gathering on March 1, Omar said:

> I want to talk about the political influence in this
> country that says it is okay for people to push for al-
> legiance to a foreign country. I want to ask: Why is it
> OK for me to talk about the influence of the NRA,
> of fossil fuel industries or Big Pharma, and not talk
> about a powerful lobbying group that is influencing
> policy?[280]

An outpouring of individuals and organizations vilified Omar
once again. Jewish Congressman Eliot Engel (D-NY) said, "it's
unacceptable and deeply offensive to question the loyalty of fellow
American citizens because of their political views, including support
for the Israel-U.S. relationship. ... Representative Omar's comments
leveled that charge by invoking a vile anti-Semitic slur."[281]

AIPAC tweeted, "The charge of dual loyalty not only raises
the ominous specter of classic anti-Semitism, but it is also deeply
insulting to the millions upon millions of patriotic Americans,
Jewish and non-Jewish, who stand by our democratic ally, Israel."[282]

Representative Juan Vargas (D-Calif.) blamed Omar for
perpetuating "anti-Semitic stereotypes," and added, "questioning
support for the U.S.-Israel relationship is unacceptable."[283]

Congresswoman Nita Lowey (D-NY) tweeted, "anti-Semitic
tropes that accuse Jews of dual loyalty ...must ...be roundly
condemned."[284]

Omar answered her critics: "I should not be expected to have
allegiance/pledge support to a foreign country in order to serve my
country in Congress or serve on committee."[285]

Not indebted to special interest groups, Jewish senator Bernie
Sanders defended Omar as "a leader with strength and courage."[286]

The Congressional Black Caucus questioned the wisdom of
singling out a Muslim woman of color while ignoring the bigotry of
Republicans and Donald Trump.[287]

Speaker Pelosi scheduled a vote on a resolution condemning anti-

Semitism and the "insidious, and pernicious history" of Jews being accused of dual loyalty.[288] Although the resolution did not mention Omar by name, it was a retort to her comments. Uncomfortable with the Speaker's narrowness, progressive democrats pressured her to expand the resolution to include anti-Muslim bigotry, white supremacy, and other forms of hatred.

On March 1, a poster associating Omar with 9/11 appeared in the rotunda of the West Virginia Capitol.[289] Democrat Mike Pushkin, who is Jewish and a member of the West Virginia House of Delegates, compared the poster to 1933 Berlin. He asked his fellow delegates to join him in condemning it. Not one Republican did so.[290]

Three weeks later, Omar gave an address at the Council on American-Islamic Relations (CAIR), where she spoke about the "right to a dignified existence and a dignified life" and the bombings of schools and mosques that have taken place in the US since 9/11.[291] She also explained that her use of criticism "is based on what country is violating basic human rights":

> As Muslims, we are called on to stand up for justice and to speak the truth, even if it is against ourselves, our parents and our close relatives …it is important …to make sure that we 're not only holding people that we don't like accountable. *We must also hold those that we love … accountable* [emphasis added].[292]

If those who claim to love Israel held it accountable, there would have been peace long ago.

Omar also called Trump's Muslim ban, "a very hateful policy that has now been fully implemented."[293] She bemoaned

> a world leader in the White House who publicly says Islam hates us, who fuels hate against Muslims, who thinks it is OK to speak about a faith and a whole community in a way that is dehumanizing, vilifying …He knows that there are people that he can influ-

ence to threaten our lives, to diminish our presence,
but what we know …is that love trumps hate[294]

In what turned out to be her most controversial remark, the
congresswoman noted that in the aftermath of 9/11, Muslim-
Americans began "to lose access to [their] civil liberties [because]
some people did something…"[295] Her use of language did not
capture the gravity of that tragic day, but anyone listening to
the speech knew there was no intent on her part to devalue the
tragedy. On April 11, the Rupert Murdoch-controlled, pro-Trump
New York Post retaliated by taking her words out of context and
associating her with terrorism. Splashed across the front page was
the headline, "REP. ILHAN OMAR: 9/11 WAS 'SOME PEOPLE
DID SOMETHING,'" beneath which was a photo of the twin
towers engulfed in flames and these words: "Here's your something.
2,977 people dead by terrorism."

Fearful of a violent backlash, New York's Muslims reacted with
alarm. Debbie Almontaser, secretary of the board of directors for the
Yemeni American Merchant Association in Brooklyn, announced
a boycott of the newspaper and said, "What the *New York Post* is
doing is endangering the lives of American Muslims and people of
color."[296] The Association demanded the *Post* apologize to Omar
and New York's Muslim-American community.[297]

Another Yemeni, Mohammed Alsebri said, "I was shocked. How
a newspaper in New York City would do a front page like that is
crazy… [I]gnorant people will read these words and attack any
Muslim, just like they did after 9/11."[298]

Invigorated by *The Post*'s front page and lusting for revenge,
on April 12, Trump tweeted a video clip of Omar saying, "some
people did something" juxtaposed with footage of the twin towers
burning in the background and a message, "WE WILL NEVER
FORGET!"[299] Picked up by Trump's base the tweet went viral.

Omar responded, "No one person – no matter how corrupt,
inept, or vicious – can threaten my unwavering love for America. I

stand undeterred to continue fighting for equal opportunity in our pursuit of happiness for all Americans."[300]

On Sunday the 14th, Omar reported an increase in death threats, many of which were ascribed to Trump's video tweet.[301] Speaker Pelosi noted that Capitol Police and the Sergeant-at-Arms were conducting a security assessment to ensure the safety of Omar, her staff, and her family.[302] The Speaker added: "The president's words weigh a ton, and his hateful and inflammatory rhetoric creates real danger. President Trump must take down his disrespectful and dangerous video."[303] He did not. A cybersecurity expert found "hundreds of direct threats" to Omar, primarily from white men and women.[304]

In criticizing Israel, Omar's use of language revealed an unfamiliarity with American and Jewish society and with figures of speech that have come to be associated with anti-Semitism, though she did show a willingness to learn from her Jewish colleagues, most of whom are unfamiliar with her background. What could be more healing and gratifying than if Omar's colleagues were to cultivate an interest in learning from her about the pain and heartache the powerless endure when the powerful deny them basic human rights? Those who reject legitimate criticism of Israel have shown little if any misgivings over Israel's refusal to accept responsibility for its mistreatment of Palestinians, more than seven million of whom are refugees.[305] Their willful blindness and indifference to human suffering are far more consequential than Omar's unfamiliarity with their feelings.

Indelicate though it may have been, Omar's "*it's* [emphasis added] all about the Benjamins" comment was not as cavalier as some want to believe. On February 14, 2019, just a few days after her tweet, the Murdoch-owned *Wall Street Journal* tweeted, "Aipac, the pro-Israel lobby, raises more than $100 million a year, which it spends on lobbying politicians for U.S. aid and sending members of Congress to Israel."[306] None of the legislators who were so quick to castigate Omar reacted to the *Journal*, but nobody will ever confuse it with a brown-skinned, hijab-wearing, female Muslim immigrant. It is almost axiomatic that politicians will look the other way if doing so boosts their political prospects, and success requires money. During the 2016 presidential campaign, the top five Clinton and top two Trump donors were Jewish. But the greater truth is that "*it's*" more about the presumption of limited identities than it is about money.

Omar is also correct that some people are guilty of dual loyalty. Do Omar's critics think because Jews have been unfairly accused of this behavior in the past, they can never be guilty of it in the present? Do they think it is impossible to be dually loyal if one is a Jew and that it is anti-Semitic even to think so? The truth is never anti-Semitic, nor is it anti-anyone. If the truth discriminates against Jews, what does that say about Jews? And how should we expect the world to judge American Jews when they consider themselves exempt from dual loyalty allegations even when they put the government of Israel's needs ahead of the needs of the United States? I always felt a greater allegiance to Israel than to the US even though Zionism was never discussed at home and was rarely discussed at synagogue. What my community discussed was how the world's indifference to the Holocaust made Israel a moral necessity. I now see that the overriding moral necessity is to recognize that all human beings are deserving of equal rights and that we are part of one interconnected family whose true nature transcends politics, religion, ideology, race, or nationality.

Foreseeable as they were, Jewish congress members' reactions to Omar's statements reveal how seductive core identities can be. During his four-and-a-half decades of public service, Senate minority leader Chuck Schumer, the most influential Jewish vote in Congress, has been a consistent voice for liberal values. But when it comes to Israel his willful blindness obligates him to disregard those values: "Of course, we say it's *our* land, the Torah says it, but [Palestinians] don't believe in the Torah. So that's the reason there is not peace."[307] That's the reason he voted, along with Eliot Engel and the Republicans, against the Iran nuclear deal (JCPOA). Swayed by Benjamin Netanyahu's more than twenty-five years of verbal attacks on Iran, and his false alarms that the Islamic Republic was approaching nuclear weapons capability, Schumer's justification was that Iran posed a threat to Israel.[308] If Iran posed a threat to Israel—not the other way around—why would Schumer have preferred a status quo in which Iran was only a few months away from producing a nuclear weapon when the JCPOA, which contains several provisions that last from ten to twenty-five years, postponed that eventuality by at least a decade?[309] If he thought of Iran as a threat to any country other than Israel, he would not have subscribed to the irrational thinking that characterizes the Republican party, home to a sizeable number of Islamophobes and dispensationalists. Schumer voted against the deal because he is Jewish. Why else would a Jewish legislator have a history of forsaking his liberal and democratic values in exchange for policies that deny Palestinians the most fundamental of rights; and why else would that legislator be so negligent as to avoid learning documented facts about Israel-Palestine—documentation that would disabuse him of his idealistic images of Israel and help him regain his customary sense of justice and decency? Schumer did not look at the deal through the eyes of an American loyal to the United States. He looked at the deal through the eyes of a Jew loyal to Israel. Dual loyalty was at the heart of Schumer's vote against the JCPOA and his criticism of Omar.

The emotional attachments that accompany identity are hard to let go of. They blind us to reality and seduce us into making selfish evaluations. The minority leader's willful blindness will backfire on him. Like the probable consequences of the Anti-Semitism Awareness Act, anger over Israel's license to conduct itself in ways that bring censure to other countries will generate enemy images of the Jewish people and arouse anti-Semitism.

What about Christians, who are so blinded by their devotion to preparing the Holy Land for Christ's return they do not notice or care that the indigenous people have been deprived of their human rights? They too practice dual loyalty, as do most legislators in the twenty-seven states that defied the Constitution by voting for bills that grant immunity from accountability to a lone country. These Americans are frightened of or beholden to the Israel lobby, but before they or anyone can show genuine loyalty to Israel or to the Jewish people, they first need to show loyalty to the truth. Then they will see the wisdom in holding the Jewish state accountable to the same laws and conventions they expect other countries to obey.

Omar's comment that supporters of Israel are "hypnotized" is compelling because it implies unconsciousness and willful blindness. Rather than finding it offensive, if supporters mustered the decency to inquire into Israel-Palestine, most would become aware of the offensiveness of their own beliefs. Likewise, by attacking her for telling the truth, they proved her right. Omar offered them a mirror of their minds, but they were blind to its reflection. If the veil of ignorance were to fall from their eyes, they would see that in the name of humanity they defend inhumanity; in the name of justice, they defend injustice; and that their accusations of anti-Semitism are foils that disguise their insensitivity and prejudice toward the Palestinian people and the Muslim world.

In 2011, an arm of the Gallup organization published a poll that compared the attitudes of Muslim-Americans with Americans of other religious affiliations. The poll asked, "Some people think that for the military to target and kill civilians is sometimes justified, while others think that kind of violence is never justified. What is your opinion?" Seventy-eight percent of Muslims, 39 percent of Catholics, 38 percent of Protestants, and 43 percent of Jews answered that it is *never* justified for the military to kill civilians, while 21 percent of Muslims, 58 percent of both Catholics and Protestants, and 52 percent of Jews agreed that it is *sometimes* justified.[310]

When the poll changed "the military" to "an individual person or a small group of persons," 89 percent of Muslims, 71 percent of both Catholics and Protestants, and 75 percent of Jews said the killings were never justified.[311]

17
Clarifying One-Sided Arguments

The whole world is against us
Never mind, we'll overcome
....
And everybody who's against us
Let him go to hell
– 1969 song referring to the
Israeli collective spirit.[312]

We were here before you, and we will
be here after you. – Avi Dichter[313]

I N THIS CHAPTER, I DISCUSS a few of the arguments that constitute the Israeli narrative. I understand that by bringing them into alignment with historical documentation, I am venturing into forbidden terrain. My chutzpah in breaking the taboo that insulates Israel's self-image from the truth has already gotten me in trouble with loyalists, whose tribal thinking interferes with their ability to empathize with the other. They reject my promise that impartial research combined with self-inquiry can release them from a pathological fear of the other and the illusion of victimhood. Their rejection does not imply faithlessness in the power of inquiry; it implies that they are not in touch with either their fear or their victimhood. Their state of denial leads them to accuse me of dishonesty and one-sidedness for exposing the dishonesty and one-sidedness of their positions. Not only are their accusations projections, they are disingenuous because as long as they refuse to research the subject, they have no way of determining who is or is not being one-sided. Facts and logic are often the first casualties in emotionally charged debates. The tendency to believe what we want to believe and to ignore or reject what we do not want to believe is so forceful as to drown out common sense and rational thinking. Whenever research contradicts cherished beliefs, loyalists fabricate, deny, or take history out of context. No matter if they block all paths to peace, they will then incorporate these fabrications and denials into the chronicle of Israel-Palestine. Loyalists are driven by an internal logic that ignores the dehumanization demanded by Israel's matrix of control over the lives of Palestinians. In *A Durable Peace: Israel and Its Place Among the Nations*, Benjamin Netanyahu portrays this matrix as "a liberal policy aimed at radically improving the lives of the Arabs."[314] Few Palestinians would concur that living as stateless residents under military occupation has improved their lives, and no reasonable person familiar with the history would find value in Netanyahu's statement.

———————

The arguments below have persisted for decades and are so deep-seated that loyalists extol them as indelible truths. Formidable obstacles to peace and products of a misguided compulsion to be right, they preserve a false sense of self. For example, in the 1950s, while ignoring peace overtures from Colonel Nasser, David Ben-Gurion labeled the Egyptian president, "the Hitler of the Middle East," a catchphrase that made a deep impression on me as a young member of a community still haunted by memories of the Holocaust. The images Ben-Gurion's language conjured in my imagination contributed to a distrust of Arabs and an irrational fear for my people's survival.

Years before Nasser came to power or Israel became a state, Jewish leaders had targeted one Arab in particular, Haj Amin al-Husseini, Grand Mufti of Jerusalem, and a fierce opponent of Zionism.

Husseini came to symbolize the Arab thirst for the extermination of the Jewish people. Palestinians, however, did not choose him for Grand Mufti. Under Ottoman rule, it was traditional for a Muslim electoral college to nominate three candidates for *Mufti* of Jerusalem.* Husseini, who was in his mid-twenties, was not among the nominees, but in 1921 British High Commissioner Herbert Samuel bypassed tradition, invented the office of *Grand* Mufti of Jerusalem, and named the young man to the post.[315] Behind the scenes, Husseini's selection was the work of Ernest T. Richmond, a member of the British High Commissioner's secretariat and a declared enemy of Zionist policy.[316]

In 2012, Prime Minister Netanyahu branded al-Husseini "one of the leading architects" of the Final Solution.[317] Three years later, while speaking before the 37th Zionist Congress, Netanyahu distorted history:

> Hitler didn't want to exterminate the Jews at the time, he wanted to expel the Jews. And Haj Amin al-Husseini went to Hitler and said, "If you expel them, they'll all come here." "So what should I do with them?" he asked. He said, "Burn them."[318]

The backlash to Netanyahu's speech was severe. Isaac Herzog, opposition leader in the Knesset, demanded Netanyahu retract his claim "immediately, as it minimizes the Holocaust, Nazism and … Hitler's part in our people's horrible disaster."[319]

Yad Vashem chief historian Dina Porat said Netanyahu was "completely erroneous, on all counts."[320]

Husseini did hate Jews, probably because of what they had done to his people, but his efforts to build a pro-Nazi movement among Palestinians never gained any traction. The prime minister's depiction of Husseini as responsible for the Holocaust and as an evil embodiment of Palestinians has reinforced the belief within much of Jewish society that today's Palestinians are yesterday's Nazis.

---

* Palestine was part of the Ottoman Empire from 1517 to 1917.

Character assassination and the fear it triggers give leaders platforms from which they can market racist policies as necessary for national security, no matter how self-destructive the policies are and how insecure they make Jews feel.

Haj Amin al-Husseini is a name few American Jews have heard of, but he holds a conspicuous place within the halls of Yad Vashem which, besides being a memorial to the victims of the Holocaust, is a depository of biographical material on the criminals who plotted to eradicate world Jewry. In its four-volume *Encyclopedia of the Holocaust*, published in 1990, the entry on Husseini is longer than the entry on Adolf Eichmann, longer than the entries on Heinrich Himmler and Reinhard Heydrich combined, and more than twice the length of the entries on Joseph Goebbels or Hermann Goering. The only biographical material that surpasses Husseini's in length, and only by a small margin, is Adolf Hitler's.[321]

———

One of Israel's founding myths is that Arab leaders instructed Palestinians to flee their homes during the 1948 Nakba. Therefore, Israel is not responsible for the Palestinian refugee problem. Anyone who makes this claim must think that if Arab leaders had not instructed Palestinians to flee, the Jewish military would have allowed them to stay. If that had been the case, Israel's Palestinian population would have exceeded its Jewish population and the Zionist dream of a Jewish state would have died. In 1959, Oxford University-educated historian Walid Khalidi proved the claim to be a falsehood. Two years later, Irish scholar and UN diplomat Erskine Childers independently corroborated Khalidi's findings.[322] By examining the archives of Arab governments and newspapers and the reports of the CIA and the BBC, which monitored and transcribed every Arab radio broadcast of 1948, both men proved that Arab leaders never gave such instructions. To the contrary, they broadcast appeals to Palestinians *not* to flee their homes. There were even times they threatened to punish anyone who left their village or city.[323]

Benny Morris's research supports Khalidi and Childers: "There is no evidence that the Arab states and the AHC [Arab Higher Committee] wanted a mass exodus or issued blanket orders or appeals to flee."[324]

In June 1948, the Arab section of Israel's Intelligence Service produced a paper titled, "Migration of Eretz Yisrael Arabs between December 1, 1947 and June 1, 1948." It said, "Without a doubt, [direct Jewish hostile actions against Arab communities] were the main factor in the population movement."[325]

When asked by the UN to account for its claim that Palestinian flight was encouraged by Arab leaders, the Israeli Foreign Ministry library could not produce a scintilla of supporting evidence.[326] False information like this has influenced westerners to dismiss the Nakba and accuse the aggrieved as the side responsible for distorting evidence and disseminating propaganda.

With the adoption of General Assembly Resolution 273 on May 11, 1949, the United Nations admitted Israel into its membership, contingent upon its promise to obey international law, including all current and future UN resolutions, without exception. Resolution 273 noted that "[Israel] unreservedly accepts the obligations of the United Nations Charter and undertakes to honour them from the day when it becomes a member of the United Nations." It also referenced UN General Assembly Resolution 194, which resolves that "refugees wishing to return to their homes and live at peace with their neighbours should be permitted to do so at the earliest practicable date." Unfaithful to its promises, Israel has barred a Palestinian return. In July 1950, the Knesset passed the Law of Return, which gives Jews from anywhere in the world the right to occupy lands "stolen"—to use Ben-Gurion's language—from their lawful inhabitants.

———

Another argument loyalists use to defend Israel's actions involves Jewish acceptance and Palestinian rejection of the UN Partition Plan, Resolution 181, which the UN General Assembly adopted on November 29, 1947. As alluded to earlier, Israeli loyalists, a majority of whom consider the United Nations an anti-Semitic body, defend the Jewish state's refusal to comply with resolutions that criticize its behavior, yet they have no compunctions in citing this resolution as evidence of Israel's sincerity in wanting to make peace.* It is important to remember that the ego-identity will ignore logic and fair play and use almost any tactic to justify its self-righteousness.

Compromised by its failure to obtain the consent of the majority population, Resolution 181 granted 56 percent of British Mandate Palestine, including 80 percent of the coastline, to the Jewish people, who made up 30 percent of the population and owned less than 7 percent of the land. It granted 43 percent of the land to the Palestinians and designated the remaining 1 percent, Jerusalem and Bethlehem, as a corpus separatum under the authority of the United Nations.

Although passage of 181 was but a partial realization of a Greater Israel, it was also vindication for years of effort by Zionists who eagerly accepted a 700 percent increase in the land they controlled.† David Ben-Gurion and Chaim Weizmann had long emphasized the necessity of settling for whatever territory the international community was prepared to hand over to the Jewish people. Weizmann: "The Jews would be fools not to accept [partition] even if [the land they were allocated] were the size of a table cloth."327

In 1937, Ben-Gurion wrote to his son Amos: "[E]very increase in power facilitates getting hold of the country in its entirety.

---

* From June 2006 to June 2016, of the 135 resolutions adopted by the UN Human Rights Council that were critical of countries, sixty-eight were critical of Israel. From 2012 through 2015, the UN General Assembly adopted ninety-seven resolutions criticizing countries. Eighty-three of them criticized Israel. (UN Watch, unwatch.org/un-israel-key-statistics).

† Greater Israel refers to the World Zionist Organization's plan for a Jewish state that would extend from the Nile to the Euphrates and include historic Palestine and parts of Syria, Jordan, and Lebanon.

Establishing a [small] state …will serve as a very potent lever in our efforts to redeem the whole country."[328]

A year later, Ben-Gurion added, "No Zionist can forego the smallest portion of the Land of Israel."[329]

He promised, "[A]fter we become a strong force, as the result of the creation of a state, we shall abolish partition and expand to the whole of Palestine."[330]

The takeover of Palestine had always been Zionism's aim. In 1895, Theodore Herzl wrote in his diary:

> We shall try to spirit the penniless population across the border by procuring employment for it in the transit countries, while denying it any employment in our own country… Both the process of expropriation and the removal of the poor must be carried out discreetly and circumspectly.[331]

In conjunction with denying employment, Herzl proposed starving Palestinians and forcing them into exile.[332]

The Jewish Agency established its first Population Transfer Committee in 1937 to develop strategies to rid the land of Palestinians. Ben-Gurion: "I support compulsory transfer. I don't see anything immoral in it."[333] On December 20, 1940, Joseph Weitz, director of the Jewish National Fund's Lands Department, wrote:

> [I]t must be clear that there is no room is this country for both peoples… If the Arabs leave it, the country will become wide and spacious for us… The only solution is a land of Israel, without Arabs… There is no room here for compromises… Not one village must be left, not one [bedouin] tribe.[334]

The Agency set up additional Population Transfer Committees in 1941 to make sure there would be no break in the work of removing Palestinians.[335]

One month after the UN voted for partition, Ben-Gurion pledged to Mapai, his political party, that the borders established by 181 were not final.[336] Another month later, Moshe Sharett promised that Israeli territory would be determined by "possession," not Partition.[337] Neither man's pledge came as a surprise to either American or British intelligence, both of which knew the Zionist leadership was committed to expansion. By February and March 1948, the CIA had determined that the Zionists wanted to "set up a Jewish state in all of Palestine and Transjordan."[338]* Before Ben-Gurion proclaimed Israel's establishment on May 14, 1948, the US State Department predicted:

> [T]he Jews will be the actual aggressors against the Arabs. However, the Jews will claim that they are merely defending [themselves]. In the event of such Arab outside aid the Jews will come running to the Security Council with the claim that their state is the object of armed aggression and will use every means to obscure the fact that it is their own armed aggression against the Arabs inside which is the cause of Arab counter-attack.[339]

The first Arab-Israeli War began on May 15, 1948. By the time Israel signed its 1949 armistice agreements with Egypt on February 24, Lebanon on March 23, Jordan on April 3, and Syria on July 20 it had taken possession of 78 percent of Palestine.

Israel has never defined its borders. As Sharett foresaw, beginning in 1967 it has adjusted its de facto borders to accommodate the movement of Jewish settlers and the expansion of illegal settlements in the West Bank, where Jewish residents have full rights of citizenship and Palestinian residents have none. These rights are founded on religious identity, not on the place of one's birth. Israel's settlement enterprise betrays its promises to the United Nations.

---

* In 1949, the Hashemite Kingdom of Transjordan, commonly referred to as Transjordan, changed its name to the Hashemite Kingdom of Jordan, now commonly referred to as Jordan.

It also betrays its commitment to the *Fourth Geneva Convention*, which was adopted in August 1949 to prevent a repeat of war crimes like those carried out by the Nazis and which Israel ratified in 1951. Article 49 states, "The occupying power shall not deport or transfer parts of its own civilian population into the territory it occupies."

───────────

While testifying before the Peel Commission in the 1930s, Ben-Gurion swore that no earthly institution had a mandate to decide the borders of the Jewish homeland and that the Bible, not the British Mandate for Palestine, was the Jewish people's mandate.[340]* As prime minister two decades later, he introduced a grand strategy to reshape the Middle East and ensure Israel's continuation. He recommended partitioning Jordan between Israel and Iraq, annexing southern Lebanon and creating a Christian Maronite state in the north, and replacing Nasser with a pro-western leader.[341] In his excitement, he went so far as to call for a "Third Kingdom of Israel."[342] These fantasies were unacceptable to both the United States and the Soviet Union, who contemplated expelling the new nation from the UN.[343]

Another former prime minister, Yitzhak Shamir stressed that Judea and Samaria "are an integral part of the Land of Israel, neither 'captured' in 1967 nor 'returnable' to anyone."[344] He exhorted: "The sacred work [of expanding settlements] must not stop. It cannot stop. It is the heart of our existence and life."[345]

Just as he considered Jews the natural rulers of Israel, the West Bank, and Gaza, Shamir considered Jordan the proper homeland of the Palestinian people.[346] Ariel Sharon agreed and urged the overthrow of Jordan's King Hussein to make way for a Palestinian state.[347]

───────────

* The 1936–1937 Royal Palestine Commission, headed by Lord William Peel, was appointed by the British government to investigate the causes of the Arab-Jewish conflict. In July 1937, after concluding that "the gulf between the two races is thus already wide and will continue to widen if the present Mandate is maintained," it recommended that mandatory Palestine be partitioned into two countries.

Menachem Begin considered partition "illegal" and "invalid."[348] In 1948, he declared that partition "will not bind the Jewish people. Jerusalem was and will forever be our capital. Eretz Israel [the Land of Israel] will be restored to the people of Israel. All of it. And forever."[349]

The "Peace and Security" chapter of the Likud Party platform asserts the following non-negotiable principles that are in accord with the ideas of Ben-Gurion, Shamir, Sharon, and Begin, the latter three members of Likud:

> The Government of Israel flatly rejects the establishment of a Palestinian Arab state west of the Jordan River.
>
> The Jordan Valley and the territories that dominate it shall be under Israeli sovereignty. The Jordan River will be the permanent eastern border of the State of Israel.
>
> Jerusalem is the eternal, united capital of the State of Israel and only of Israel.
>
> The Jewish communities in Judea, Samaria, and Gaza are the realization of Zionist values. Settlement of the land is a clear expression of the unassailable right of the Jewish people to the Land of Israel and constitutes an important asset in the defense of the vital interests of the State of Israel. The Likud will continue to strengthen and develop these communities and will prevent their uprooting.
>
> Israel rejects out of hand ideas raised by Labor Party leaders concerning the relinquishment of parts of the Negev to the Palestinians.

Speaking at a ceremony commemorating the fiftieth anniversary of Israel's victory in the 1967 Six-Day War, Prime Minister Netanyahu declared: "In any agreement, and even without an agreement, we will maintain security control over the entire territory west of the Jordan River."[350]

A cursory review of its history of expansion and the declarations of its leaders should convince any reasonable person that the 78 percent of Palestine that Israel has controlled since the end of the Arab-Israeli war has never been enough to satisfy its territorial ambitions. Yet, in their compulsion to be right, Israel's loyalists imagine their founding fathers were satisfied with 56 percent of Palestine and a divided Jerusalem, and that Jewish acceptance and Palestinian rejection of partition proves the Jewish side has always wanted peace and the Palestinian side has never wanted peace. Therefore, it's the Palestinians' fault they live under occupation. It's their fault that Israel continues to seize more and more of their land.

Unacquainted with the history, most loyalists do not know, nor do they want to know, that within a week of its passage, Ben-Gurion violated 181 by situating the Chief Rabbinate and other national institutions in Jerusalem.[351] They are also willfully blind to the fact that a Jewish state under partition would have had an initial 49 percent Arab minority that would have become a majority within a few years. To think Jewish leaders would have accepted such an outcome is an exercise in self-delusion. The only remedy for this "demographic problem" was the ethnic cleansing of the Palestinian population. Galvanized by 181's passage, between December 1, 1947 and May 1, 1948, the Jewish army forced 175,000 Palestinians from their homes.[352] By the time Israel and Syria signed the last of the 1949 armistice agreements, 750,000 Palestinians were homeless. Between November 29, 1947 and the end of August 1949, 133 new Jewish settlements were constructed on land Resolution 181 had allocated for a Palestinian state.[353]

The Palestinian leadership was keenly aware of longer-term Zionist objectives, which contributed to its anxiety about partition. Palestinians could only agonize that an organization, "committed to maintaining international peace and security, developing friendly relations among nations and promoting … human rights" was about to give away 56 percent of their homeland to a minority population that owned a fraction of the land.[354] They knew a price had to be paid for the Holocaust and that they, not Europe, would pay it. Anticipating their anguish, in 1944 David Ben-Gurion said, "There is no example in history of a people saying we agree to renounce our country, let another people come and settle here and outnumber us."[355]

Twenty-five years earlier, Zeev Vladimir Jabotinsky, leader of the Revisionist Zionist movement and founder of the Irgun said:

> Every native population, civilized or not, regards its lands as its national home, of which it is the sole master, and it wants to retain that mastery always; it will refuse to admit not only new masters but even new partners or collaborators.[356]

The added awareness that 181 would never have garnered the votes needed to pass if the United States, under intense pressure from the Zionist lobby, had not delayed the vote exacerbated Palestinian anguish. President Harry Truman:

> The facts were that not only were there pressure movements around the United Nations unlike any-thing that had been seen there before, but that the White House, too, was subjected to a constant bar-rage. I do not think I ever had as much pressure and propaganda aimed at the White House as I had in this instance. The persistence of a few of the extreme Zionist leaders–actuated by political motives and en-gaging in political threats–disturbed and annoyed me.[357]

In hindsight, and cognizant that Israel was intent on preserving a substantial Jewish majority population while expanding "into the whole of Palestine," the Palestinian leadership could have yielded to the inevitable and accepted partition. Although their self-sacrifice would have had little or no effect on the Zionist goal of "redeeming" the land, it would have backed the United States into a corner where it might have felt disposed to exercise greater caution before overlooking and enabling the unceasing violations of international law that have resulted from the Jewish side's exploitation of UN Resolution 181.

The Zionist project's artful planning laid the groundwork for a bleak future for millions of Palestinians and for a protracted and infuriating debate between those who believe in equal rights for all people and those who believe in equal rights for some people. By absolving the Jewish side and blaming the Palestinian side for the years of anguish spurred by 181, this argument, like so many others, distorts the history and diminishes the prospects for peace.

18
Ego Before God

Only an internal revolution can have the power to heal our people of their murderous sickness of causeless hatred (for the Arabs).

It is bound to bring complete ruin upon us. Only then will the old and young in our land realize how great was our responsibility to those miserable Arab refugees, in whose towns we have settled Jews who were brought here from afar, whose homes we have inherited, whose fields we now sow and harvest, the fruits of whose gardens, orchards and vineyards we gather, and in whose cities, that we robbed, we put up houses of education, charity and prayer, while we babble and rave about being the "People of the Book and the light of the nations." – Martin Buber[358]

I F, AS DAVID BEN-GURION SWORE, the Bible is the Jewish people's mandate and if, as Gilad Erdan said, "it doesn't matter what the nations of the world say," then Israel's commitments to international law are subservient to its territorial ambitions.

In Genesis 15:18, God speaks to Avram: "'Unto thy seed have I given this land, from the river of Egypt unto the great river, the river Euphrates.'"

In Genesis 26:3, God speaks to Yitz'chak (Isaac): "Stay in this land, and I will be with you and bless you, because I will give all these lands to you and to your descendants. I will fulfill the oath which I swore to Avraham your father."*

In Genesis 28:13, God speaks to Ya'akov (Jacob): "I am *Adonai*, the God of Avraham your [grand]father and the God of Yitz'chak. The land on which you are lying I will give to you and to your descendants."[359]

The 2013 *Israeli Democracy Index*, a public opinion poll, found that almost 65 percent of Israeli Jews believe "very strongly" or "quite strongly" that they are the "chosen people."[360] It also found that their "sense of 'chosenness' entails the exclusion of others."[361]

The Pew Research Center reports that 61 percent of Israeli Jews and 40 percent of American Jews believe God promised the land of Israel to the Jewish people.[362] Pew also found that 82 percent of white evangelical Protestants share this belief.[363]

That the descendants of Ishmael and Isaac's father are all Jews and that God would take land from one people and give it to another is a fantasy that replaces God with ego-identity and poisons religion with personal prejudice. Both recipe and excuse for selfish behavior, this interpretation of God's will maneuvers religion onto an anti-evolutionary trajectory that rejects both self-awareness and devotion to the divine principle of ego-transcendence. To adopt it is to have lost touch with one's deeper values, without which there can be no relationship with God.

When God's word is so authoritative that a solitary nation among a community of nations has license to renege on its binding agreements, it would be the height of hypocrisy for that nation's supporters to neglect God's word concerning any other matter. If they

---

* When God entered into His covenant with Avram, he promised to make him the father of a great people. In recognition, He changed Avram to Avraham. Avram means "exalted father," while Avraham means "father of a multitude."

can celebrate the dispossession of an entire people, surely they can observe Shabbos, keep kosher, and obey all 613 mitzvoth. Neither requests nor suggestions, mitzvoth are God's commandments. In the truest sense, their observance helps Jews transcend the limits of the separate self and guides them to a higher awareness. In Leviticus 20:22, God says, "You are to observe all my regulations and rulings and act on them, so that the land to which I am bringing you will not vomit you out." Among these regulations and rulings are prohibitions:

> Exodus 20:14: *Thou shalt not covet thy neighbor's house... nor any thing that is thy neighbor's.*
>
> Leviticus 19:11: *Ye shall not steal; neither shall ye deal falsely, nor lie one to another.*
>
> Leviticus 19:13: *Thou shalt not oppress thy neighbor, nor rob him.*
>
> Deuteronomy 16:19: *You shall not pervert justice.*

Israel's occupation of Palestine and its duplicity regarding its promises to the nations of the world demand an answer to the following question: what, according to Judaism, are the Jewish people chosen for? Are they chosen to covet, steal, lie, oppress, rob, and pervert justice, or are they chosen to rectify injustice, to be a blessing to the world, a light unto the nations; to reflect God's goodness and perfection by observing His mitzvoth; to "make a dwelling place for G-d in the lowly realm [of our physical world]."[364]

If Judaism is a divine revelation that aspires to elevate the consciousness of humankind, then adherents must understand that its most sacred principles place a higher value on human life than on emotional or messianic attachments to land, no matter how holy they imagine that land to be. A former Israel cabinet minister and member of the Knesset, Orthodox scholar and chief rabbi of Norway Michael Melchior says:

I believe those who have created priorities where love of the land supersedes love of man and of peace are distorting the Torah. I believe that those who censor the Torah of such concepts as the natural morality of man, as the belief that God has created every human being in His image, and as the basic human right to respect and dignity which stems from this belief, are desecrating the Holy name of God... I have often challenged my rabbinical colleagues to show me one single source from the "Jewish Bookshelf," the Bible, the Talmud, the Rambam, the Shulchan Aruch, or the immense traditional rabbinical literature, which rules that you cannot give up land in order to obtain peace. They have never been able to do so.[365]*

Rabbi Schlomo Yitchaki (1040-1105 A.D.), known by the acronym *Rashi* (**RA**bbi **SH**lomo Itzhaki), was the most famous commentator on the Talmud and Hebrew Bible of the Middle Ages. He taught:

Where the Torah tells about the creation of the first human being ...the earth from which Adam was formed was not taken from one spot but from various parts of the globe. Thus, human dignity does not depend on the place of one's birth nor is it limited to one region.[366]

---

* Rambam is an acronym for Moses Maimonides (1135–1204), who was a Sephardic philosopher and one of the greatest Torah scholars in Jewish history. The *Shulchan Aruch*, composed by Sephardic Rabbi Joseph Caro and published in 1563, is the most widely consulted manual of *halacha* (Jewish law) in Judaism.

19

Democracy or Ethno-Nationalism?

This country exists as the fulfillment
of a promise made by God Himself. It
would be ridiculous to ask it to account
for its legitimacy. – Golda Meir[367]

We send the children to the army,
to the territories and get back
animals. That is the result of the
occupation. – Israeli journalist and
anchorwoman, Oshrat Kotler[368]

The beginning of all wisdom is to call
things by their proper names, for if
things are not called by their proper
names, then what is said is not what is
meant, and if what is said is not what
is meant, then that which ought to be
done is left undone. – Confucius

JUSTIFYING ISRAEL'S DISPOSSESSION OF THE Palestinian
people by asserting that God promised the land to the Jewish
people, while proclaiming that Israel is "the only democracy in
the Middle East," epitomizes profound confusion. Imagine telling
non-Jews anywhere in Israel-Palestine they live in a democracy. This
proclamation professes a moral superiority while diverting attention

from anti-democratic policies that betray a moral inferiority. No definition of Israel's political structure can disguise the inequality that is perpetuated by the very people who make this proclamation.

The largest private landowner in Israel, with holdings equal to 13 percent of the country, the Jewish National Fund was established in 1901 to purchase and develop land on behalf of the Jewish people. JNF's website lauds its achievements:

> Over the past century, the JNF family has planted over 240 million trees, built over 180 dams and reservoirs, developed over 250,000 acres of land, created more than 1,000 parks throughout Israel and educated students around the world about Israel and the environment.[369]

JNF's trees, lands, and parks, two-thirds of which are planted on the tops of Palestinian villages, are off-limits to the 2.25 million Israeli citizens who are not Jewish and whose past Israel has erased from its history books.[370]

Adalah, the Legal Center for Arab Minority Rights in Israel, has compiled a database of over sixty-five laws that discriminate against Palestinian citizens in Israel proper and the West Bank: "These laws limit the rights of Palestinians in all areas of life, from citizenship rights to the right to political participation, land and housing rights, education rights, cultural and language rights, religious rights, and due process rights during detention."[371]

In June 2018, three members of the Joint List, an alliance of Israel's four Arab-dominated political parties, introduced a bill in the Knesset, "to anchor in constitutional law the principle of equal citizenship while recognising the existence and rights of the two, Jewish and Arab, national groups living within the country."[372*] The Knesset presidium disqualified the bill before it could be placed on the agenda, the first time in the past two Knesset terms—about five

---

* The Joint List is comprised of Hadash (the Democratic Front for Peace and Equality), Balad (National Democratic Assembly), Ta'al (Arab Movement for Renewal) and the United Arab List.

years—that a bill has not reached the floor.* The formal basis for the disqualification was Article 75(e) of the Knesset bylaws, which states, "The Knesset presidium shall not approve a bill which, in its view, rejects Israel's existence as the state of the Jewish people…"[373] Legalizing equal citizenship does not reject Israel's existence as the state of the Jewish people. What it does is to challenge the assumption that some groups are more entitled than others.

A substantial number of Jews and Christians around the world accept at face value Israel's boast about its "democratic values." AIPAC, Israel's proxy in the US, gushes: "Israel is a unique sanctuary of democracy, freedom and pluralism in the Middle East, protecting its citizens' rights while upholding the core values it shares with America."[374] This description is a hallucination. A Pew Research Center survey found that 48 percent of Israeli Jews believe Arabs should be "expelled or transferred from Israel," and 79 percent believe Jews "should be given preferential treatment over Arabs."[375] Their intolerance explains the sixty-five laws that discriminate against Israel's non-Jewish population. Had the United States Congress not outgrown a comparable mindset, it would never have passed the Civil Rights Act of 1964.

————————

To better comprehend the reality of Israel-Palestine we need to be cognizant of the misleading language Israel's propagandists have popularized for generations. The first step would be to recognize that Israel's self-identification as a democracy rests upon two fundamental misconceptions: 1) the laws that apply to Palestinian citizens of Israel proper are identical to those that apply to Jewish citizens; and, 2) the territories Israel has occupied for more than a half-century are not a part of the state.

What kind of democracy legislates discrimination against its own citizens on the basis of religious affiliation or gives a few hundred

---

* The Knesset presidium consists of the speaker and deputy speakers, who decide which bills the full Knesset will consider.

Jewish residents of the West Bank city of Hebron full citizenship, while denying citizenship to two hundred thousand Palestinian residents?

The legal system Israel has installed in the West Bank grants Jews the same rights their counterparts in Israel proper enjoy, while subjecting Palestinians to military law. Under military law, when the prosecution charges a Palestinian with a crime, it prevails in court 99.74 percent of the time; and when it has no evidence of a crime being committed, it uses a practice known as administrative detention that allows it to arrest Palestinians and sentence them to prison terms of up to six months, with an indefinite number of extensions possible.[376] Israeli authorities sometimes inform detainees they have secret evidence against them their lawyers are not privy to, and that they are imprisoning them for security reasons. With this uneven application of the rule of law, Israel has used its legal system to imprison Palestinians for years without trial. Detainees include college students, human rights activists, journalists with no record of violence, and even children.

Between June 1967 and December 2012, eight hundred thousand Palestinians saw the insides of prison cells.[377] Some served or are serving lengthy prison terms for crimes which, if committed by Jews, would not warrant a police investigation. Palestinian children, robbed of the same opportunities Jewish children take for granted, sometimes throw stones at Israeli tanks, soldiers, and settlers. Given the heavy-handedness of the legal system, these acts of resistance and defiance in the face of hopeless odds often lead to severe consequences for the children and their families. In 2015, the Knesset passed a law that sentences Palestinians to prison terms of up to twenty years for throwing stones at civilian vehicles when proof of harmful intent exists and ten years without proof.[378] The law has no provision that punishes Jews for throwing stones.

Torture often follows arrests. In 2018, Amnesty International concluded:

Israeli soldiers and police and Israel Security Agency

officers subjected Palestinian detainees, including children, to torture and other ill-treatment ...particularly during arrest and interrogation. Reported methods included beatings, slapping, painful shackling, sleep deprivation, use of stress positions and threats.[379]

UNICEF determined that the military detention system's ill-treatment of children, "appears to be widespread, systematic and institutionalized throughout the process, from the moment of arrest until the child's prosecution and eventual conviction and sentencing."[380]

Since 1967, Israel has arrested over fifty thousand Palestinian children.[381] The most common justification for the arrests is stone-throwing.[382] Quoting Military Court Watch, the US State Department wrote, "90 percent of Palestinian children arrested by the IDF during the year were hand-tied, 84 percent blindfolded, 58 percent subjected to physical abuse, and 91 percent denied access to a lawyer prior to questioning."[383]

Human Rights Watch: "Palestinian children are treated in ways that would terrify and traumatize an adult."[384]

Defense for Children International-Palestine estimates that law enforcement uses physical violence on 73 percent of children after arrest.[385] In a majority of cases, neither the children nor their parents know why they are arrested or where they are being taken.[386] Once arrested, soldiers blindfold and handcuff them, make them sit or lie down on the floor of the transport vehicle, and beat them.[387] On the way to interrogation centers, they leave children in the rain, cold weather, or hot sun for hours without food, water, or access to toilets.[388] At the centers, where no lawyers are present, soldiers threaten them with sexual harassment, beatings, and longer sentences. They tell the children they will demolish their houses and arrest their parents, and they force every child to sign an Arabic-language document they do not allow them to read that says they have informed them of their rights.[389;390] Regardless of their guilt or innocence, interrogators intimidate and manipulate kids into signing confessions.[391] This is standard Israeli procedure, so standard that not one of one thousand complaints filed against Israeli officers since 2001 has led to a criminal investigation.[392]

Civilians often behave worse than the police or IDF. Israel provides subsidies for housing, water, rent, and transportation to encourage Jews to settle in Palestinian territory. Resentful they have to share the land with Palestinians, settlers have carried out hate crimes, almost always with impunity, and sometimes in the presence of soldiers, who do nothing to stop them. By indulging their behavior, the Israeli government has turned the settlers into a de facto occupation force with a directive to drive out Palestinians and make room for Jews. For the period beginning in 2006 and ending in August 2013, OCHA, the United Nations Office for the Coordination of Humanitarian Affairs, recorded 630 settler-related incidents leading to Palestinian deaths or injuries and 1,344 incidents that caused damage to Palestinian property or land.[393] For 2018, the United Nations verified that the toll on Palestinian children at the hands of soldiers and settlers was fifty-nine dead and 2,756 injured.[394]

Under the pretext that their training, scholarship, and certification authorize them to apply the law with intelligence, logic, and integrity, Israeli judges rubber-stamp these travesties of justice, which makes them accomplices in systemic racial domination. The final scene in the 1961 movie, *Judgment at Nuremberg* takes place in a jail cell. German judge Herr Janning, played by Burt Lancaster, has been convicted of using his authority to facilitate the dispossession of Jews and others of their property, their humanity, and their lives. At his request, the chief judge at the trials, played by Spencer Tracy, pays him a visit. Janning expresses his respect for the chief judge's competence and fairness, then says: "Those people, those millions of people. I never knew it would come to that. You must believe it. You must believe it."

The chief judge replies: "Herr Janning, it came to that the first time you sentenced a man to death you knew to be innocent."

The irony of comparing Israel's judicial system to the Nazis' does not escape me, but as stated earlier, when we objectify people and rob them of their humanity, we lose our own humanity. Then, any behavior is possible.

———————

During my 2010 visit to Israel-Palestine undergraduates at Birzeit University near Ramallah in the West Bank told me that Israel prohibits student groups of any kind on or off campus, and that students who defy the prohibition risk arrest and administrative detention. Confused, I asked them what would happen if they formed a Hebrew language group or a group that studied Judaism or Jewish history. The undergraduates stressed that the nature of the group was irrelevant to Israeli authorities. With forty activity groups to choose from, students at the Hebrew University of Jerusalem have no such problem.

20
Strategies of Dispossession

*"Ethnic cleansing" is a purposeful
policy designed by one ethnic or
religious group to remove by violent
and terror-inspiring means the civilian
population of another ethnic or religious
group from certain geographic areas.
To a large extent, it is carried out in
the name of misguided nationalism,
historic grievances and a powerful
driving sense of revenge.* – Letter
Dated 24 May 1994 from the U.N.
Secretary-General to the President
of the Security Council.[395]

*Judaism is not a religion of space and
does not worship the soil. So, too,
the State of Israel is not the climax
of Jewish history, but a test of the
integrity of the Jewish people and
the competence of Israel.* – Rabbi
Abraham Joshua Heschel[396]

I SRAEL IS THE ONLY COUNTRY in the world that uses home
demolitions to collectively punish a population under its rule.[397]
Since 1967, it has demolished over forty-eight thousand Palestinian

homes but not one Jewish home.[398] Among the reasons for the demolitions are: the inhabitants of a home are friends, neighbors, or relatives of someone suspected of a security offense; they built their homes on land Israel covets for settlements; they built them without permits.[399] From 2010 through 2014, the Israeli government approved 1.5 percent of Palestinian permit requests.[400]

In August 2017, an Israeli court ordered six residents of the "unrecognized" Bedouin village of al-Araqib in the southern Negev region to reimburse the state 262,000 shekels ($75,660) for the cost of demolishing their homes and 100,000 shekels ($28,878) for the state's legal fees.[401] Israeli policy requires that homeowners pay the costs of demolition, so the least expensive option is to demolish their homes themselves. This practice of singling out non-Jews brings to mind a familiar saying: "The only way to deal with the Palestinians is to *humiliate* them."

The Negev's population was almost 100 percent Bedouin during the first half of the twentieth century, but Israeli forces drove out 90 percent during the 1948 war. Today, the Bedouin population is two hundred thousand, of which half live in thirty-five villages Israel classifies as illegal, which disqualifies them from receiving basic services such as electricity, paved roads, and running water. Al-Araqib residents say they have owned the land since it was a part of the Ottoman Empire. Beginning in 2010 and continuing into August 2019, Israeli bulldozers have demolished their village 149 times.[402]

In 2010, I visited a Palestinian village in Israel's northern district where I met a married couple who had built their house on a plot of land the husband inherited from his father. A few years after they moved in, Israeli authorities served them with a demolition order. The reason for the order was that a boundary of a future Jewish-only settlement overlapped the couple's land by one foot. Although the deed to the land had been in the family for decades, and the couple had obtained the proper construction permits years before architects drew up plans for the settlement, authorities claimed the homeowners were in violation of Israeli law. The remedy was to tear the house down. Any fair-minded person can recognize that Israel concocted its legal interpretation to enable the commission of a crime: the theft of an innocent family's homestead. If the couple was guilty of anything, it was for failing to foresee the future when they decided to build a house. The Israeli government, however, envisaged the future years earlier. Its vision has always been to take as much land as possible while removing as many Palestinians as possible, even if doing so violates its international commitments. UN Resolution 181 stipulates:

> No expropriation of land owned by an Arab in the Jewish State …shall be allowed except for public purposes. In all cases of expropriation full compensation as fixed by the Supreme Court shall be paid previous to dispossession.[403]

———

On March 14, 1950, the Knesset took advantage of the 1948 Palestinian exodus by passing the Absentees' Property Law, which is still in effect. The law defines an absentee as a non-Jewish property owner who, between November 29, 1947—the day the UN passed Resolution 181—and September 1, 1948, was in:

> ii) [Lebanon, Egypt, Syria, Saudi Arabia, Trans-Jordan, Iraq or the Yemen] or in any part of Palestine outside the area of Israel, or (iii) was a Palestinian citizen and left his ordinary place of residence in Palestine (a) for a place outside Palestine or (b) for a place in Palestine held at the time by forces which sought to prevent the establishment of the State of Israel or who fought against it after its establishment.[404]

During this period, residents who, for any reason, left their homes for areas not yet under IDF control were classified as absentees. The custodian could then seize their property and turn it over to the

Jewish National Fund or give it to a Jew, often a European who had recently arrived in Israel. The fact that residents may have returned to their homes within a few hours was not a mitigating factor. Israel seized about four million dunams, or 60 percent of arable Palestinian-owned land—double the amount of Jewish-owned land at the time of Israel's creation—in this innovative manner.[405*] The seizures included ten thousand shops and stores, most of the olive orchards and vegetable and fruit crops, and half the citrus groves.[406] Of the 370 settlements Israel established between 1948 and the beginning of 1953, 350 were built on land stolen from Palestinians through this acquisitive law.[407] By 1954, a third of Israel's Jewish population was living on absentee property.[408]

The seizure of a family's homestead is not always enough to satisfy the designs of the Absentees Property Law, which also decrees that the absentee hand over to the custodian the right to any property or money owed to the absentee.[409] To make sure the law produces its desired result, the Knesset has indemnified the custodian from having to prove he based his decisions on accurate information. If he errs in classifying someone an absentee, his decision still stands.[410] In actuality, the law legalizes the practice of ethnic cleansing and facilitates the dispossession of the native people.

In March 1953, Israel passed its Land Acquisition Law, which focused on the remaining Palestinian population, those who did not meet the definition of absentee. This law legalized the confiscation of land that was uncultivated after 1948 as well as land that was cultivated but untitled as of April 1952.[411]

In March 2017, Israeli officials issued demolition orders for every home and structure, including the mosque, clinic, and local elementary school, in Khan al-Ahmar, a Bedouin village five miles northeast of East Jerusalem, and situated in the West Bank between the settlements of Kfar Adumim and Ma'ale Adumim. The Israeli

---

* A dunam equals one thousand square meters, slightly less than a quarter-acre.

Civil Administration ruled the structures illegal because residents built them without permits. Villagers had applied for permits, but the civil administration denied their applications due to the lack of a master zoning plan. They had submitted a master zoning plan three years earlier, but it was rejected over questions about land ownership, a rationale that gives Israel's government the flexibility to expel non-Jews whenever it wants. The village then submitted five alternative master plans, but they went nowhere when courts decided not to review them.[412] Villagers live in tents and corrugated tin shacks instead of structures made of wood or concrete, materials Israel prohibits. The elementary school accommodates children from five villages and is built out of tires and mud.

Khan al-Ahmar's residents are members of the Jahalin Bedouin tribe, who were expelled from their ancestral lands in the early 1950s and relocated to what was then the village of Kfar Adumim. In the late 1970s, when it was convenient for Israel to turn Kfar Adumim into a Jewish-only settlement, it expelled the Jahalin again, resettling them in Khan al-Ahmar.

Khan al-Ahmar is one of the few Palestinian villages still standing in E-1, a twelve square kilometer zone. The eviction of 173 Bedouin from the village, half of whom are children, will make room for both Kfar Adumim and the larger settlement of Ma'ale Adumim to expand their boundaries. The expansion will create an Israeli corridor extending from the Mediterranean Sea through Jerusalem to the Jordan River. Bifurcating Palestinian territory and sealing off East Jerusalem from the rest of the West Bank, it will prevent the establishment of a contiguous Palestinian state. When the expansion is complete, Israel's supporters will be hard-pressed to repeat their claim that the failure to negotiate a two-state solution is due to Palestinian intransigence. Eid Abu Khamis, spokesman and leader of the Bedouin community: "If Khan al-Ahmar falls so will Al-Aqsa, as well as the entire peace process."[413*]

* The Al-Aqsa Mosque is built on top of the Temple Mount (Haram esh-Sharif or Noble Sanctuary) in the Old City of Jerusalem and is the third holiest site in Islam after the Kaaba in Mecca and the Prophet's Mosque in Medina.

Israel plans to transfer Khan al-Ahmar's residents to Al-Jabal West, a centralized village it created in 1997 to house evicted Bedouin tribes. Al-Jabal West sits next to the biggest garbage dump in the West Bank, where trucks dispose of 700 tons of waste each day and where no sane human being would want to live. Environmental studies show "high levels of toxic gases, which pose an immediate threat to residents."[414] Since the site has no housing, the state says it will supply the new residents with tents until such time it allows them to build houses.[415] It has apportioned one-sixteenth of an acre to each family, enough space for a dwelling, but not enough for the family's sheep, dogs, or donkeys.[416] Israel is cheating the Bedouin out of their traditional way of life.

Although the US government has not addressed Israel's designs, which the latter has taken as consent, in November 2017, Bernie Sanders, Elizabeth Warren, and eight other US senators, all democrats, wrote to Prime Minister Netanyahu asking him not to demolish Khan al-Ahmar. They admonished, "Your government's efforts to forcibly evict entire Palestinian communities and expand settlements throughout the West Bank not only directly imperil a two-state solution, but we believe also endanger Israel's future as a Jewish democracy."[417]

Six months later, seventy-six well-intentioned members of the United States House of Representatives, again all democrats under the illusion that Israel and the Trump administration are interested in "Palestinian dignity" and in "two-states for two peoples," wrote to the prime minister asking him to halt the planned demolitions of Khan al-Ahmar, Susya, and other Bedouin villages. The lawmakers: "The destruction and displacement of such communities would run counter to shared US and Israeli values, while further undermining long-term Israeli security, Palestinian dignity and the prospects for peacefully achieving two states for two people."[418]

In June 2018, a letter signed by 300 legal scholars, elected officials, academics, artists, faith leaders, and activists from Israel and around the world cautioned the Israeli government that "Forcible transfer

– by direct physical force or by creating a coercive environment that makes residents leave their homes – is a war crime."[419]

A month later, the European Union warned Israel that its demolitions and "plans for new settlement construction ...exacerbate threats to the viability of a two-state solution and further undermine prospects for a lasting peace."[420] It added that it "expects the Israeli authorities to reverse these decisions and fully meet its obligations as an occupying power under International Humanitarian Law."[421]

UN Special Coordinator for the Middle East Peace Process Nikolay Mladenov tweeted: "Israel should stop such actions and plans for relocating Bedouin communities in the occupied West Bank. Such actions are contrary to international law & undermine the two-state solution."[422] The next day, the U.K., France, Germany, and Italy protested the demolition of Khan al-Ahmar.[423] Diplomats from those and eight other European Union countries attempted to enter the village and visit the school, but Israeli police blocked them. On July 11, Israel sealed all entrances with cement blocks and turned away a Palestinian mobile medical unit that had come to care for ill patients.[424]

In August, the State Prosecutor's Office promised that if every member of the Jahalin tribe signed a written agreement not to resist eviction, instead of moving them next to the garbage dump, it would move them next to a sewage treatment plant, a site the state has marked as off-limits to Jews because of the danger the plant poses to human health.[425] On September 4, 2018, the High Court rescinded all earlier injunctions blocking the eviction and gave Israeli authorities the green light to proceed with the demolition at their discretion.[426] The ruling sets a precedent for the expulsion and demolition of other Bedouin villages. A week later, the European Parliament passed a resolution warning, "the demolition of Khan al Ahmar and the forcible transfer of its residents would constitute a grave breach of international humanitarian law."[427] On September 23, Israeli civil administration officials handed out notices to the villagers "asking" them to demolish their habitats by October 1, 2018.

The notices made clear that if villagers refused the administration's "request," local authorities would enforce the court's ruling.[428]

To prevent Palestinians, journalists, and demonstrators from entering or exiting the village, on September 28 Israel declared Khan al-Ahmar a closed military zone.[429] Anxious to assist their government in ridding the area of Bedouin, on October 2 and again on October 15, settlers from Kfar Adumim flooded Khan al-Ahmar's lands with wastewater.[430] On October 17, Fatou Bensouda, Prosecutor of the International Criminal Court, cautioned Israel that "extensive destruction of property without military necessity and population transfers in an occupied territory constitute war crimes under the Rome Statute."[431]* Along with the diplomatic pressure Israel was already up against, Bensouda's intervention almost certainly prompted Attorney-General Avichai Mandelbit to announce in late October that Israel's "Security Cabinet [had] granted an extension of several weeks in order to exhaust the negotiations for evacuation by agreement."[432] Prime Minister Netanyahu assured his right-wing base the delay was for a short time.

Deriding the extension as a "shameful capitulation," and criticizing Netanyahu's "policy of selective law enforcement against Jewish settlement in Judea and Samaria," right-wing NGO Regavim said, "[the cabinet's] decision reeks of cowardice and makes a laughingstock of Israel's sovereignty and commitment to law and order."[433]†

Education Minister Naftali Bennett, head of Bayit Yehudi (Jewish Home), opined: "In a state which *abides by the rule of law* [emphasis added], the law is enforced even if there is opposition or threats from the international community."[434]

---

* The *Rome Statute* of the International Criminal Court established four core international crimes: genocide, crimes against humanity, war crimes, and aggression. Neither Israel nor the United States is a signatory to the Statute, which has been ratified by 118 countries.

† A non-profit association, Regavim monitors and initiates legal action against what it considers illegal construction and land seizures by Palestinians and Bedouin in Israel and the West Bank. (Ariel David, "Why Is an Israeli Pro-settler Group Campaigning for Brexit," *Haaretz*, June 19, 2016).

Regavim and Bennett's outrage exposes the narcissism at the heart of Israel's psychology. In their worldview, laws that expedite nationalist objectives are essential, while laws that would insure the civil rights of Palestinians are unworthy of consideration.

In June 2019, at the request of the Trump administration, the Israeli government postponed the village's evacuation until at least December 2019.[435]

Besides emptying entire villages, Israel's Population, Immigration and Border Authority has arbitrarily revoked the citizenship of hundreds, perhaps thousands, of Bedouin.[436] Alleging "erroneous registration," with a simple keystroke unelected clerks have sentenced them to legal limbo and, probably, a lifetime without the protections citizenship affords.[437] Many of the newly stateless, for whom there is no appeals process, were born within the borders of Israel proper and have voted in elections and paid taxes their entire adult lives. Some served in the IDF and some are children of a parent who served in the IDF.[438] Israeli law holds that only the High Court has the power to revoke citizenship, but the actual implementation of the law and the protections it provides apply to Jews only.

The Bedouin are not the only group whose rights are in jeopardy. When Israel annexed East Jerusalem in 1967, it created a permanent residency status for the city's Palestinian inhabitants, 95 percent of whom are not Israeli citizens, which means they have no political or civil rights and cannot vote in Knesset elections.[439;440] Classifying their residency status as *permanent* illustrates Israel's deceptive use of language because their status is subject to revocation if they move abroad for seven or more years or obtain citizenship or residency in another country. In 1995, Israel toughened its requirements so that Palestinians who move abroad for any length of time—including to Gaza and the West Bank—and cannot prove their center of life is in Jerusalem also risk having their status revoked.[441] From the start of the occupation in 1967 through 2016, Israel has revoked the residency permits of at least 14,595 Palestinians, most for failing to prove their center of life was in Jerusalem.[442] About eighty-six thousand Palestinians, including dependent children, have left the city.[443] This figure does not include the two hundred and thirty thousand Palestinians since 1967 whose requests for registration, residency, and family unification have been turned down.[444] A study by Israeli Professor Yael Ronen, "did not find any examples or cases where a country took over an area and applied its sovereignty without enabling in an active way the residents of that area to become its citizens."[445]

In March 2018, the Knesset passed a law giving the interior minister absolute authority to strip Palestinian Jerusalemites of their residency if he determines they are guilty of any of the following: 1) endangering public safety; 2) the acquisition of residency through false information; 3) breach of loyalty. If no country accepts the violator, the interior minister must grant them an alternative status. Under international law, an occupying power has neither the right to enforce loyalty constraints upon members of an occupied population nor the authority to revoke their status as permanent residents. Knesset member Esawi Freige of Meretz reacted to the legislation:

> Since 1967 there has been a campaign to empty East Jerusalem of its Palestinian residents. We see this in the entrance of Border Police to the neighborhoods, in the conduct of government institutions, and in laws like this, and to hell with human rights and international law.[446]

In the pre-dawn hours of July 22, 2019, hundreds of IDF soldiers stormed the Wadi al-Hummus area of the Sur Bahir neighborhood, just outside the municipal boundaries of East Jerusalem. They threw families out into the streets and demolished twelve residential buildings containing seventy to one hundred apartments. Israel said the buildings were security risks because they were too close to its separation wall—erected on land Israel stole from Palestinians—

and were built without Israeli permits. Palestinians countered that the buildings were in Area A and the Palestinian Authority had issued permits for their construction.* Under the terms of the Oslo Accords, the PA has full jurisdiction over Area A and Israel has none.[447] The European Union advised Israel to stop the "illegal" demolitions, warning they undermine "the viability of the two-state solution and the prospect for a lasting peace."[448] Kuwait, South Africa, and Indonesia submitted a request to the UN Security Council to condemn this latest breach of international law, but the United States vetoed the effort.[449] The PA called the demolitions a "war crime" and "ethnic cleansing."[450]

Israel controls 86 percent of East Jerusalem's geographical area where two hundred thousand settlers live on land confiscated from Palestinians.[451] Its laws, policies, and judicial rulings give it a foundation, no matter how spurious, to create facts on the ground, extend Jewish sovereignty over all of Jerusalem, and shrink the non-Jewish population of East Jerusalem. One-third of Palestinian homes throughout East Jerusalem were built without permits, making them, like the erstwhile buildings in Sur Bahir, candidates for demolition, and their one hundred thousand inhabitants candidates for displacement.[452] Since 1967, the Israeli government has built fifty-five thousand housing units for Jews and six hundred for Palestinians.[453] Although 37 percent of Jerusalem's population is Palestinian, the Israeli government has set aside a mere 8.5 percent of the city (equal to 15 percent of East Jerusalem) for their housing.[454]

---

* The Palestinian Authority, also known as the Palestinian National Authority, was formed out of the 1993 Oslo Accords to govern the Gaza Strip and Areas A and B of the West Bank.

21

Legalizing Discrimination

From the place where we are right
flowers will never grow in the
Spring. – Yehuda Amichai

O N J ULY 18, 2018, THE Knesset passed the *Basic Law: Israel the Nation State of the Jewish People.** With its pronouncement that "the exercise of the right to national self-determination in the State of Israel is unique to the Jewish people," the nation-state law enshrines a right to discriminate against Palestinians and other minorities and annuls the promise of Israel's *Declaration of the Establishment of the State of Israel* to "ensure complete equality of social and political rights to all its inhabitants irrespective of religion, race or sex." The minority is 25.5 percent of Israel's total population.[455] Jews now have legal justification for barring non-Jewish families from living in their communities. Accenting its bias, the nation-state law affirms the "ingathering of the exiles," a Jewish right of return to Israel, while ignoring that same right for Palestinians.

The law thumbs its nose at the decades of effort the world community has expended trying to find a solution to the Israel-Palestine tragedy: "The state views the development of Jewish

---

* In Israel, a Basic Law elucidates the state's underlying principles. Although Israel does not have a constitution, its Basic Laws are analogous to amendments to the US Constitution.

settlement as a national value and shall act to encourage and promote its establishment and strengthening." Some experts interpret this provision as applicable only to Israel proper, but given Israel's longstanding refusal to define its borders, adhering instead to Golda Meir's doctrine that "the borders [of Israel] are where Jews live, not where there is a line on a map," the vague language affirms an exclusive right for Jews to colonize the West Bank.[456] Until now, Israeli law has regarded outposts as illegal, though enforcement has been lax, but settler activists can now argue the nation-state law supersedes earlier laws. Six weeks after its passage, the Jerusalem District Court ruled that the Mitzpeh Kramim outpost, which was built on private Palestinian land, could be legalized.[457] Justice Minister Ayelet Shaked celebrated: "This is a precedent-setting, extremely significant verdict. It means the state isn't saying anymore that settlements must be evacuated, but that we'll find a way to legitimize them, to enable settlements' development and growth."[458]

Underlying these legal gymnastics is Israel's continued abdication of its responsibilities under international law. The *Fourth Geneva Convention* and the International Court of Justice are unequivocal that colonizing the West Bank is illegal. Illegal as well is Israel's annexation of East Jerusalem, yet the new law reiterates its July 1980 Basic Law that "Jerusalem, complete and united, is the capital of Israel."*

Recognizing Hebrew as Israel's official language, and downgrading Arabic from a national language, the law sends a message to Israel's Arab population that their government doesn't want them. Intentionally or not, it discriminates against Israel's Mizrahi Jewish population, fifty of whom have asked the High Court of Justice to nullify the law, which they accuse of "strengthening the impression that Jewish-Arab culture is inferior …and anchoring the identity of the State of Israel as anti-Arab."[459]†

Likening the "ideal of Zionism" to his dream of a white, American "ethno-state," Richard Spencer, a leader of the alt-right movement

---

* Israel's annexation of East Jerusalem has never been recognized by a single country.
† Mizrahi Jews come from the Middle East, North Africa and parts of the Caucasus.

in the US, and a self-described "white Zionist," said the law shows "a path forward for Europeans."[460]

In the weeks leading up to the vote on the nation-state bill, the Knesset passed a series of laws that forbid organizations from criticizing the occupation in public schools and that deny LGBT men access to state-subsidized surrogacy services. Another recently-passed law blocks Palestinians from litigating land disputes in the High Court, which means they will have to take their appeals to lower courts, which are known to be less sympathetic to their plight.

In 1935, Nazi Germany passed the first in a series of laws devised to disenfranchise Jews and deny them basic rights. The Nuremberg Laws prohibited Jews from voting and from marrying or having sexual relations with persons of German blood. Jewish lawyers could not practice law and Jewish doctors could not administer to non-Jews. Six years later, the Third Reich escalated its persecution of Jews when it opened its death factories in Poland.

Months after the Knesset passed the nation-state law, television celebrity and model Rotem Sela commented to her 830,000 Instagram followers: "When the hell will someone in this government let the Israeli public know that this is a country for all its citizens and that every person is born equal. And also, that the Arabs are human beings."[461]

Prime Minister Netanyahu responded:

> Dear Rotem Sela, I read what you wrote. First of all, an important correction: Israel is not a state for all its citizens. According to a basic law we passed, Israel is the nation-state of the Jewish people – and the Jewish people only.[462]

At a cabinet meeting later that week, Netanyahu said: "I want to respond to a few people who are confused. The state of Israel is not a nation-state of all its citizens; other minorities have a national representation in other countries."[463] Meretz leader Tamar Zandberg upbraided the nation-state law as "an act of sabotage against Israeli law that replaced equality with racism."[464] Zandberg must know that Israel has always chosen racism over equality and that the new law does not inject racism into an egalitarian society. What it does is to legitimize a pre-existing and deep-seated practice of racism into an Ethnocracy. Zandberg and other lawmakers are no longer in a position to hide behind Israel's self-image as a democratic state. They have to come to terms with the fact that no Israeli government has ever been willing to let the image become a reality. By a vote of seventy-one to thirty-eight, on December 12, 2018, the Knesset reinforced that tradition when it rejected a bill introduced by Zandberg's party. *The Basic Law: Equality* stipulated, "The State of Israel shall maintain equal political rights amongst all its citizens, without any difference between religions, race and sex."[465]

Risking accusations of anti-Semitism, American Jewish organizations reacted to the nation-state law's passage. The New Israel Fund called it "racist" and "discriminatory."[466] NIF CEO Daniel Sokatch said it was "tribalism at its worst" and "a danger to Israel's future."[467] Fourteen American Jewish organizations sent a letter to Isaac Herzog, at the time the head of the Jewish Agency, warning him that the law will "give constitutional protection to policies that could discriminate against minorities, including women, Palestinian citizens, racial minorities, LGBT people, non-Orthodox Jews, Muslims, Druze, Christians and others."[468]

Rabbi Rick Jacobs, president of the Union for Reform Judaism, said, "It will make Israel an open target on the world stage for all those who seek to deny the Jewish people our right to a homeland."[469] I agree with Jacobs and the others, but if their concern for Israel's future is sincere, they ought to use their status within the Diaspora to insist that Israel stop denying the Palestinian people their right to a homeland.

A tribute to the illusion of identity, the nation-state law highlights the ultra-nationalistic and theocratic character of Israel, foments the most extreme of identity politics, and makes Jewish supremacy a bedrock principle. If they don't already, many countries will regard the assertion that Israel is a democracy and a state for all of its citizens as hypocrisy. Gideon Levy describes Israel's hierarchy of importance:

> Israel is representing a new scale of rights: At the top are Jews who kill Arabs (serving in the army), after them come Jews who do not serve in the army, followed by Druze who serve, Bedouin who serve, Circassians who serve, Christians, who are relatively good Arabs, and at the bottom, Muslim Arabs, who are not entitled to rights in the Jewish state.[470]

As long as their minds are steeped in prejudice, confusion, and fear, leaders and their political bases will continue to suppress elements within their society that seek to transform tribal thinking into "deep soul-searching about the nature of man." The likely result of their efforts is that tribalism in Israel will prove unstoppable and that history will repeat itself. Earlier, I said it would be more accurate if, instead of defining itself as the nation-state of the Jewish people, Israel defined itself as the nation-state of "the right-wing Jewish people." This law removes any doubt that is the case.

22

Aliyah

*This sort of "Zionism" blasphemes
the name of Zion; it is nothing
more than one of the crude forms of
nationalism, which acknowledge no
master above the apparent (!) interest
of the nation. –* Martin Buber[471]

A S LONG AS MY NEED to defend my identity dominated my
worldview, I blamed anti-Semitism for the twentieth century
expulsion of eight hundred thousand Jews from their homes
in Arab countries; and I refused to believe that until the late
1940s, Arabs and Jews had experienced 2,500 years of relatively
peaceful coexistence. Had I valued historical context, I would have
understood the expulsion of Jews as an anti-Zionist—not an anti-
Semitic—reaction to the 1947 UN Partition Plan and the 1947-8
expulsion of Palestinian Arabs. Former nun and religious scholar
Karen Armstrong:

> Hatred of the Jews became marked in the Muslim
> world only after the creation of the state of Israel in
> 1948 and the subsequent loss of Arab Palestine. It is
> significant that Muslims were compelled to import
> anti-Jewish myths from Europe …because they had
> no such traditions of their own.[472]

A few days before the vote on partition, Heykal Pasha, the head of the Egyptian delegation to the General Assembly, cautioned:

> The United Nations...should not lose sight of the fact that the proposed solution might endanger a million Jews living in the Moslem countries... If the United Nations decides to partition Palestine, it might be responsible for the massacre of a large number of Jews.

> If Arab blood runs in Palestine, Jewish blood will necessarily be shed elsewhere in the Arab world...[473]

Iraqi Foreign Minister Fadil Jamali agreed with Pasha's admonition: "Any injustice imposed upon the Arabs of Palestine will disturb the harmony among Jews and non-Jews in Iraq; it will breed inter-religious prejudice and hatred."[474]

Rather than acknowledging the obvious, that the expulsion of Palestinians led to the expulsion of Jews, Israel's loyalists change the subject to Jewish suffering and victimhood, making it appear that both peoples suffered equally. I do not want to understate the pain that Jews in Arab countries went through, but in the context of the events that unfolded in the twentieth century Middle East, there is no moral equivalence between Palestinian and Jewish suffering. Changing the subject to Jewish suffering distorts history by implicating Palestinians as responsible for the expulsion of Jews from Arab lands. Other than being beneficiaries of sympathy from their fellow Arabs, Palestinians played no such role.

In 2012, Israel's government initiated an *I am a Refugee* campaign to instruct Israeli diplomats and Jewish refugees and their descendants to use any relevant forum, including the internet, to remind people about Jewish flight from Arab lands.[475] The campaign's goal is not to achieve restitution for Jewish refugees. It is to drown out the voices of generations of Palestinian refugees who seek the same rights Jews sought when they established their state.

Former Speaker of the Knesset and past Minister of the Police and Internal Affairs Shlomo Hillel, who immigrated from Iraq, said,

"I don't regard the departure of Jews from Arab lands as that of refugees. They came here because they wanted to, as Zionists."[476]

At a hearing before the Knesset, former MK Ran Cohen, who was born in Baghdad, testified, "I am not a refugee. I came at the behest of Zionism, due to the pull that this land exerts, and due to the idea of redemption. Nobody is going to define me as a refugee."[477]

Yemeni-born Jew Yisrael Yeshayahu, who served as Speaker of the Knesset from 1972 to 1977, disputes the notion he is a refugee: "We are not refugees. [Some of us] came to this country before the state was born. We had messianic aspirations."[478]

There is no question that Arab countries discriminated against Jews, but as Hillel, Cohen, and Yeshayahu point out, a large number who emigrated were guided by Israeli appeals for them to make aliyah.* Many had time to gather their possessions and, once in Israel, one hundred fifty thousand moved into homes that belonged to Palestinians.[479] Nowadays, with the state's blessing, Jewish settlers confiscate Palestinian homes in East Jerusalem, Hebron, and other towns and cities.[480]

---

* Aliyah is a Hebrew word meaning ascent or going up. It refers to Jewish immigration to Palestine and, later, to Israel.

23

Intransigence

The argument has to be to Israel, "Yes, you're giving up physical security but you are gaining a state of peace – better relations, the intangible aspects of security." – Henry Kissinger[481]

I intend to issue an opinion soon, according to which the International Court of Justice in the Hague has no authority to discuss the Israeli-Palestinian conflict because there is no Palestinian state. – Avichai Mandelbit, Attorney-General of Israel, November 26, 2018.[482]

To understand the historical relationship between Israel and the Palestinian people, we need to juxtapose the myth of Palestinian intransigence with the myth of Israel's readiness to trade land for peace. In 1977, Nahum Goldmann said:

> Israel has never presented the Arabs with a single peace plan. She has rejected every settlement plan devised by her friends and by her enemies. She has seemingly no other object than to preserve the status quo while adding territory piece by piece.[483]

As mentioned earlier, David Ben-Gurion ruled out peace talks with Egypt's President Nasser, who tried to communicate with the Israeli prime minister through British, Maltese, and Quaker emissaries. In 1962, Nasser told *London Times* editor Dennis Hamilton, "If I could meet with Ben-Gurion for two–three hours we would be able to settle the Israeli-Arab conflict."[484]

In 1949, Syria offered to take in three hundred thousand Palestinian refugees as part of a comprehensive plan that included economic cooperation. UN mediator and future Nobel Peace Prize laureate Ralph Bunche pleaded with Ben-Gurion to respond to the Syrians, but the prime minister was uninterested. At the Lausanne Conference in the same year, Israel denied responsibility for the Palestinian refugee problem, blaming the Arab states instead. Before the 1967 Six-Day War, Prime Minister Eshkol forbade Director of Mossad Meir Amit from traveling to Egypt for peace talks.[485] In the next six years, the Jordanians held thirty-two secret meetings with Israel, nineteen of which were attended by King Hussein, who offered a full peace with the "personal authority" of Nasser. The king stressed, "Our sole demand upon Israel is the withdrawal of its armed forces from all territories occupied in the June 1967 war, and the implementation of all other provisions of the Security Council Resolution."[486] Hussein also left open the possibility of minor reciprocal border adjustments, but his efforts proved fruitless as Golda Meir, who was prime minister from 1969 to 1974, took Foreign Minister Abba Eban's advice to engage the king in a "futile discussion."[487;488] She and her colleagues welcomed Eban's strategy of delay and confusion, which took "the shape of a consistent foreign policy of deception."[489] Eban, who delighted in his mastery of *takhsisanut*—Hebrew for deception or deviousness—admitted to his Labor Party's Expanded Political Committee that Israel was not engaged in a peace process, but in a struggle to maintain the status quo of permanent control over the West Bank.[490]

Moshe Dayan said, "The question is not, What is the solution? but, How do we live without a solution?"[491] On another occasion, he said:

There should be no Jew who says, "that's enough," no-one who says "we are nearing the end of the road."… It is the same with the land… Your duty is not to stop; it is to keep your sword unsheathed, to have faith, to keep the flag flying. You must not call a halt – heaven forbid – and say "that's all; up to here…" For that is not all. [492]

In 1969, William Rogers, President Richard Nixon's secretary of state, presented a peace plan for the Middle East based on UN Resolution 242.* Prime Minister Meir rejected it as "a disaster for Israel."[493] A year later, she forbade Nahum Goldmann from speaking to Nasser, claiming, "There's no one to talk to."[494]

Israel has never honored the terms of the 1978 Camp David Accords, which grant "full autonomy" to the Palestinians, and for years insisted that peace was impossible because of Yasser Arafat, who died in 2004. Secretaries of State George Schultz and James Baker, during the Reagan and George H. W. Bush years, saw their attempts to find solutions go nowhere when Israel refused to curtail its settlement activity. With a directness unusual for American officials when dealing with Israel, Baker testified before the House Foreign Affairs subcommittee on foreign operations:

Nothing has made my job of trying to find Arab and Palestinian partners for Israel more difficult than being greeted by a new settlement every time I arrive. I don't think that there is any bigger obstacle to peace than the settlement activity that continues not only unabated but at an enhanced pace.[495]

Israel has also never responded to the Arab Peace Initiative,

---

* Adopted on November 22, 1967, UN Security Council Resolution 242 emphasizes "the inadmissibility of the acquisition of territory by war and the need to work for a just and lasting peace in which every State in the area can live in security," calls for Israel to withdraw from territories occupied in 1967, and affirms "the necessity for achieving a just resolution to the [Palestinian] refugee problem."

introduced in 1982 at the Arab League conference in Fez, Morocco, updated in 2002, and reiterated in 2012. The Initiative would end the Arab-Israeli conflict, normalize relations with the entire Arab and Muslim worlds—fifty Muslim governments, of which twenty-two are Arab—and provide security for "all the states of the region." It also gives Israel a veto over a Palestinian right of return. Israel's leaders must believe they are more secure in *not* making peace with border nations Syria and Lebanon, their latest arch-enemy Iran, and every Muslim nation on Earth than they are in making peace. The Initiative is still on the table and was re-introduced in 2013–14 by US Secretary of State John Kerry during his unsuccessful attempt to broker an agreement between the Palestinians and Israelis.

In 2002, the George W. Bush administration outlined a Roadmap for Peace that would have resolved the Israel-Palestine issue. Both sides accepted, but the Israelis attached such extreme requirements to their acceptance that they may as well have rejected it outright. Among their requirements were that all of Jerusalem remain under Israeli control, a specification negotiators knew would be indefensible to the Muslim world. Israel also insisted on a Palestinian "waiver of any right of return of refugees to Israel" and stipulated that there would be "no discussion of Israeli settlement in Judea and Samaria;" that "the Roadmap cannot state that Israel must cease violence and incitement against the Palestinians;" and that there would be "no reference to the key provisions of UN Resolution 242," specifically, the "inadmissibility of the acquisition of territory by war," and the "withdrawal of Israeli armed forces from territories occupied in the [1967] conflict."[496] Prime Minister Sharon said he would accept a demilitarized Palestinian state, but only on 42 percent of the West Bank, minus security areas, and 70 percent of the Gaza Strip.[497] Sharon's message to the Americans was that Israel's acceptance of the Roadmap depended upon the unconditional surrender of the Palestinian people and an end to their rights under international law.

A glaring example of disinformation and myth-making is the failed Camp David Summit of 2000. Israeli Prime Minister Ehud Barak's announcement that he wanted to negotiate a peace deal elicited surprise among the Americans and Palestinians. Barak had not reached out to the Palestinians for an exchange of ideas and was ignoring his government's obligations under the Oslo Accords to free Palestinian prisoners and withdraw IDF personnel from three Palestinian villages. Although both President Clinton and Yasser Arafat considered Barak's initiative premature, Arafat and his advisers fretted Israel would malign them as obstructionists if they didn't cooperate, so they came to Camp David to negotiate the 22 percent of Palestine they had not given up when they signed the Oslo Accords.

A day or two after the talks broke down, I watched an interview with chief US negotiator Dennis Ross in which he said Barak had made an unprecedented offer to the Palestinians of 95 to 97 percent of the West Bank and all of Gaza. Ross explained that the Palestinian delegation had accepted the offer, but that Arafat reversed his position a day later, coming up with one excuse after another to justify his about-face. All my life I had worried that the Arabs would never allow Israel to live in peace and now, just as an old era was about to end and a new one about to begin, Arafat had reverted to character, at least the character assigned to him over the years by Israeli and western media, and snatched a momentous and historic outcome from me and my people. At first crestfallen, Ross's words served to validate my belief that the Jews had "no partner for peace" because the Palestinians wanted to drive us into the sea. Doubt was erased from my mind and the certainty that I had been right all along tempered my disappointment and provided me a measure of consolation. Barak's offer was proof that my people, generous to a fault, were willing to accommodate an intransigent people.

My reaction to Camp David was consistent with millions of Jews, all of us hoodwinked by a public relations campaign that ascribed qualities to each side that would have been more accurate had they been ascribed to the other. Through a process of identification I had not yet uncovered, I had allowed Israel to become my surrogate. Not only did Ross's words vindicate Israel, most importantly, they vindicated me.

Before the Summit began, Clinton had promised Arafat he would not blame him if it failed, yet he joined Ross in doing just that. The most credible explanation for the president's betrayal is that he wanted to help Barak in his approaching re-election campaign against Ariel Sharon.

Years later, American and Israeli negotiators at Camp David exposed Clinton and Ross's insincerity in putting the onus on Arafat. Barak, for example, had locked himself in his room and would only meet with Arafat one time, but only on the condition they discuss nothing of substance.[498] The prime minister's approach was of great importance because it was his idea to hold the Summit, the whole point of which was to negotiate with Arafat and resolve the Arab-Israeli conflict. Ross himself admitted that the Israeli team at Camp David never provided the Palestinian team with either a written proposal or a single map, while other negotiators explained that the Israelis had pushed the Palestinians to make the small backwater village of Abu Dis their capital in place of Jerusalem.[499] I spent time in Abu Dis in 2010. There wasn't much to see but tin shacks, a few shops, mostly empty roads, and the looming presence of the separation wall that separates the townspeople from Jerusalem. The proposal to replace Jerusalem with Abu Dis was a cynical message from the Israelis that the Palestinian people should be satisfied with the few crumbs Israel might toss their way.

One of the negotiators, Ned Walker, a former ambassador to Israel, explained: "Of the ideas discussed at Camp David ... there is no way in hell the Palestinian people would have accepted this thing."[500]

Aaron David Miller, a negotiator who served six Secretaries of State as an adviser on the Arab-Israeli peace process, quoted Barak's chief negotiator at Camp David: "[I]n the words of ... Shlomo Ben-Ami the prime minister's idea of the concessions required of Israel for such a sweeping accord 'fell far short of even modest Palestinian expectations.'"[501]

In 2006, Ben-Ami admitted, "If I were a Palestinian I would have rejected Camp David as well."[502] He explained that before his team left for Camp David, Barak had shown him a map of two states in which Palestinians would receive 66 percent of the West Bank.[503] Barak never shared that or any other map with the Palestinian team, but the 66 percent he revealed to Ben-Ami was a far cry from the "generous offer" he made to Arafat. What was authentic was the promise he made to the residents of Ma'ale Adumim in September 1999 to "strengthen" their presence and, "'Every house you have built here is part of the state of Israel - forever - period!'"[504] During his tenure as prime minister, the settler population in occupied territory increased by 90 percent.*

A few months after Camp David, President Clinton presented his parameters for peace. An improvement over anything offered by the Israelis, they became the focus of the January 2001 negotiations at Taba, Egypt. The Clinton parameters proposed that 80 percent of Jewish settlers remain in 209 settlements on about 10 percent of West Bank land. Jimmy Carter explained that the 10 percent figure was misleading because it did not account for zones, eight hundred meters in diameter, that would surround each settlement and be inaccessible to Palestinians; roadways connecting one settlement to the next and to Jerusalem, life arteries, ranging in width from five hundred to four thousand meters that provide settlements with sewage, water, communications, and electricity; about one hundred military checkpoints that "block routes going into or between Palestinian communities, combined with an uncountable number of other roads that are permanently closed with large concrete cubes or mounds of earth and rocks."[505] Were this added infrastructure taken into account, the land left to the Palestinians would have approximated the 66 percent of the West Bank Barak had shown Ben-Ami.

---

* Barak's term of office lasted from July 6, 1999 to March 7, 2001.

Clinton also called for Israel to retain control over portions of East Jerusalem and the Jordan River Valley. Palestinians would have no "direct access eastward into Jordan," and the West Bank would be divided "into at least two non-contiguous areas and multiple fragments," some of which were uninhabitable or unreachable.[506] Even with these inducements, the Israeli government had twenty pages of reservations.[507] Barak ended the talks when polls showed that Ariel Sharon would thrash him in Israel's approaching national election. General Amnon Lipkin-Shahak, a former Israeli Chief-of-Staff and member of Barak's negotiating team, admitted: "Taba was bullshit... Taba was not aimed to reach an agreement. Taba was aimed to convince the Israeli Arabs to vote."[508]

In December 2003, the Swiss government sponsored the Geneva Accords, a comprehensive peace treaty drafted by past members of the Israeli and Palestinian negotiating teams. Based on the Clinton parameters, the Roadmap, and the Arab Peace Initiative, the Accords covered all aspects of the Israel-Palestine dispute and received broad support from both the Israeli Left and world leaders, but Prime Minister Sharon ridiculed the plan and called Yossi Beilin, the Israeli side's chief negotiator, a traitor.

In 2011, Qatari-based *Al Jazeera* published a collection of 1,700 confidential documents that dealt with negotiations for a two-state solution. Referred to as the *Palestine Papers*, they divulge what has been plain to impartial observers for decades: Israel does not negotiate in good faith. The *Papers* also clarified that the Palestinians have been far more flexible in negotiations than reported by the media. For example, in Taba in 2001 and Annapolis in 2007, the Palestinians were open to the possibility of ceding to Israel jurisdiction over most of East Jerusalem and a right to land occupied by illegal settlements. They accepted Israel's demand for a demilitarized Palestinian state and considered placing the Noble Sanctuary (Haram esh-Sharif) under the authority of an independent commission. Negotiators were even on the verge of surrendering their right of return and annulling UN Resolution 194. Saeb Erekat, the PA's chief negotiator, told US Mideast envoy George Mitchell: "19 years after the start of the process, it is time for decisions. Negotiations have been exhausted... Palestinians will need to know that 5 million refugees will not go back."[509] These unheard-of concessions had the potential to ignite a backlash throughout the Muslim world, but they were still not good enough for the Israelis. In November 2007, Foreign Minister Tzipi Livni acknowledged Palestinian frustrations:

> I understand the sentiments of the Palestinians when they see the settlements being built. The meaning from the Palestinian perspective is that ... the Israel policy is to take more and more land day after day and that at the end of the day we'll say that it is impossible; we already have the land and cannot create the state.[510]

Livni later modified her comment by explaining that she had described, "the policy of the government for a really long time, [but at the end of 2007 it was] still the policy of some of the parties but not the government."[511]

Livni may have come up with that explanation while heading Prime Minister Ehud Olmert's negotiating team. At the Annapolis Conference in November 2007, Olmert acknowledged: "If the day comes when the two-state solution collapses, and we face a South African-style struggle for equal voting rights (also for the Palestinians in the territories), then, as soon as that happens, the State of Israel is finished."[512]

In 2008, Olmert introduced the most far-reaching peace proposal ever put forward by an Israeli leader. Key features included Israeli withdrawal from 93.7 percent of the West Bank and, contingent upon the Palestinian Authority retaking control from Hamas, full Palestinian sovereignty over the Gaza Strip. To offset its retention of 6.3 percent of the West Bank, he offered a desert area equivalent in size to 5.8 percent of the West Bank. The proposal was unsatisfactory to the Palestinians because it denied their people a right of return, though there was room for negotiation, and did not provide for a contiguous state with East Jerusalem as capital. Olmert's plan was doomed from the start. His term was nearing its end, he had no political backing from senior Israeli politicians, and he was under investigation for bribery and corruption. United States President George W. Bush and Secretary of State Condoleezza Rice warned him his proposal would fail. Bush also warned PA President Mahmoud Abbas that "any deal Olmert negotiated would be dead simply because he was its sponsor."[513] Likewise, Livni and Defense Minister Ehud Barak told Abbas not to accept the plan.

Abbas believed that if Olmert had stayed in office, the two sides could have resolved the outstanding issues within four or five months.[514] His team wanted to continue negotiations after Olmert was replaced by Benjamin Netanyahu on March 31, 2009, but the new prime minister was not interested, just as he was not interested in discussing three proposals Abbas relayed to him through longtime negotiator and *Jerusalem Post* columnist Gershon Baskin, the founder of the Israel-Palestine Center for Research and Information (IPCRI).[515]

On July 9, 2009, historian Benzion Netanyahu admitted what anyone familiar with his son's career knows: "He doesn't support [a Palestinian State]. He supports [proposing] the sorts of conditions that they [the Arabs] will never accept."[516]

Former Shin Bet director Yuval Diskin: "[The Netanyahu] government has no interest in talking with the Palestinians, period. It certainly has no interest in resolving anything with the Palestinians, period."[517]

Another past Shin Bet head, Carmi Gillon: "The state of Israel is run by a bunch of pyromaniacs led by an egomaniac to its ultimate destruction."[518]

While campaigning in early 2015, Netanyahu vowed he would never permit a Palestinian state or the removal of a single settlement. In a May 2015 speech to the Knesset, he echoed Moshe Dayan: "I'm asked if we will forever live by the sword. The answer is yes."[519]

On August 28, 2017, speaking at the West Bank settlement of Barkan, Netanyahu echoed David Ben-Gurion's nationalist fervor:

"This is the land we inherited from our forefathers. This is our land. We have returned here to remain for eternity. There will not be any more uprooting of settlements in the Land of Israel."[520]

I have not forgotten Yitzhak Rabin, considered by many a transformative leader who recognized that living in peace with the Palestinians was in Israel's best interests.* Transformative or not, one month before his assassination on November 4, 1995, Rabin told the Knesset the Palestinians would have an "entity" that would be "less than a state."[521] He called for a "united Jerusalem …as the capital of Israel, under Israeli sovereignty," and declared, "The security border of the State of Israel will be located in the Jordan Valley, in the broadest meaning of that term."[522] In the broadest meaning of that term, the Jordan Valley encompasses 30 percent of the West Bank and contains the northern Dead Sea, the Jordan River basin, and some of the country's richest water resources. Rabin also promised "not to uproot a single settlement in the framework of the interim agreement, and not to hinder building for natural growth."[523] His assurances explain why he dismissed settlers who came to him with offers to vacate their homes in return for compensation and why, in his final term as prime minister, the settler population in the West Bank grew at a faster rate than under previous prime ministers. It explains why, in the wake of Baruch Goldstein's murder of twenty-nine Palestinian worshippers at Hebron's Ibrahimi Mosque (known to Jews as Machpelah or the Cave of the Patriarchs) in 1994, Rabin did not seize the moment and bring his nation into compliance with UN Security Council Resolution 904, which calls on Israel "to implement measures, including, *inter alia*, confiscation of arms, with the aim of preventing illegal acts of violence by Israeli settlers." Instead, his government imposed harsh security measures that restricted Palestinian movement, allowed settlers to dominate areas near the mosque, turned buildings into military sites and housing units for settlers, shut down Shuhada Street, the main avenue

---

* Rabin served as Israeli prime minister from 1974 to 1977 and 1992 to 1995.

leading to the mosque, and drove thousands of Palestinian residents from their homes.

———————

Seventy years of supposed peace talks suggest the longstanding complaint that Palestinian intransigence is the chief obstruction to peace is a projection that describes Israel's posture. With the possible exception of Olmert, Israel's participation has been a display of *takhsisanut*, a deception to conceal its determination to seize as much land as possible while ethnically cleansing as many Palestinians as possible. Instead of falling for the myth of Israel's eagerness to sacrifice land for peace, its loyalists need to accept the actuality of Israel's willingness to sacrifice peace for land.

In 1980, Major General Shlomo Gazit, a former director of Israeli Military Intelligence, told British journalist Alan Hart, "the trouble with us Israelis is that we have become the victims of our own propaganda."[524]

Gazit also said, "If we had a government consisting of only former Directors of Military intelligence we would have had peace with the Palestinians long ago."[525]

24

The Ongoing Theft of Land and Resources

It's important to say [that] this
land is ours. All of it is ours. We
didn't come here to apologize for
that. – Tzipi Hotovely, Deputy
Minister of Foreign Affairs[526]

HOME TO FIVE THOUSAND RESIDENTS, the Palestinian village
of Ni'lin lies twenty-six kilometers west of Ramallah in the
West Bank. At one time its land area equaled fifty-eight thousand
dunams, but as the 1948 war ended, Israel annexed forty thousand
dunams.[527] After its victory in the 1967 war, Israel seized an
additional eight thousand dunams on which it built the settlements
of Kiryat Sefer, Mattityahu, and Maccabim plus a military base,
checkpoints, and Jewish-only roads to serve the existing settlements
of Nili and Na'ale.[528]

Ninety-three percent of Ni'lin sits in Area C, with the rest in
Area B. Area C makes up 61 percent of the West Bank and contains
most of the West Bank's agricultural land, minerals, and water. Only
4 percent of the Palestinian population of Israel-Palestine resides in
Area C, with many having been pushed out to make room for Jewish
growth. Israel's civilian and security administration has jurisdiction
over Area C, which makes it easy to commandeer Palestinian
resources for the benefit of the Jewish population.

Area B, which comprises 21 percent of the West Bank and is mostly rural, falls under the Palestinian Authority's civilian administration with Israel in charge of security. The Oslo Accords prohibit Jewish settlement in Area B, but Jewish outposts in Area C have expanded onto private Palestinian land in Area B. As stated earlier, Area A, the rest of the West Bank, contains the major Palestinian cities and is under Palestinian civilian and security administration.

———————

In 2004, a Ni'lin farmer walked out to inspect his fields only to encounter Israeli bulldozers uprooting his beloved olive trees, his family's primary source of income. The bulldozers were preparing the terrain for a separation wall the Israeli cabinet had authorized in 2002 during the Second Intifada.* The cabinet's rationale for building a wall was to prevent Palestinian violence. A suicide attack at the Park Hotel in the city of Netanya on March 27, 2002 had killed thirty Israelis at a Passover celebration. Given the circumstances, the rationale was plausible, though not forthcoming. Haggai Alon, a past senior adviser to the Defense Ministry, divulged that the route the IDF was setting was designed to prevent the establishment of a Palestinian state.[529]

Justice Minister Tzipi Livni admitted the wall would be, "the future border of the state of Israel" and, "by means of its rulings on the separation fence the High Court was sketching the borders of the state."[530]† Emphasizing her point, Livni said, "One does not have to be a genius to see that the fence will impact the future border."[531]

Another discrepancy in the Israeli cabinet's security explanation is that seventy thousand Palestinians with permits cross through the wall's checkpoints to work in Israel every day and another thirty

---

* The Second Intifada (Intifada is Arabic for "shaking off") began on September 28, 2000, a few months before Ariel Sharon's election as Israel's prime minister, when Sharon and one thousand police officers made an unwelcome visit to the Noble Sanctuary, known to Jews as the Temple Mount. The February 8, 2005 Sharm el-Sheikh Summit, where Palestinians and Israelis agreed to end hostilities, marked the end of the intifada.

† The Israeli government prefers to use the word "fence" as opposed to "wall."

to fifty thousand enter by scaling walls and scrambling through drainage pipes.[532]

The wall redraws the 315 km (195 miles) Green Line, the Jordanian-Israeli armistice line that demarcates Israel proper from occupied Palestinian territory. When completed, its length will be 708 km (440 miles). Eighty-five percent of its route will weave through Palestinian territory, separating farmers from their fields and olive groves and annexing their land for current and future Jewish settlement. In 2004, the International Court of Justice ruled, "The destruction of homes, the demolition of the infrastructure, and the despoilment of land, orchards and olive groves that has accompanied the construction of the wall cannot be justified under any pretext whatsoever."[533]

The land's despoilment channels rainwater and raw sewage into streams near Palestinian villages, which sit at lower elevations than settlements. In 2016, settlements with no sewerage systems emptied nineteen million cubic meters of raw sewage onto Palestinian land, poisoning their crops.[534] Sewage contaminates drinking water, desiccates olive trees, attracts insects and rodents, and endangers the lives of humans and animals. Over the years, soldiers and settlers have uprooted two-and-a-half million fruit trees and eight hundred thousand olive trees.[535]

Israel's government has turned over control of the West Bank's water resources to Mekorot, a state-owned company that routinely siphons Palestinian wells and springs to Jewish vineyards, dairy farms, settlements, outposts, and greenhouses. In sum, Israel extracts 82 percent of Palestinian groundwater for use within its borders and settlements.[536] Jewish settlers irrigate 70 percent of their cultivated land, while Palestinians are only able to irrigate 6 percent of theirs.[537] In February 2019, authorities cut off the water supply to eighteen thousand villagers in Beit Furik and Beit Dajan.[538]

During the first half of 2016, Israel demolished over fifty water and sanitation structures in the West Bank.[539] In April 2017, IDF soldiers entered the Palestinian village of Bardala in the northern Jordan Valley, shut off its water outlets, destroyed the main pipelines that carry water to its farms, and confiscated 168 meters of steel pipe belonging to the village and its farmers.[540]

While claiming its withholding of water is legal because Palestinian villages do not have the permits Israel requires for them to build a water infrastructure, when villages apply for permits, Israel rejects their applications. This forces Palestinians who can afford it to buy expensive tankered water and those who cannot to mount cisterns on their roofs to collect rainwater. Israel's Civil Administration retaliates by issuing demolition orders for non-permitted cisterns and bans Palestinians from repairing old wells or digging new ones. Its strategy is to make life so unbearable, people will evacuate their villages for less coveted areas of the West Bank and leave the door open for more Jewish colonization.

In Jewish settlements in the Jordan Valley, per capita consumption of water is 450 liters per day, while Palestinian per capita consumption in central and northern parts of the Jordan Valley averages sixty liters daily.[541] According to the World Health Organization (WHO), between fifty and one hundred liters of water per person per day are necessary to meet basic needs, such as drinking, washing, hygiene, and sanitation.[542] In Nablus in 2017, residents had access to drinking water once every ten to fourteen days.[543] Villages in the Jenin, Hebron, and Salfit governorates have gone forty days in a row without running water.[544]

If Palestinians had jurisdiction over their water resources, health would be a priority, but under Israeli rule 44 percent of children in rural areas of the West Bank suffer from diarrhea, the world's biggest killer of children under five years of age.[545]

———————

With bulldozers threatening Ni'lin, its citizens mobilized to stop Israel from shaving off another two thousand five hundred dunams from the ten thousand dunams that were still accessible. The village took its complaint to Israel's High Court, where it lost. In 2008, residents began holding weekly nonviolent demonstrations opposing their occupier's land grab.* At a demonstration on April 14, 2017, an Israeli border policeman shot village leader Muhammed Amira with a sponge-tipped bullet.[546] Not as safe as they sound, sponge tips are made of hard, synthetic rubber. They can inflict serious injury and are lethal at close range. An ambulance transported the forty-seven-year-old to the Sheba Medical Center outside of Tel Aviv, where he was shackled to his bed and treated for internal bleeding. Israeli police claim he was throwing stones. Amira and other Ni'lin residents deny the charge.

I met Muhammed during my visit to the region in June 2010. He was a farmer until Israel confiscated his land. He then found work as a teacher at the local elementary school. As we walked together, this gentle father of four told me a story that at first warmed my heart but ended up shocking my senses. One day, one of his students, ten-year-old Ahmed Musa, came to class with a drawing of two flags, one Israeli, the other Palestinian. In front of the classroom, Muhammed asked the boy why he had drawn the picture. When Ahmed replied, "Why can't we all live together in peace," all the kids in the room jumped to their feet and cheered.

During a demonstration on July 29, 2008, the boy was alone in an olive grove when Israeli Border Police officer Omri Abu spotted him and shot him in the head.[547] Ahmed died a few days later. During his funeral service, Israeli forces attacked mourners as they went to bury Ahmed, shooting one man in the head three times at close range. After laying in a coma for three days, the man died.[548] On May 25, 2010, an Israeli court indicted Abu for negligent manslaughter. Acquitted of that charge on October 30, 2012, he was convicted on a lesser charge of negligent use of arms.[549] I heard but cannot substantiate that he was sentenced to one week of house arrest.

Muhammed also told me about an attempt he made during one of Ni'lin's demonstrations to have a heart-to-heart talk with an Israeli commander. Hopeful he could bond with the Israeli as one

---

* Ni'lin is one of many Palestinian villages that hold or have held demonstrations protesting Israel's theft of their land and other human rights violations.

father to another, he tried to share his dream of a better world for Palestinian and Israeli children. With his three-and-a-half-year-old son in his arms, Muhammed outlined the benefits both sides would enjoy if they made peace. The commander reacted by grabbing the boy and tossing him into the cactus bushes. Committed to nonviolent resistance, Muhammed kept his composure. After the incident, his son began expressing intense anger toward his entire family. I believe Muhammed will teach the boy to transform his anger into civil disobedience toward those who are blinded to the humanity of little children.

Muhammed has led Ni'lin's demonstrations since they first began. Moved by the righteousness of his people's struggle, Europeans and Americans, Jews and Christians come to the village to lend their hearts and their voices. In 2009, hoping to educate his people on the historical pressures behind Israel's animosity toward Palestinians, Muhammed helped bring an exhibition of the Nazi Holocaust to Ni'lin.

He has talked young Palestinians out of throwing stones at soldiers. Yaron Ben-Haim, an Israeli activist, who has taken part in the demonstrations, said that Muhammed "has never thrown a stone in his life."[550]

Knesset member Jamal Zahalka of the Joint List:

> Imagine bringing before a truly just judge the stone thrower as well as those responsible for him throwing the stones. Who would the judge put in jail? The one destroying (the stone thrower's) home, expropriating lands, killing his brother, or the boy who threw a stone?[551]

25
Operation Cast Lead

The Israel Defense Forces has to expand the fighting ... to destroy the water and electricity infrastructure, the roads, the transportation and communications, and send Gaza back to the Middle Ages.
– Israeli Interior Minister Eli Yishai[552]

We need to flatten entire neighborhoods in Gaza. Flatten all of Gaza. The Americans didn't stop with Hiroshima – the Japanese weren't surrendering fast enough, so they hit Nagasaki, too. There should be no electricity in Gaza, no gasoline or moving vehicles, nothing. – Gilad Sharon[553]**

DESPITE ISRAEL'S REFUSAL TO PREPARE the soil for peace to blossom, its supporters, who "only want to live in peace," insist that the Jewish state has no choice but to defend itself against an enemy that resents its existence. If life is intolerable for Gazans, Gazans have only themselves to blame. If they fire rockets into Israel, Israel will respond in kind. The facts are more complex, so

---

* Gilad Sharon is the son of Ariel Sharon.

it would be useful to examine a few statistics, followed by a brief review of Operation Cast Lead.

For the period from September 2005 through May 2007, Human Rights Watch compared the number of Palestinian rockets launched against Israel to the number of Israeli rockets launched against Gaza. Palestinian groups fired 2,696 rockets that "on impact produce a small explosion with little shrapnel." The IDF fired 14,617 artillery shells, many of which were "extremely deadly" high explosive 155 mm shells.[554] If loaded with TNT, these shells can spread two thousand fragments in all directions with a lethal radius of fifty to one hundred and fifty meters and a casualty radius of one hundred to three hundred meters.[555]

In another study, this one covering the nine *years* ending on December 31, 2008, the Intelligence and Terrorism Information Center at the Israel Intelligence Heritage and Commemoration Center (IICC) found that Palestinian groups fired 8,088 projectiles into Israel.[556] Compare those figures to the nine *month* period ending in June 2006, during which Israel fired 7,700 projectiles into Gaza.[557]

In 2010, I visited Sderot, an Israeli town in the western Negev. Less than a mile from the Gaza border, Sderot has been a frequent target of rocket launches. As I walked around, I noticed that the impressions left in the ground by the home-made rockets were both shallow and narrow. I remember thinking, *These glorified firecrackers would have to land within five to ten yards from me to cause injury.*

It is one thing to strike back against a nemesis of similar strength who repeatedly inflicts harm upon oneself or one's loved ones. It is a whole other thing to react with aggression when faced with monumentally disproportionate odds. The Palestinians I have met are not suicidal, but given the tragedies and humiliations they have suffered, it would be foolish not to expect some to have been driven to revenge, even to the point of giving no thought for their own lives or the lives of their fellow citizens. Compare their numbers to the 91 to 95 percent of Israel's Jewish citizens who cheered on Operations Cast Lead (December 27, 2008 to January 18, 2009),

Pillar of Defense (November 14-21, 2012), and Protective Edge (July 8, 2014 to August 26, 2014).

———————

From January 1, 2008 through June 18, 2008, Gazans fired 2,278 rockets and mortars at Israel.[558] On June 19, 2008, the sides signed a six-month lull, or ceasefire. Hamas agreed to stop its projectile attacks into Israel and Israel agreed to open the border crossings and end its airstrikes and other acts of aggression against Gaza. From June 19 to November 4, Palestinian rocket and mortar firings fell to thirty-eight (eight of which landed in Gaza).[559] There were no Israeli casualties during this period. The IICC: "The lull was sporadically violated by rocket and mortar shell fire, carried out by rogue terrorist organizations …Hamas was careful to maintain the ceasefire."[560]

Hamas's restraint was not enough to pacify Israel and keep it from violating the ceasefire. On November 4, 2008, IDF Forces snuck into Gaza and killed seven Hamas members, allegedly because they were digging a tunnel into Israel to kidnap Israeli soldiers. Claiming the tunnel was defensive, Hamas responded with a wave of rocket attacks. At an Israeli cabinet meeting on December 21, director of Shin Bet Yuval Diskin advised his colleagues, "Make no mistake, Hamas is interested in maintaining the truce."[561]

Uninterested in Diskin's message, on Shabbos day, December 27, 2008 at 11:30 a.m., a time when the streets are filled with civilians, Israel launched an air offensive against the Gaza Strip. Without warning, Apache helicopters, unmanned drones, and F-16 fighter jets bombed one hundred locations, killing 229 people and wounding 700.[562] Most casualties were civilians. An Israeli analyst noted, "The IDF, which planned to attack buildings and sites populated by hundreds of people, did not warn them in advance to leave, but intended to kill a great many of them, and succeeded."[563]

Two weeks later, on another Saturday, Israeli officials blocked humanitarian supplies from entering Gaza. The explanation they gave for their inaction was that they did not want to violate the Shabbos.[564]

On November 5, 2012, I entered the Gaza Strip as a member of an Interfaith Peace-Builders delegation. During our one-week stay, we visited a block in the center of Gaza City that Israel had bombed four years earlier on December 27. As we stood on the corner, our guide recounted that on that day, he and his son had been standing on the very spot we were then standing on when a loud explosion startled them. Turning toward the sound, they watched a woman as she flew through the air, her body smashing against the side of a building and falling lifeless to the sidewalk.

On January 10, 2009, while hostilities were still raging, Efraim Halevy reminded his colleagues, "If Israel's goal were to remove the threat of rockets from the residents of southern Israel, opening the border crossings would have ensured such quiet for a generation."[565]

Halevy also said:

> [Hamas is] ready and willing to see the establish-ment of a Palestinian state in the temporary borders of 1967... They know that the moment a Palestinian state is established with their cooperation, ...[t]hey will have to adopt a path that could lead them far from their original ideological goals.[566]

The Israeli Air Force boasted that 80 percent of the bombs it blasted Gaza with were precision-guided, with 99 percent hitting their targets.[567] For three weeks, until a January 18, 2009 truce, these precision-guided armaments destroyed hospitals, clinics, concrete factories, water and wastewater treatment facilities, fishing harbors, agricultural lands, mosques, and schools. When the fighting ended, 1,400 Palestinians, including 344 children, were dead. Amnesty International found that "much of the destruction was wanton and resulted from direct attacks on civilian objects as well as indiscriminate attacks that failed to distinguish between legitimate military targets and civilian objects."[568] B'Tselem, Human Rights Watch, the International Red Cross, National Lawyers Guild, and

UNICEF joined Amnesty in accusing Israel of war crimes and possible crimes against humanity. B'Tselem: "Whole families were killed; parents saw their children shot before their very eyes; relatives watched their loved ones bleed to death; and entire neighborhoods were obliterated."[569]

The International Organization for the Elimination of all Forms of Racial Discrimination (EAFORD) wrote, "Israel made no effort to allow civilians to escape the fighting."[570]

The United Nations Fact-Finding Mission on the Gaza Conflict, headed by South African judge Richard Goldstone, a lifelong Jewish loyalist, concluded:

> The operations were carefully planned in all their phases. Legal opinions and advice were given throughout the planning stages and at certain operational levels during the campaign. There were almost no mistakes made according to the Government of Israel. It is in these circumstances that the Mission concludes that what occurred in just over three weeks at the end of 2008 and the beginning of 2009 was a deliberately disproportionate attack designed to punish, humiliate and terrorize a civilian population ...[and] radically diminish its local economic capacity...[571]

———————

An old man in Gaza stood on a corner holding a placard on which were written these words:

> You take my water, burn my olive trees, destroy my house, take my job, steal my land, imprison my father, kill my mother, bombard my country, starve us all, humiliate us all but I am to blame: I shot a rocket back.[572]

26

Do You Sleep with Your Shoes On?

*We each decide whether to make
ourselves learned or ignorant,
compassionate or cruel, generous or
miserly. No one forces us. No one
decides for us, no one drags us along one
path or the other. We are responsible
for what we are. – Maimonides*[573]

A T THE INSISTENCE OF THE George W. Bush administration, on January 26, 2006, the Palestinian National Council, the legislative body of the PLO, held elections in the West Bank and Gaza Strip to select a new government. In a resounding upset, Hamas won seventy-four of 132 seats, ending forty years of domination by the more moderate Fatah Party, which captured forty-five seats. International monitors certified the elections as free and transparent. While voters viewed Hamas as relatively incorrupt, they viewed Fatah as Israel's subcontractor in occupied territory. The unexpected results frustrated American and Israeli expectations that Fatah would retain its governance over the Palestinian people. In an assault on democracy, Israel, with Bush's blessing, arrested thirty-three of Hamas's newly elected legislators, most without charge.*

---

* According to a joint report by the Palestinian Prisoner Society, Addameer (Arabic for *Conscience*), and the Prisoners Commission, since the 2006 elections through December 2018, 40 percent of the members of the Palestinian parliament have been held in administrative detention without charge or trial. (Middle East Monitor, "40% of Palestinian lawmakers detained by Israel since 2006 elections," December 19, 2018).

189

On March 29, 2006, Ismail Haniyeh, who had headed Hamas's candidate list and whom Israel did not arrest, was sworn in as prime minister of the Palestinian Authority. Over the next several months, instead of cooperating to form a stable government, Hamas and Fatah escalated tensions. On February 1, 2007, Fatah fired rocket-propelled grenades and mortars on the Islamic University in Gaza City, setting it on fire. Hamas struck back with attacks on a series of police stations. President Abbas, who preferred a unity government to civil war, arranged to meet with Hamas Political Bureau Chief Khaled Mashaal in Mecca, Saudi Arabia, where the two leaders agreed that the new government, with Haniyeh as prime minister, would reserve influential posts for Fatah members. The reconciliation between the two factions brought relief to their members but alarm to the Israeli and American governments, both of which classify Hamas as a terrorist organization and want to see it isolated. Secretary of State Condoleezza Rice flew to Ramallah and told Abbas to vacate the vote and hold new elections. Abbas acquiesced to Rice's request but did not carry it out. His inaction may have been providential for the US. Had there been a second set of elections, an outcome comparable to the first would have embarrassed Rice and President Bush by forcing them to either nullify the election results and expose their hypocrisy or accept a democratic government led by a "terrorist organization."

In the meantime, the United States supplied Fatah with scores of military radios and combat vehicles and thousands of assault rifles. In June 2007, uneasy with Fatah's enhanced fighting capabilities, Hamas launched a preemptive strike that overthrew the unity government in five days and allowed it to take control of Gaza and possession of most of Fatah's American-supplied equipment. A month later, David Wurmser resigned his post as Vice-President Dick Cheney's chief Middle East adviser.[574] Accusing the Bush administration of "engaging in a dirty war in an effort to provide a corrupt dictatorship [led by Abbas] with victory," Wurmser did not believe Hamas had any intention of taking over the Gaza Strip: "It looks to me that what happened wasn't so much a coup by Hamas but an attempted coup by Fatah that was pre-empted before it could happen[575]

In a similar vein, a senior Israeli intelligence figure remarked, "When Hamas preempts [a putsch], everyone cries foul, claiming it's a military putsch by Hamas–but who did the putsch?"[576]

The split between Hamas and Fatah was welcome news to the Israeli leadership, which opposed a Palestinian government that refused to collaborate with its policies. Another benefit was that Hamas's isolation in Gaza meant it would not compete with Fatah in the West Bank. With US approval, Israel set up a blockade of Gaza, which is illegal under international law and in effect as of this writing. Israel admits the blockade is "a form of economic warfare."[577] In a 2008 cable, US embassy officials in Tel Aviv wrote:

> Israeli officials have confirmed …on multiple occa-
> sions that they intend to keep the Gazan economy on
> the brink of collapse without quite pushing it over
> the edge [with the aim of having Gaza's economy]
> functioning at the lowest level possible consistent
> with avoiding a humanitarian crisis.[578]

Unperturbed with the humanitarian crisis in Gaza, and ignoring warnings from the International Red Cross, United Nations, and WHO that the crisis was intensifying, in June 2017, at Mahmoud Abbas's request, Israel cut electricity down to two-and-a-half hours daily, with blackouts sometimes lasting more than twenty-four hours. After the cuts went into effect, my friend Rana, who has spent her entire life in Gaza, wrote: "No security. No water. No electricity. No salary. No medicine. No milk." Abbas wanted to weaken Hamas's power in the Gaza Strip and demonstrate to President Trump his commitment to fighting "terrorism." By doing his bidding, Israel compromised its responsibilities under article 56 of the *Fourth Geneva Convention*:

> To the fullest extent of the means available to it, the
> Occupying Power has the duty of ensuring and main-

taining, with the cooperation of national and local authorities, the medical and hospital establishments and services, public health and hygiene in the occupied territory.

Fourteen hospitals and sixteen health facilities were at risk of partial or total closure.[579] Without refrigeration, blood and vaccines were on the verge of spoiling. Obstetric facilities, operating rooms, hemodialysis centers, and emergency departments had to discontinue critical services.[580] Kidney dialysis machines, breathing regulators, respirators, and other medical devices were inoperable.

In early July 2017, Rana told me that babies lying in their cribs were dying. OCHA's "Humanitarian Needs Overview" reported, "An estimated ten thousand newborn infants out of fifty-five thousand born every year are acutely vulnerable and in need of transfer to nursery and neonatal intensive care units for specialized life-saving treatment."[581] One week later, Rana wrote: "Thirty hours without electricity. Everything is ruined. Dying in the very hot weather." In its July 2017 report, "Gaza Ten Years Later," the United Nations noted, "An 11 year-old child has not experienced more than 12 hours of electricity in a single day in his/her lifetime."[582]

The blockade has left its mark on land, air, and sea. Sardines, Gaza's primary catch, make their habitats at least six nautical miles from shore while breeding grounds of larger fish are at least eight NM from shore. The Oslo Accords approved a fishing range of twenty NM, but Israel unilaterally reduced it to six, though its naval vessels sometimes open fire on and intercept fishing boats as little as one NM from shore. In the first eight months of 2018, Israel carried out 233 attacks on Gazan fishermen, killing one, injuring fifteen, detaining forty-one, and confiscating thirteen boats.[583]

A typical Israeli exercise is the "swimming procedure," in which armed sailors force fishermen to undress, dive into the sea, even in hazardous weather, and swim to the Israeli ship. Blindfolded, handcuffed, and interrogated, the navy transports them and their boats to the Israeli port of Ashdod. Authorities eventually send the fishermen back to Gaza, but they impound their boats, well aware they are depriving them of a living and making life intolerable for their families. What is the point of this animus? The fishermen have no weapons and 95 percent live below the poverty line.[584] All they are doing is struggling to eke out a meager living. The only reasons the Israeli navy harasses them is to accommodate the sadistic tendencies of the seamen or their commanders and to remind the fishermen that the State of Israel is master over their lives and can do whatever it wants whenever it wants. Each time a fisherman puts out to sea, he risks arrest, injury, or death.

Limited fishing zones combined with Israel's imperious behavior have devastated the fishing industry, once among the most prosperous in Gaza. In 2000, the Gaza Strip had ten thousand registered fishermen. Today that figure is four thousand and half are grounded because Israel bans the materials they need to repair their boats. In this same period, the Strip's population has grown from 1.13 million to two million. Fewer fishing boats lead to reduced supply, which makes protein expensive and imperils the health of Gaza's population.

Targeted bombings have destroyed Gaza's water infrastructure and sewage facilities and poisoned the water and soil with depleted uranium and other compounds. Even so, Israel will not allow Gaza's Water Authority to repair or rebuild its water treatment plants. In November 2013, the *New York Times* wrote that 3.5 million cubic feet (99 million liters) of raw sewage spills into the Mediterranean Sea every day.[585] That figure is expected to grow to over 4.2 million cubic feet by 2020.[586] The Palestinian Environmental Quality Authority warns that sewage has contaminated over half of Gaza's beaches, while Medical Aid for Palestinians says 73 percent of the shoreline is "dangerously polluted."[587;588] Swimming is prohibited in areas where "the sea is full of floating excrement."[589] In July 2017, a five-year-old Palestinian boy fell ill and died after swimming.[590]

Fifty percent of Gaza's population receives water for domestic use eight hours every four days, 30 percent for eight hours every three days, and 20 percent for eight hours every two days.[591] The

UN: "No one remembers a time in recent memory when drinkable water reliably appeared out of the tap."[592] Sewage and salt pollute 97 percent of Gaza's water.[593] As a result, 50 percent of the Strip's children suffer from parasitic infections and 41 percent from diarrhea.[594;595] Blue baby syndrome, pediatric cancer, marasmus (severe malnutrition), gastroenteritis, salmonella, and typhoid fever are at dangerous levels.[596] Viral hepatitis, diarrhea, and acute bloody diarrhea are the leading causes of death from infectious disease. Clean water is so scarce that surgeons refrain from washing their hands before performing surgery.[597]

In August 2017, I learned that Rana's family pays fourteen dollars every four days for tankered water, six times the standard rate for regular tap water.[598] With his master's degree in Management and Human Resources Development, Rana's husband earns nine dollars daily, but he hasn't been able to find work for more than twelve days each month, so his highest monthly wage amounts to $110. No buses run near the family's home, so Tamer spends thirty-five to forty dollars per month for roundtrip transportation. His net income of seventy to seventy-five dollars does not even cover the family's water needs, let alone rent and food. Without help from friends, Rana, Tamer, and little Rannie would be homeless. Still, with Gaza's overall unemployment rate at 43 percent, the highest in the world, and youth unemployment at 60 percent, they are among the lucky ones.

With these hardships, it is confounding that Israel, a world leader in water technology, continues to block the construction of a desalination plant that would provide water to two hundred thousand Gazans.[599] Israel's desalination, water recycling, and conservation policies have made it the only country in the world whose deserts are shrinking due to an abundance of water.[600] Not a single Israeli experiences water scarcity.[601] *Scientific American* writes that "Israel has more water than it needs."[602] The obvious conclusion one can draw from the facts is that Israel is poisoning the people of Gaza.

Ten percent of Gazan children under five suffer from chronic malnutrition, while 7.1 percent are "moderately stunted" in height.[603;604] Overall, one in five has post-traumatic stress disorder. Among children exposed to heavy bombardment during Operation Protective Edge, the rate for PTSD is 54 percent.[605] These children exhibit flashbacks, nightmares, difficulty sleeping, and other symptoms.[606] Prostate and other cancers, kidney disease, osteoporosis, and high blood pressure are all over-represented in the general population.

Israel does not allow sanitation trucks inside Gaza, causing tons of garbage to pile up on the streets. Nor does it allow building materials, medical devices, or medicine. Years of bombings have destroyed the flower, citrus, and olive industries, once essential to Gaza's economy. Doctors work seventy hours per week for an average salary of $280 per month.[607]

Israel has allocated 30 to 50 percent of Gaza's arable land for buffer zones. Accessible only to occupation forces, the zones extend along Israel and Gaza's common land borders. According to the IDF, they are supposed to penetrate three hundred meters into Gaza, but studies document the shooting and killing of farmers as much as two kilometers from the border. Oxfam researcher Mohammed Ali Abu Najela: "Nearly every week, there are reported cases of farmers being shot at."[608] Najela quoted an aphorism Gazans attribute to Israeli soldiers: "If I can see you, I will shoot you."[609] When we teach young and often bored soldiers that "it's a mitzvah to kill Arabs," and when there are no consequences for their behavior, the temptation for some to test their long-range shooting skills is hard to resist.

With the uncertainties farmers face, it is maddening they must also contend with toxic herbicides. Hired by Israel's Defense Ministry to kill off weeds, private aviation companies fly crop dusters that spray both sides of the Israel-Gaza border.[610] The wind blows westward and deposits chemical residue as much as 2,200 meters into Gazan territory. The Red Cross says the spraying has "totally destroyed" crops between 100 and 900 meters from the border.[611] Israeli authorities are not naïve. They know the direction the wind blows and they know herbicides seep into the soil, pollute the water, and destroy more than just weeds. They also know that the chemicals in the herbicides, glyphosate, oxyfluorfen, and diuron, can be dangerous to human health, yet they refuse to discontinue their use, nor are they willing to compensate farmers for their losses.[612;613] The World Health Organization classifies glyphosate "as probably carcinogenic to humans," while the US National Library of Medicine at the National Institutes of Health says, "exposure to diuron may exert harmful effects on fetal development and damage human health."[614;615]

In a society at risk of starvation, the poisoning of crops is alarming. With only enough food allowed in to keep residents at a subsistence level, 80 percent of Gaza's residents depend on the United Nations Relief and Works Agency for food aid. During my delegation's visit, we inspected an UNRWA food storage warehouse in Gaza City. Its entire inventory was made up of bags of white rice, white flour, white powdered milk, and white sugar, along with bottles of oil. In no way do these foods constitute a nutritious diet. Food deprivation is a major reason 39.1 percent of pregnant women and 50 percent of children up to the age of two suffer from anemia.[616]

As we toured the devastation left in the wake of Operation Cast Lead, we witnessed piles of rubble dotting the landscape, the exteriors of still-standing buildings riddled with holes from mortar attacks, and foul-smelling sewage spilling out onto the streets. The once elegant airport, bombed in 2001 and 2002 and again during Cast Lead, was a wasteland of torn up runways and ragged blocks of concrete.

My delegation visited the Rafah refugee camp in the southern Gaza Strip. Donkey carts, banged-up little motorcycles, and rusted old cars crept along narrow, dirt streets bordered by crumbling walls made of cinder block and mud. I spent an hour with a resident of the camp, a man in his mid-thirties, who told me that both his mother and two-year-old daughter had needed medical treatment Gaza's hospitals were not equipped to provide. His family applied for medical permits so they could travel to Israel, East Jerusalem, or the West Bank, but officials rejected their applications. A short time later, the mother and daughter died, two more casualties of Israeli indifference to Palestinian life.

In 2017, Israel prevented eleven thousand sick people from making their scheduled medical appointments.[617] Bureaucrats automatically reject applications for medical permits from Hamas members and their relatives, a cynical excuse for preventing sick people from getting the medical care they need. Hamas, after all, has been Gaza's dominant political party for years, so most residents have at least one relative who is a member.

Many of the ill have died waiting for authorities to approve or reject their applications. Delays can last for weeks or months. Some applicants never receive a response. Ghada Majadala and Mor Efrat of Israeli Physicians for Human Rights noted, "A non-reply does not enable patients to use their right to appeal a refusal if one is given. Not replying for many months attests to a policy of contempt for the patients' suffering."[618]

PHR's director, Ran Goldstein: "The fact that patients sometimes don't get answers for months is cruel and the weakest population pays the price."[619]

In August 2018, Gaza's al-Rantisi hospital halted all chemotherapy treatment due to a shortage of medication. Forty-five chemotherapy drugs out of its stock of sixty were depleted.[620] Israel will not allow patients to leave Gaza to buy these drugs and it won't allow hospitals to import them. The hospital warned that the unavailability of one drug, Neubogen, "highly threatened" the lives of eight thousand cancer patients.[621]

———————

In 1970, the Israeli government established the Gush Katif bloc of settlements on the southwestern edge of the Gaza Strip. Bordered by the Mediterranean Sea in the northwest, Egypt and the city of Rafah in the southwest, and Khan Yunis and Deir al-Balah in the east and northeast, Gush Katif covered 25 percent of Gaza's land area.

My new acquaintance explained that in the settlement's early days, the shortest distance between settler houses and the seaward side of his refugee camp was six hundred meters, but settlers kept building within that space until the distance shrank to five meters. The settlers never sought permission to construct homes on land that was not legally theirs, nor did they pay for the land. Their conviction that God gave the land to the Jewish people and that Palestinians are squatters was enough to justify their covetousness as a fulfillment of God's will. Settlers sometimes cite the Book of Numbers 33:55:

> But if ye will not drive out the inhabitants of the land from before you, then shall those that ye let remain of them be as thorns in your eyes, and as pricks in your sides, and they shall harass you in the land wherein ye dwell.

My Gazan friend told me the settlers made it dangerous, if not impossible, for him and his friends to walk on the beach or swim in the Mediterranean. A feeling of nausea washed over me when he told me the settlers were so hateful that every half hour he and his friends would stop what they were doing and thank Allah they were still alive.

———————

Israel has fostered the illusion that the 2005 unilateral withdrawal from Gaza of Gush Katif's 8,500 settlers, known as the *Disengagement Plan of Prime Minister Ariel Sharon*, was evidence of Sharon's sincerity in wanting to make peace. George W. Bush, who was out of his league in his dealings with the prime minister, wrote to Sharon that the "steps described in the plan will mark real progress toward realizing my June 24, 2002 vision, and make a real contribution towards peace."[622] Bush never understood that Sharon's refusal to coordinate the withdrawal with the Palestinian Authority was at odds with the Roadmap for Peace. He mistook the Gaza disengagement as a step forward, when it was in fact a continuation of Sharon's longstanding goal of politicide, the extinguishment of all prospects for an independent Palestinian political entity: "My plan is difficult for the Palestinians, a fatal blow. There's no Palestinian state in a unilateral move."[623]

Chief adviser Dov Weisglas elaborated on Sharon's plan: "The disengagement is actually formaldehyde. It supplies the amount of formaldehyde that's necessary so that there will not be a political process with the Palestinians."[624]

Weisglas reiterated that the disengagement ended negotiations over Jerusalem, borders, and refugees, thereby preventing any chance for a peace treaty:

> Effectively, this whole package that is called the Palestinian state, with all that it entails, has been removed from our agenda indefinitely. And all this with authority and permission. All with a presidential blessing and the ratification of both houses of Congress.[625]

On November 8, 2012, random Israeli machine gunfire erupted in the village of Abassan Kabira in the southern Gaza Strip, fatally wounding thirteen-year-old Hamid Abu Daqqa as he was playing soccer on the narrow dirt road in front of his house. The next day, my delegation attended the boy's funeral, a sad and dignified occasion. Afterwards, Hamid's playmates took us to the spot where he was shot. Sustaining wounds to his chest, Hamid had stumbled over to the front door of his house before collapsing, his Real Madrid tee shirt soaked in blood. Ronaldo, Real Madrid's superstar, was Hamid's favorite soccer player. By the time paramedics showed up, the youth was comatose. He died before the ambulance reached the hospital.

One-and-a-half kilometers from the Israeli border, Abassan Kabira is near a buffer zone. In conversations with residents, I learned that Israeli tanks, drones, and helicopters enter Gaza as often as six days a week. Once inside the border, they fire in all directions to scare away anyone in the area.

After saying goodbye to Hamid's friends, my fellow delegates and I began walking back to our bus when we came upon a house in the final stages of construction. Some of us climbed to the roof to take in a view of the border area, which was marked by a grove of trees, beyond which sat Israeli tanks. Coming down and continuing our walk, we arrived at the bus where a group of villagers was waiting to speak with us. With my Gazan friend Khalil translating, a middle-aged woman asked me, "Do you sleep with your shoes on?" I realized this was a rhetorical question, so I replied by asking if she slept with her shoes on. She explained that Israel's incursions into Gaza are so terrifying that many residents sleep with their shoes on so they can jump out of bed at a moment's notice and run to safer areas. During the next couple days, the residents I spoke with confirmed that this phenomenon is widespread throughout the Gaza Strip.

Years of control by a ruthless power have traumatized Gaza's two million residents. Locked inside one of the most populated spots on Earth, a Hell realm with not enough water, electricity, or employment, they are unindicted prisoners serving indeterminate sentences with nothing to look forward to—no money, no food, no future. Former British Prime Minister David Cameron has called Gaza a "prison camp" and "a giant open prison."[626] Cameron is correct, though with a median age of 17.2, the Gaza Strip is predominantly a children's prison camp.[627]

As early as 1907, Ben-Gurion and other Jewish immigrants organized boycotts to starve Palestinians and drive them from the land.[628] Sixty years later, at the end of the Six-Day War, Prime Minister Levi Eshkol made a similar suggestion with regard to

Gaza: "Perhaps if we don't give them enough water they won't have a choice, because the orchards will yellow and wither."[629] Another fifty-two years have passed and Ben-Gurion and Eshkol's suggestions have become Israeli policy. But Palestinians are steadfast in their determination not to surrender their rights. Their spirit of sumud (steadfastness) gives them the courage to continue resisting the oppressive conditions Israel subjects them to every day of their lives.

27

Yetzer Hara: The Evil Inclination

I and the public know
What all schoolchildren learn,
Those to whom evil is done
Do evil in return.
– W.H. Auden, "September 1, 1939"

I still say we have the most moral
army in the world. – Ehud Barak[630]

F OR MOST OF MY LIFE, it went without saying that Israel's armed forces were the most moral in the world. I didn't need its leaders to affirm the obvious. I just knew it, but when they did affirm it, I felt a sense of pride along with gratitude that my people were superior to other people. If someone tried to contradict my dogma with tales of attacks on schools, hospitals, mosques, and other civilian structures, I maligned their information as anti-Semitic propaganda. My confidence was based on a life-long conviction that Jews were by nature both innocent and just, then comparing those qualities to what little I knew about Arabs, most of which came from biblical stories that portrayed them as sworn enemies of my people. It never entered my mind that I might be biased or could learn something of value if I took the time to research the history. The difference between Jewish honor and Arab enmity was self-evident.

My good fortune is that the awakening in July 2006 transformed my view of the world and motivated me to correct the benighted arguments I once cherished. That includes sharing my insights so that others, many as misinformed as I had been, might also recognize that blind acceptance of the Israeli narrative makes peace impossible. Together, we could examine the history in a neutral light and uncover the factors that induce us to fuel conflict, even when we think we are contributing to peace. In the years since the awakening, my research has concentrated on Israeli sources, including the Ministries of Defense, Internal Security, and Foreign Affairs, the writings of Israeli prime ministers, and the Israeli state, Central Zionist, and IDF archives.

Earlier, I mentioned that compulsory transfer of the indigenous people was a tenet of the Zionist movement. Neither Ben-Gurion nor other Zionist leaders were under any illusions they could achieve their goals through peaceful efforts; and if they were so single-minded that they were prepared to turn their backs on half the Jewish children of Germany if they could bring the other half to the new Jewish homeland, there was little they would not do.

During the 1948 War of Independence, Ben-Gurion said, "A small reaction to [Arab hostility] does not impress anyone. A destroyed house – nothing. Destroy a neighborhood and you begin to make an impression."[631]

In his diary, Ben-Gurion recorded Palmach commander, General Yigal Allon's intentions:*

> There is a need now for strong and brutal reaction...
> If we accuse a family – we need to harm them with-
> out mercy, women and children included. Otherwise
> this is not an effective reaction. During the operation
> there is no need to distinguish between guilty and not
> guilty.[632]

Military historian Aryeh Itzhaki, director of the IDF archives in the 1960s, tried to convert Israeli discourse from denial to reality:

---

* The Palmach were the guerrilla strike force of the Haganah.

[A] generation has gone by and it is now possible to face up to the ocean of lies in which we were brought up. In almost every town conquered in the War of Independence acts were committed that are defined as war crimes, such as blind killings, massacres, and even rapes.[633]

Itzhaki's definition of a massacre:

[The] deliberate killing of between 50 and 250 victims in a single episode, whether these are civilians, including old people, women, and children (often by blowing up houses with the occupants locked inside), or civilians and Palestinian soldiers who had been taken prisoner and were killed with a bullet to the back of the head before being thrown into a common ditch.[634]

Throughout Israel's history, the commission of war crimes has not disqualified the guilty from advancing their careers. Commanding officers and the political leadership often abet cruel behavior in occupied Palestinian territory. Instead of being court-martialed and dismissed from the IDF, Ariel Sharon was afforded the personal protection of David Ben-Gurion. In time, he ascended to his nation's highest office. Before they were prime ministers, Menachem Begin and Yitzhak Shamir were heads of Jewish terrorist groups, the Irgun and Stern Gang.

In 2006, Prime Minister Ehud Olmert bragged: "The IDF is the most moral army in the world. It does not and never has made a policy of targeting civilians."[635]

Ze'ev Schiff, who Olmert undoubtedly was familiar with, was described by the BBC as "the most respected military analyst in Israel."[636] At his funeral in 2007, former Defense Minister Moshe Arens eulogized: "His articles were read by statesmen and politicians, generals and reservists and they knew that he wrote the stark truth."[637]

Schiff's truth: "the Israeli Army has always struck civilian populations, purposely and consciously …the Army …has never distinguished civilian [from military] targets …[but] purposely attacked civilian targets."[638]

Olmert must also have known that the IDF's rules of engagement prohibit soldiers from interfering with settlers, even while they are harassing Palestinian civilians. IDF soldiers accompany parents and their children to Palestinian areas where the youngsters throw stones, spit at, and scream at Palestinian kids walking home from school. The state empowers its soldiers to enforce the law on Palestinians, but not on Israelis. Rather than protecting Palestinian children from settler violence, they facilitate it. Throwing stones at Jews is terrorism, but throwing stones at Palestinians is a national pastime. Former soldier Ido Even-Paz:

> [T]here is no way [for a soldier] to behave ethically in occupied territory. It's a system in which Palestinians are always treated as inferior, always viewed as the enemy, whoever they are. Every day, the job is to inflict collective punishment. We were told explicitly that we were waging psychological war, that we were there to intimidate them. In the middle of the night we raided families' homes, chosen randomly, waking up frightened children.[639]

Selective memory and repression help us to maintain self-images of decency and righteousness. When he praised the IDF's morality, the killings, massacres, and rapes Aryeh Itzhaki acknowledged never crossed Olmert's mind, even though both of his parents were members of the Irgun. Olmert also drew a blank on Ariel Sharon, whom he succeeded as prime minister when the latter suffered a stroke that left him in a vegetative state for the remaining eight years of his life. Sharon may have been an exaggerated symbol of the Israeli military, but he was no aberration. If he were, his career would have ended in the 1950s.

In late 2008, when word came in that Jewish settlers in Hebron had thrown rocks at civilians, had shot and wounded three of them, and had set cars, fields, and buildings on fire, Olmert said:

> As a Jew, I was ashamed at the scenes of Jews opening fire at innocent Arabs in Hebron. There is no other definition than the term "pogrom" to describe what I have seen. We are the sons of a nation who know what is meant by a pogrom, and I am using the word only after deep reflection.[640]

I am glad Olmert had the decency to make that statement and that he had the emotional intelligence to recognize the parallel between the persecution of Palestinians and the persecution of Jews, but I wish he had said *as a human being* he was ashamed. Not only is it unnecessary to identify as a Jew to feel compassion for another human being's pain, it was "as a Jew" that Olmert had been oblivious to Palestinian suffering. Like the rabbi I referred to in chapter two, Olmert, at least for a moment, was able to get in touch with his common humanity.

A more recent example of Israeli authorities' tolerance for violence from their side occurred on May 24, 2016 in the Tel Rumeida neighborhood of Hebron when IDF medic Elor Azaria executed Abdel Fattah al-Sharif as he lay on the road, barely conscious, critically wounded, and surrounded by Israeli soldiers. Before shooting him, Azaria told the soldiers that al-Sharif, who had attacked and injured an Israeli soldier, "needs to die."[641] The incident was filmed, leading to worldwide headlines that forced Israel to put the medic on trial. Convicted of manslaughter, Azaria was sentenced to eighteen months in prison, a lesser punishment than Palestinian children get for throwing stones. After the sentencing, his family and supporters hugged him, hailed him as a hero, and sang Hatikvah, Israel's national anthem. Extreme right-wing groups held rallies where they chanted, "He is a hero! Release him – Kill the Arabs!"[642]

A majority of Israelis believe Azaria deserved no prison time, and a significant number believe the rule of law should not encumber acts of "heroism" like the killing of a Palestinian assailant, even if the assailant is unconscious at the time.[643] In their veneration of him, Azaria's admirers ignore the oath the medic swore to care for the wounded and to consider his "actions with understanding, wisdom, and love of humanity."[644] Instead of acting as a medic, Azaria acted as an executioner.

Upset with the prison sentence, Prime Minister Netanyahu and other Knesset members asked IDF Chief-of-Staff Gadi Eisenkot to pardon Azaria. Eisenkot did not go that far, but he reduced the sentence to fourteen months, noting that Azaria was a "combat soldier and a warrior [who had] endured a lot."[645] How much more do Palestinians have to endure before Israelis treat them with a fraction of the compassion they lavished upon Azaria?

In November 2017, Avigdor Lieberman beseeched President Reuven Rivlin to pardon Azaria. The only remaining official with that authority, Rivlin declined, noting that Azaria, who had not begun his sentence until August of that year, was eligible for release as early as February 2018. Journalist Bradley Burston described the public's reaction to Rivlin's decision as "a level of extreme-right venom that approached the ferocity of the public-arena hate storm which directly preceded – and led to – the 1995 assassination of then-prime minister Yitzhak Rabin."[646] Burston singled out Benjamin Netanyahu for this latest hate storm, just as journalists had singled out Netanyahu for the hate storm against Rabin.

After serving nine months of his sentence, Azaria was discharged for good behavior on May 8, 2018. When he returned home, Israelis greeted him with signs saying, "It's so good to have you home, soldier of us all," and, "Welcome home, Elor the hero."[647]

Transportation and Intelligence Minister Israel Katz wrote, "I appeal to President Reuven Rivlin to act now to delete Elor's criminal record so he can integrate into civilian life…"[648]

Culture Minister Miri Regev said, "I wish for Elor and his

family to return to a normal way of life. There remains just one more objective: to wipe Elor's criminal record."[649]

Education Minister Naftali Bennett tweeted, "Elor, it's good to have you home."[650]

Two months later, Azaria returned to the scene of his crime, where jubilant settlers gave him a warm welcome. As they raised a toast, he raised the Israeli flag.[651] A month later, Azaria said:

> I am at peace with what I did, I acted properly and followed my inner truth. I did the right thing and this affair shouldn't have become what it did… There is no doubt that if you took me back to those seconds in Hebron …I would act exactly the same all over again because that is what had to be done.[652]

––––––––––––

For decades, settlers, under the watchful eye of the IDF, have assaulted Palestinian farmers, poisoned their crops, dropped sheep and chicken carcasses into their wells, cut down their olive trees, attacked their livestock, shot at them, and spray-painted mosque and church walls with slurs like, "Death to the Arabs" and, "Jesus is a monkey." Except for cases that attract widespread attention, the settlers have license to act with near impunity as their political and religious leaders encourage the sense of entitlement and paranoia that incites their behavior in the first place. In July 2015, in an appalling act of violence, two settlers firebombed the Duwabshe home in the northern West Bank village of Duma. Eighteen-month-old Ali was burned alive. A few weeks later, his parents, Saad and Riham, succumbed to their wounds. With burns covering 80 percent of his body, Ali's four-year-old brother Ahmad was the lone survivor. Before bombing the house, the settlers spray-painted the Star of David and the Hebrew words, "Vengeance" and "Long live the Messiah" on its outer walls.[653]

Politicians, many of whom had incited violence in the past,

denounced the crimes, but the government refused to pay compensation to the Duwabshe family.[654] Avigdor Lieberman explained that Jewish victims of Palestinian violence are entitled to compensation, but Palestinian victims of Jewish violence are not.[655]

The malevolence of two despicable settlers should not lead us to denigrate an entire group, but when a child's incineration becomes a rallying cry, decent people, especially Jews who are vocal in their defense of Israel, have to sit up and take notice. At a Jewish wedding reception in December 2015, dozens of guests were filmed dancing around a photo of the deceased infant. They were celebrating his death and praying for more revenge on Palestinians.[656] Revenge for what? For resisting settlers' demands they accept God's covenant with Abraham and turn their land over to Jews. Imagine what the reaction would be in Israel if anyone, let alone a Palestinian, had firebombed a Jewish home and killed a child.

Murderous hatred toward Palestinians is no aberration. Shmuel Eliyahu, chief rabbi of Safed, one of Judaism's four holy cities, urged the Israeli army to stop arresting Palestinians, proposing instead that "it must execute them and leave no one alive."[657*]

In 2010, rabbis Yitzhak Shapira and Yosef Elitzur from the Od Yosef Chai yeshiva in the settlement of Yitzhar near Nablus published *The King's Torah* (Torat Hamelech), *Part One: Laws of Life and Death Between Israel and the Nations*. Endorsed by prominent rabbis, this compendium of halacha explains that the sixth commandment, "Thou shalt not kill," applies only "to a Jew who kills a Jew."[658] The rabbis instruct their readers: "There is a reason to kill a child if it is clear that they will grow to harm us; in such a situation the attack should be directed specifically at them."[659]

The rabbis also teach that goyim are "uncompassionate by nature" and that attacks on them "curb their evil inclination."[660†]

The hatred religious settlers harbor for Palestinians does not

---

* The three other holy cities are Jerusalem, Hebron, and Tiberias.

† According to Judaism, man is created with two inclinations. The *yetzer hara* (literally, "the evil creation") refers to the inborn inclination to do evil, while the *yetzer hatov* refers to the inborn inclination to do good.

arise in a vacuum. It incubates within their communities and erupts in actions like the Duwabshe murders. Shapira and Elitzur may think that curbing a goy's evil inclination is an act of compassion, but fanatics who have lost touch with their inborn compassion cannot sense compassion within others. Nor do they possess the wherewithal to curb the evil inclination that so twists their humanity they consider the murders of babies manifestations of their good inclination.

On June 20, 2018, Jewish protesters gathered outside the Central District Court in Lod where a preliminary hearing for Amiram Ben-Uliel, the chief defendant in the Duwabshe arson/murder case, was to take place. A member of the Hilltop Youth, a violent, extremist, religious-nationalist settler movement, Ben-Uliel had confessed to the murders. The protesters held signs with inscriptions such as, "the people are with you." When Ali's grandfather Hussein Duwabshe walked out of the courthouse, the crowd taunted him with chants of, "Where is Ali, there is no Ali, Ali burned. Ali is on the grill" and, "Where is Ali? Where is Riham? Where is Saad? It's too bad Ahmed didn't burn as well."[661] The police stood around, doing nothing. Ben-Uliel's case is still pending.

On July 12, 2018, an Israeli court ordered Ben-Uliel's unnamed co-defendant released from detention and remanded to house arrest. Seventeen years of age at the time of the crime, prosecutors charged him with conspiracy and with helping to plan the murders.[662] On May 12, 2019, his attorneys negotiated a plea deal with the State Prosecutor's Office that dropped the murder charges but convicted him of conspiracy to commit arson. Prosecutors promised not to ask for a prison sentence greater than five-and-a-half years.[663] The Duwabshe family derided the deal as "unfair," adding, "it encourages the settler gangs to commit more crimes."[664]

The police had arrested another suspect, Meir Ettinger, within three days of the arson attack, but declined to charge him for the Duwabshe case. Implicated in a string of hate crimes, Ettinger was released after ten months in detention.[665] He is the grandson of the late Meir Kahane, an extremist rabbi whose motto was "Arabs out!"

Assassinated in 1990, the Brooklyn born Kahane was the founder of Kach (Thus), an ultra-nationalist political party that lobbied for the restoration of the biblical nation of Israel. Rejecting its racist platform, in 1988 Israel's High Court banned the party from the Knesset. In 1994, after Kahane admirer Baruch Goldstein carried out his mass murder at the Ibrahimi Mosque, the Rabin government passed a law outlawing Kach as a terror organization.

With Prime Minister Netanyahu's backing, Kahane's nationalistic ideas have spread to the point that they have incarnated in a new political party, Otzma Yehudit (Jewish Power), whose members former senior Mossad and IDF intelligence official Yossi Alpher calls, "extremist hate-mongers who literally worship at the tomb of Baruch Goldstein."[666] Like Kach and the prime minister himself, Otzma Yehudit opposes a Palestinian state. Its goals are to restore Israeli sovereignty over the Temple Mount, nullify the Oslo Accords, annex the entire West Bank, and get rid of Palestinians who do not pledge loyalty to Israel. Netanyahu has promised that if re-elected he will give control over the Department of Education to these bigots, ensuring that a new generation of Israeli schoolchildren will be taught to deny the humanity of the other and, in so doing, lose touch with their own humanity.

There is no evidence the Duwabshe case has stimulated any soul-searching within the Israeli government. Minister of Justice Ayelet Shaked met twice with the families of five minors arrested in October 2018 for throwing stones at Palestinian vehicles and for causing the death of a forty-seven-year-old woman.[667] She told one mother to "stay strong."[668] Israel will not imprison these youths, deport them, or demolish their homes or the homes of their relatives, nor will it impose a closure on their settlement.

28

The Insanity of War

*First use force, and if force
doesn't work, use more force. –*
Popular Israeli Saying[669]

*That since wars begin in the minds
of men, it is in the minds of men
that the defences of peace must be
constructed.* – From the Preamble
to the UNESCO Constitution

IN NOVEMBER 2012, HOSTILITIES BETWEEN Hamas and Israel
were on the verge of exploding. Gazans were battering Israel
with home-made rockets, while Israel was continuing its routine
of sending tanks, helicopters, drones, and airplanes into the Strip.
The death of Hamid Abu Daqqa added to the tension. Hopeful they
could avoid another confrontation, negotiators from the two sides
met in Egypt, where they committed to a ceasefire with a starting
date of November 12. The calm lasted two days. On November 14,
Israel launched an airstrike that killed Ahmed al-Jabari, the leader
of Hamas's military wing, along with his bodyguard, a cameraman,
a seven-year-old girl, and five bystanders.

Israel rather disingenuously claimed the assassination was
necessary to stop rocket attacks and punish Hamas. Jabari was
responsible for ensuring that Hamas and Gaza's other militant
factions observed ceasefires with Israel. He had also been in charge

of safeguarding Hamas captive Corporal Gilad Shalit and for returning him home safely. At the time of his death, Jabari was in possession of a copy of the ceasefire agreement. Gershon Baskin, who helped draft the document, reacted: "The Israeli decision to kill Ahmed Jabari was total insanity. Jabari was behind enforcing all of the recent ceasefire agreements. He sent his troops out to stop the rockets and was prepared to reach a long-term ceasefire."[670]

Insanity possesses its own logic. Dr. Mustafa Barghouti, a former candidate for the presidency of the Palestinian National Authority, illuminated the likely thinking behind the assassination:

> It is certain that Benjamin Netanyahu, Ehud Barak, and Avigdor Liberman wanted to use Palestinian and Israeli blood as propaganda for the coming elections in January 2013. They could not start a war with Iran so they instead refocused their sights on Gaza. They are using this war to gain support from the Israeli electorate as well as to divide Palestinian people and crush their will to resist; yet another confirmation that the government of Israel is a government of war, not a government of peace.[671]

Jabari's death was the opening salvo in Operation Pillar of Defense, an eight-day air offensive on Gaza that claimed the lives of 174 Palestinians, 101 of whom were civilians, including thirty-three children and thirteen women.[672] Four Israeli civilians and two soldiers also lost their lives.

On November 18, Israeli forces dropped a large bomb on the Dalu family house in Gaza City's heavily populated Nasser neighborhood, destroying it and executing their target, Mohamed Jamal al-Dalu, a low-ranking police officer and alleged "terror operative." Five women and four children, all members of the Dalu family, were collateral damage as were an elderly woman and a young man in the house next door. At least nine other civilians were wounded and three nearby houses destroyed or badly damaged. While Israel has never produced evidence to substantiate its allegation that Mohammed was a terrorist, relatives and neighbors said he was not a member of any armed group. Denouncing the airstrike as "a clear violation of the laws of war," Human Rights Watch pointed out, "Even if al-Dalu …was a legitimate military target under the laws of war, the likelihood that the attack on a civilian home would have killed large numbers of civilians made it unlawfully disproportionate."[673]

One would think a nation that brags its military is the most moral in the world would be vigilant in guarding against violations of international law and unswerving in its observance of ceasefire agreements. Anyone who has studied Israel's history knows that idealistic notions of its pursuit of peace pale in comparison to its insatiable appetite for land. They would not be surprised if a statistical analysis of ceasefires exposed Israel's facade of morality as fraudulent. In their study, "Reigniting Violence: How Do Ceasefires End," professors at MIT, Tel Aviv University, and Harvard disprove the myth that the IDF is a defensive force that reacts to Palestinian aggression:

> [It] is overwhelmingly Israel that kills first after a pause in the conflict: 79% of all conflict pauses were interrupted when Israel killed a Palestinian, while only 8% were interrupted by Palestinian attacks (the remaining 13% were interrupted by both sides on the same day)… Indeed, of the 25 periods of nonviolence lasting longer than a week, Israel unilaterally interrupted 24, or 96%, and it unilaterally interrupted 100% of the 14 periods of nonviolence lasting longer than 9 days.[674*]

If peace were a serious aim, Israel's government would admit that its control over the day-to-day lives of Palestinians is behind

---

* The professors are Nancy Kanwisher, a professor of Cognitive Neuroscience at MIT; Anat Biletzki, professor of Philosophy at Tel Aviv University; and Johannes Haushofer, a Ph.D. candidate in Neurobiology at Harvard when the analysis was written. He is now associate professor of Psychology and Public Affairs at Princeton University.

the frustration and hopelessness that lead to acts of violence. International law recognizes the natural human response to resist the inimical designs of foreign entities. The occupied are under no obligation to cooperate with their occupiers, but fabricating an image of Palestinians as antagonistic to peace serves Israel's goal of Judaizing Palestine. With help from the western media, it has disseminated this hasbara for decades. As an example, most of its defenders believe Palestinian hatred of Jews was the spark that set off the First Intifada, which began in 1987. That is what I once thought, but when I delved into the facts, I learned that no Israeli soldiers were killed in the intifada's first year.[675] Palestinians eschewed violence and embraced tactics such as the boycotting of Israeli products, nonpayment of taxes, general and local strikes, graffiti, raising the Palestinian flag, symbolic funerals, renaming streets and schools, and community-based schooling. They also printed leaflets advocating peaceful resistance and a two-state solution. Israel's rejoinder to the nonviolent civil disobedience was exemplified by IDF Chief-of-Staff Yitzhak Rabin's order to his soldiers to break the arms and legs of Palestinian activists.[676] During the intifada's first nine months, Israeli soldiers killed over two hundred Palestinians, wounded thousands, and incarcerated seven thousand with a minimum of judicial procedure.[677]

In the summer of 2014, twenty months after Pillar of Defense, Israel launched Operation Protective Edge, its most devastating invasion to date. For seven weeks, the IDF overwhelmed the Gaza Strip with 20,000 high explosive artillery shells, 14,500 tank shells, 6,000 missiles, and 3,500 naval shells. The onslaught destroyed kindergartens, hospitals, healthcare facilities, sports fields, electricity substations, apartment buildings, and whole city blocks.[678] The air force dropped one hundred one-ton bombs on Shuja'iya alone, one of many neighborhood districts in Gaza City.[679] The UN Human Rights Council calculated that of 2,251 Gazans killed, 1,462 were civilians, including 551 children and 299 women.[680] More than eleven thousand, among them 3,540 women and 3,436 children, sustained injuries, with 10 percent suffering permanent disability.[681] Sixty-seven Israeli soldiers and six Israeli civilians died.[682] At the peak of the invasion, five hundred thousand Gazans were homeless.[683] Three weeks before the sides negotiated a ceasefire, UNICEF estimated that 373,000 children had symptoms of distress, such as "fearfulness, bed wetting, clinging to parents and nightmares," that required "direct and specialized psychosocial support."[684]

As they did after Cast Lead and Pillar of Defense, human rights organizations concluded that Israel was guilty of war crimes and possible crimes against humanity. Human Rights Watch documented IDF attacks that killed and wounded scores of civilians "at or near three well-marked schools where it knew hundreds of people were taking shelter."[685]

Calling Israel's attacks "appalling," Amnesty International documented, "a failure to take necessary precautions to avoid excessive harm to civilians and civilian property… In all cases, no prior warning was given to the civilian residents to allow them to escape."[686]

Israeli human rights group Breaking the Silence collected testimonies from sixty soldiers and officers who were part of the assault. The soldiers blamed, "the IDF's policy of indiscriminate fire, which directly resulted in the deaths of hundreds of innocent Palestinian civilians."[687] They testified that their superiors ordered them "to shoot to kill every person sighted in the area."[688]

The findings of these organizations are consistent with the statements of Ben-Gurion, Allon, Itzhaki, Schiff, and other prominent Israelis. Mordecai Gur, IDF Chief-of-Staff from 1974 to 1978 was once asked, "You maintain that the civilian population should be punished?" His reply: "And how. I never doubted it, not for one moment."[689]

General Raphael Eitan was blunt: "I don't believe in peace, because if they had done to us what we did to them we'd never agree to make peace."[690]

In January 2019, Benny Gantz, IDF chief-of-staff from February 2011 to February 2015, announced a bid to unseat Netanyahu as Israel's prime minister. His campaign ad showed video footage of a Gazan neighborhood Israeli bombs had reduced to rubble. Titled, "Gaza 2014, End of Operation Protective Edge," the video bragged about the 6,231 Hamas targets and 1,364 "terrorists destroyed" under Gantz's command. It ended with, "Only the strong wins. Gantz. Israel before everything."[691] The ad was yet another example of the Israeli view that peace is a byproduct of dehumanizing the other to the point of sheer powerlessness.

During the seven weeks of Protective Edge, the first thing I did upon waking each morning was to go online and check on Rana and her family. I wanted to see if they were still alive. Israeli soldiers shot dead two of her cousins and shot and arrested another cousin. All three were trying to make their way home from the southern Gaza Strip, which was under bombardment. They were returning from the Fajr (dawn) prayer, the first of the five daily prayers that form one of the Five Pillars of Islam.* Had they reached their destination, all they would have found was rubble. None of the cousins were members of Hamas or other militant groups.

While the assault was raging, Rana appealed to the world:

> Do you know what it means to be a Palestinian? It means you are not able to move here or there; you don't have many of the basic requirements needed to live a decent life. We are even deprived of our sleep and the only thing the powers that oppress us expect us to do is to remain ignorant. How much longer will the world stay deaf? Is our blood free of charge? What crime have our children committed that they

---

* The Five Pillars are: The Shahadah (Declaration of faith); Salat (Prayer); Fasting during the month of Ramadan; Zakat (Charity or alms-giving); Hajj (Pilgrimage to Mecca).

are forced to live in hell? We are human beings, not aliens. We are exactly like you. Regardless of color, sex, nationality, or religion, we want to live like you, in peace and under good conditions.

Imagine sleeping when, suddenly, you are awakened in the middle of the night to the sounds of rockets and warplanes, and children screaming. Tell me, how are you going to deal with this situation? What would you tell your child if he came to you crying and shouting because of the bombing?

Raise your voices and stand by the truth no matter how much it costs. Our children want the same freedoms you have. They want their human rights. All the world should know what life is like here in Gaza. Only justice will heal the wounds of my people. You must not forget these crimes.[692]

29

Is Dialogue Between the Israeli and Palestinian Sides Effective?

> *The most difficult subjects can be*
> *explained to the most slow-witted*
> *man if he has not formed any idea*
> *of them already; but the simplest*
> *thing cannot be made clear to the*
> *most intelligent man if he is firmly*
> *persuaded that he knows already,*
> *without a shadow of doubt, what is*
> *laid before him.* – Leo Tolstoy[693]

WITHIN THE ISRAEL-PALESTINE DEBATE, DIALOGUE groups are a potential venue for conflict resolution and peacebuilding. In theory, participants seek common ground with their counterparts from the other side. The relationships that are formed within these groups put a human face on the *other* and transform him or her from an enemy image in one's mind to a human being with the same needs and dreams as oneself. It is impossible to use violence against our fellow humans unless we first dehumanize and objectify them. Dialogue groups are a threat to those who are wedded to the belief that the other is the source of conflict and must be neutralized.

Of the groups I have encountered—and there may be some that do not conform to my experience—participants who identify with

Israel presume a proportional relationship between theirs and the Palestinian side. With a preference for psychological comfort over historical truth, they begin with simplistic assumptions, such as that both sides have been traumatized and both have perpetrated violence. These assumptions imply the two sides bear equal responsibility for failing to arrive at a peaceful resolution. This is analogous to Afrikaners during the Apartheid era thinking they could sit down with black South Africans to discuss their relationship and the pain each side had caused, as if that could resolve their differences.

Conscious of our inner motivations or not—and I contend that most of us are not —few of us join dialogue groups believing there is something wrong with our worldviews, expecting them to be overturned, or hoping our self-images will dissolve into the nothingness whence they came. Our impulse in joining is to reinforce our personal and collective worldviews and self-images and share them with those whose views are not in accord with our own. Therefore, for these groups to be effective, it is important to nurture a commitment to self-understanding, which requires an openness to the possibility that our worldviews may not reflect the state of things as accurately as we think. Such a commitment can instill a measure of healing in all participants and establish an environment where honest and forthright dialogue is possible. Genuine commitment also requires that we recognize the clever strategies our minds use to counter challenges to our worldviews. Once we learn that the limited identity's tendency is to look at the world with an attitude of us against them, we can free ourselves from the destructive effects of dualistic thinking.

I am familiar with groups where Jews and Palestinians have been meeting for years. A few participants from opposite sides have developed strong friendships, yet the views of the Jews have hardly budged. Despite their friendships and the stories Palestinians share, not one Jewish participant has taken the next step of reading a well-documented book about their interwoven history. Instead, their inner dialogue convinces them that taking part in a group with Palestinians is prima facie evidence of their humaneness and fair-mindedness and that neither of those qualities could coexist with prejudice. Identified with Israel, they project those qualities onto the Jewish state and conclude that its policies are also humane and fair-minded. Their attachment to an idealized Israel overpowers their stated purpose in joining dialogue groups and keeps them stuck in the cycle of tribal thinking that has prevented peace for generations.

Dialogue groups are tricky because, on the one hand, it is important to keep participants involved but on the other, involvement that does not acknowledge history perpetuates delusion. Whenever groups ignore the documented history of Israel-Palestine, they fail to disabuse Israel's loyalists of the unfair notion that Palestinians never negotiate in good faith. This unexamined belief condemns them to a state of denial in which their characterization of Palestinians is undoubtedly true of themselves. Loyalists must also understand that by avoiding historical context, they rob themselves not just of the opportunity to take responsibility for their roles in the dispossession of the Palestinian people and to apologize on behalf of their people, but of the opportunity to get more in touch with their humanity and to shed the self-image of eternal victim.

Like Israel's history of negotiations, these groups often put Palestinians in positions where, if they want to share their experience with Jews who justify Israel's methods in cracking down on their people's resistance, they are expected to acquiesce to a distorted historical narrative. If they resist, they are judged as uninterested in the other side's perspective and, therefore, uninterested in peace. Constructive dialogue is impossible with anyone drawn to distortions. This is why an open mind and an adherence to self-understanding are crucial if dialogue groups are to break free from tribalism. By themselves, good intentions are not good enough. A just resolution to the Israel-Palestine tragedy requires all of us to examine our beliefs through honest research and self-reflection. Otherwise, we will never intuit our roles in the suffering of others, nor will we become sensitive to that suffering. And for those of us who identify exclusively with one side or the other, our anxiety will remain unresolved, leaving us with the dilemma of victimization: Why does the world not understand my people juxtaposed with evidence that is beyond dispute?

Afterword

*Continuing the occupation is the
single greatest threat to Israel's
safety, and to our existence as a
democracy. –* Ami Ayalon[694]

*Hope …is not the conviction that
something will turn out well, but
the certainty that something makes
sense, regardless of how it turns
out. –* Vaclav Havel, Last President
of Czechoslovakia and 1ˢᵗ President
of the Czech Republic[695]

S OME READERS WILL CRITICIZE ME for not including
Palestinian terrorism in this book, for failing to mention
hijackings and suicide bombings, attacks on Israeli soldiers and
civilians, and numerous other acts of violence that have contributed
to the distrust that exists on both sides. I do not condone any of it,
but it all has to be viewed in the context of the takeover of Palestine
and the Israeli occupation. In chapter four, I stated the obvious: a
minority of a population will use violence as the only way it knows
to retain a measure of self-respect in the face of the violence that has
been inflicted upon it for generations. That is the kind of reaction
both Ben-Gurion and Jabotinsky anticipated from the Palestinians.

As leaders of the Yishuv, it was the strategy they employed for themselves and it was the key to their success.*

My objective in this book has been to clarify history and to explain the psychospiritual dynamics at the root of suffering, conflict, and violence. If I have succeeded, then I believe I have contributed to a more comprehensive and humane understanding of the human condition in general and Israel-Palestine in particular. Thus, pointing out falsehoods, flaws, and omissions in the arguments loyalists make to defend their version of Israel's history, and then providing material information that more accurately describes the history cannot qualify as anti-Semitism or disloyalty to my heritage. Were I to remain silent, I would be enabling the armor of ignorance and denial to be passed on to the next generation; and I would be complicit in repressing sensitivity to the pain of the other; a pain my fellow Jews are at least partially responsible for; a pain I once was partially responsible for.

In a November 2003 interview, former Shin Bet directors Ami Ayalon, Carmi Gillon, Avraham Shalom, and Yaakov Peri warned that if Israel failed to make peace with the Palestinians, it would be "heading downhill towards near-catastrophe. If …we go on living by the sword, we will continue to wallow in the mud and destroy ourselves."[696]

Sixteen years later, at the 2019 J Street national conference, Ayalon, also a former commander-in-chief of the Israeli navy, predicted that the Jewish state's quest to expand its borders, build more settlements, and prevent the establishment of a Palestinian state "will isolate Israel …increase anti-Semitism around the world …and be the end of Israel as the founding fathers of Zionism envisioned it."[697†] He added:

---

* The term Yishuv refers to the body of Jewish residents in Palestine prior to the establishment of the state of Israel in 1948.

† Founded in 2007, J Street is an advocacy group, whose motto is "Pro-Israel, Pro-Peace." It is critical of the Israeli occupation, rejects a single-state solution, and lobbies for a two-state solution whereby Israel retains its majority Jewish population.

[Israelis] are in too much pain to see clearly... We need you [concerned people] to tell us the truth the way you see it ...[and] when you see the writing on the wall and we do not or cannot, you also have the duty to stand up and tell us your truth. This is the real meaning of mutual responsibility.[698]

This book is my way of standing up and telling the truth, of saving Israel from itself and the Palestinian people from the unfair and, yes, cruel treatment they have been subjected to for generations. It is a product of a commitment to separate fact from fiction and learn the documented history of the two peoples. When I first made this commitment it set in motion a release from an existential condition I was not even aware I had embodied for most of a lifetime. As denial and dogmatism gave way to an urgency to carry out objective research, I observed how a core identity affected my relationship to the world, influencing what or who I was drawn to, what or who I was repelled by, how I judged or tolerated others, and how others judged or tolerated me. No longer blind to Israel's intentions, through an unfathomable process I was liberated from the dark side of indoctrination and the bondage of unquestioned loyalty.

Nobody is intrinsically incapable of making the same commitment I made or of experiencing insights similar to the ones I experienced. The insights do not belong to me. They are everyone's inheritance. They come from the heart, where there is no separation, and they revealed themselves when I recognized my shared responsibility to alleviate suffering. Those who take the time to examine their beliefs and images will, sooner or later, discover for themselves some of the deeper things I've talked about.

I would like to summarize these heart-based insights.

1. The cause of suffering is the attachment to a presumed, limited, and mortal identity and to the beliefs and images that emanate from and reinforce that presumption.

2.   The unconscious motivation behind rejection of valid criticism is preoccupation with protecting one's presumed identity. By inquiring within, we can let go of the idealistic images we project onto nations or groups we identify with and see both their positive and negative aspects. Then we can urge them to act in accordance with the law, heal the suffering their attitudes and policies have created, live in peace with their neighbors, and work to free their cohorts from the quagmire of existential fear and confusion.

3.   The real enemy is not someone or something outside of us. The real enemy is the unexamined mind that unconsciously projects its suffering onto the *other* and then blames or scapegoats the *other* for its suffering. In truth there are no enemies. There are only people who, while suffering the consequences of their unexamined beliefs, have forgotten their common humanity.

4.   With regard to Israel-Palestine the real conflict is not Israel versus the Palestinian people or Israel versus a hostile world. The real conflict is the inability to integrate the hard-to-believe but unmistakable reality of Israel's treatment of Palestinians with unquestioned loyalty to the Jewish state. One consideration recognizes Israel's dark side. The other denies the dark side exists.

In a world so polarized and dualistic in its thinking, the Buddhist Metta (lovingkindness) prayer can remind us of our common humanity and help us to heal our wounds: "May all beings everywhere, whether near or far, whether known to me or unknown, be happy. May they be well. May they be peaceful. May they be free." Amen.

About the Author

Richard Forer grew up in in the 1950s and 1960s in Trenton, NJ, where he attended reform synagogue. His identical twin brother has been a prominent member of an Orthodox Hasidic sect since the early 1970s. Another brother is a former president of one of the largest Reform Synagogues on the East Coast. Other Orthodox members of his family live in Jewish settlements in the West Bank. Forer is a past member of the American Israel Public Affairs Committee (AIPAC). In 1996, he was certified as a practitioner of the Meir Schneider Self-Healing Method, a unique system of touch, kinesthetic awareness, and mental imagery developed by an Israeli. Forer's first book, *Breakthrough: Transforming Fear into Compassion — A New Perspective on the Israel-Palestine Conflict*, was published in 2010.

Bibliography

Al-Haq/Law in the Service of Man. *Punishing a Nation: Human Rights Violations during the Palestinian Uprising, December 1987—December 1988* (Boston: South End Press, 1990)

Armstrong, Karen. *Islam: A Short History* (New York: Modern Library Paperback Edition, 2002)

Ashton, Nigel. *King Hussein of Jordan: A Political Life* (New Haven: Yale University Press, 2008)

Begin, Menachem. *The Revolt: Story of the Irgun* (New York: Schuman, 1951)

Ben-Ami, Shlomo. *Scars of War, Wounds of Peace: The Israeli—Arab Tragedy* (Oxford University Press, 2006)

Ben-Yehuda, Nachman. *Masada Myth: Collective Memory and Mythmaking in Israel* (University of Wisconsin Press, 1996)

Benzamin, Uzi. *Sharon: An Israeli Caesar* (New York, 1985)

Biemann, Asher D., ed. *The Martin Buber Reader: Essential Writings* (New York: Palgrave MacMillan, 2002)

Carter, Jimmy. *Palestine Peace Not Apartheid* (New York: Simon & Schuster, 2006)

Chomsky, Noam. *Fateful Triangle: The United States, Israel, and the Palestinians*, Updated Edition (Chicago: Haymarket Books, 1999)

Coffin, William Sloane, ed. *The Collected Sermons of William Sloane Coffin: The Riverside Years, Volume One* (Louisville: Westminster John Knox Press, 2008)

Crenshaw, Martha, ed. *Terrorism in Context* (The Pennsylvania State University Press, 1995)

Cypel, Sylvain. *Walled: Israeli Society at an Impasse* (New York: Other Press, 2005)

Davis, Uri. *Apartheid Israel: Possibilities for the Struggle Within* (London: Zed Books, 2003)

Dreyfus, Laurence. *Wagner and the Erotic Impulse* (Cambridge: Harvard University Press, 2010)

Einstein, Albert. *Ideas and Opinions* (Crown Publishers, Inc.: New York, Fifth Printing, 1960)

Ernst, Morris L. *So Far, So Good* (New York: Harper, 1948)

Finkelstein, Norman. *Beyond Chutzpah: On the Misuse of Anti-Semitism and the Abuse of History* (Berkeley: University of California Press, 2005)

——. *Gaza: An Inquest into its Martyrdom* (Berkeley: University of California Press, 2018)

Forer, Richard. *Breakthrough: Transforming Fear into Compassion—A New Perspective on the Israel-Palestine Conflict* (Insight Press, 2010)

Fromkin, David. *A Peace to End All Peace* (New York: Henry Holt and Co., 1989)

Gay, Ninna. *Shifts: Beyond the Visible* (Author House, 2010).

Giladi, Naeim. *Ben-Gurion's Scandals: How the Haganah & the Mossad Eliminated Jews* (Glilit Publishing Co., Inc., 1992)

Golani, Motti. *Wars Don't Just Happen* (Tel Aviv, 2002)

Goldberg, Michael. *Why Should Jews Survive? Looking Past the Holocaust Toward a Jewish Future* (New York: Oxford University Press, 1995)

Goldmann, Nahum. *The Jewish Paradox* (Littlehampton Book Services, 1st Edition, 1978), translated by Steven Cox

Grodzinsky, Yosef. *In the Shadow of the Holocaust: The Struggle Between Jews and Zionists in the Aftermath of World War II* (Common Courage Press, 2004)

Hagee, John. *Jerusalem Countdown: A Prelude to War* (Front Line, 2006)

Harkabi, Yehoshafat. *Israel's Fateful Hour* (Harper Collins, 1988)

Havel, Vaclav. *Disturbing the Peace* (Vintage, 1990)

Herzl, Theodore. *The Jewish State* (New York: Dover Publications, Inc., 1988) ʾ

Hirst, David. *The Gun and the Olive Branch: The Roots of Violence in the Middle East* (New York: Thunder's Mouth Press-Nation Books, 2003)

Hutchison, E.H. *Violent Truce: A Military Observer Looks at the Arab-Israeli Conflict 1951–1955* (Devin-Adair, 1955)

Jack, Homer A., ed. *The Wit and Wisdom of Gandhi* (Dover Publications, Inc., 1979)

Khalidi, Rashid. *Under Siege: P.L.O. Decisionmaking During the 1982 War* (New York: Columbia University Press, 2014)

——. *Palestinian Identity: The Construction of Modern National Consciousness* (New York: Columbia University Press, 1997)

Kierkegaard, Soren. *Works of Love* (Princeton, NJ: Princeton University Press, 1998).

Kimmerling, Baruch. *Politicide: Ariel Sharon's War Against the Palestinians* (London: Verso Books, 2003)

Kimmerling, Baruch and Migdal, Joel. *The Palestinian People: A History* (Cambridge: Harvard University Press, 2003)

King, Mary Elizabeth, *A Quiet Revolution: The First Palestinian Intifada and Nonviolent Resistance* (New York: Nations Books, 2007)

Kissinger, Henry. *Years of Upheaval* (London, 1982)

Morelli, Mark D. and Elizabeth A., eds. *The Lonergan Reader*, (University of Toronto Press, 2002)

Marchione, Margherita. *Consensus and Controversy: Defending Pope Pius XII* (New York: Paulist Press, 2002)

McGeough, Paul. *Kill Khalid: The Failed Mossad Assassination Of Khalid Mishal And The Rise of Hamas* (New York: The New Press, 2009)

Menuhin, Moshe. *The Menuhin Saga: The Autobiography of Moshe Menuhin* (London: Sidgwick & Jackson, 1984)

Milgram, Norman, ed. *Stress and Coping in Time of War: Generalizations from the Israeli Experience* (New York: Brunnel/Mazel, 1986)

Miller, Aaron David. *The Much Too Promised Land* (New York: Bantam Dell, 2008)

Mock, Steven. *Symbols of Defeat in the Construction of National Identity* (Cambridge University Press, 2011)

Morris, Benny. *1948: A History of the First Arab-Israeli War* (New Haven: Yale University Press, 2008)

——. *The Birth of the Palestinian Refugee Problem, 1947–1949* (Cambridge University Press, 1987)

——. *The Birth of the Palestinian Refugee Problem Revisited* (Cambridge University Press: 2004)

——. *Righteous Victims: A History of the Zionist-Arab Conflict, 1881-1999* (New York: Vintage Books, 1999)

Neff, Donald. *Fallen Pillars: U.S. Policy Towards Palestine and Israel Since 1945* (Institute for Palestine Studies: 2002)

Pappe, Ilan. *The Ethnic Cleansing of Palestine* (Oxford: One World, 2006).

Patai, Raphael, ed. *The Complete Diaries of Theodore Herzl*, Volume One (New York: The Theodore Herzl Foundation, Inc., 1960)

Peters, Joan. *From Time Immemorial: The Origins of the Arab-Israel Conflict over Palestine* (Harper Collins, 1984)

Qumsiyeh, Mazin. *Sharing the Land of Canaan: Human Rights and the Israeli-Palestinian Struggle* (London: Pluto Press, 2004)

Rabkin, Yakov M. *A Threat from Within: A Century of Jewish Opposition to Zionism* (Canada: Zed Books, 2006)

Raz, Avi. *The Bride and the Dowry: Israel, Jordan, and the Palestinians in the Aftermath of the June 1967 War* (New Haven: Yale University Press, 2012)

Robinson, Shira N. *Citizen Strangers: Palestinians and the Birth of Israel's Liberal Settler State* (Stanford University Press, 2013)

Ross, Dennis. *The Missing Peace: The Inside Story of the Fight for Middle East Peace* (New York: Farrar, Strauss and Giroux, 2004) de Saint-Exupéry, Antoine. *The Little Prince* (Wordsworth Editions Limited, 1995).

Segev, Tom. *One Palestine Complete: Jews and Arabs Under the British Mandate* (New York: Metropolitan Books, Henry Holt & Company, LLC, 2000)

——. *The Seventh Million: The Israelis and the Holocaust* (New York: Henry Holt and Company, LLC., 2000)

Shapira, Anita. (Heb.) *Land and Power* (Tel Aviv: Am Oved, 1992)

Shapira, Yitzhak and Yosef Elitzur. *The King's Torah* (Torat Hamelech), *Part One: Laws of Life and Death Between Israel and the Nations* (Od Yosef Chai Yeshiva, 2009)

Shilon, Avi. *Menachem Begin: A Life* (New Haven: Yale University Press, 2012)

Shlaim, Avi. *The Iron Wall: Israel and the Arab World* (New York: W.W. Norton & Co., Inc., 2001)

——. *Lion of Jordan: The Life of King Hussein in War and Peace* (New York: Vintage Books, 2007)

Shonfeld, Reb Moshe. *The Holocaust Victims Accuse: Documents and Testimony on Jewish War Criminals* (Bnei Yeshivos: New York, 1977)

David Shulman. *Dark Hope: Working for Peace in Israel and Palestine* (The University of Chicago Press, 2007)

Suarez, Thomas. *State of Terror: How Terrorism Created Modern Israel* (Northampton, MA: Olive Branch Press, 2017)

Swisher, Clayton. *The Truth about Camp David: The Untold Story about the Collapse of the Middle East Peace Process* (New York: Nations Books, 2004)

Sykes, Christopher. *Crossroads to Israel: 1917–1948* (Bloomington: Indiana University Press 1965)

Tabarani, Gabriel G. *Israeli-Palestinian Conflict: From Balfour Promise to Bush Declaration. The Complications And The Road For A Lasting Peace* (AuthorHouseTM 2008)

Tauber, Yanki. *Beyond The Letter Of The Law* (Meaningful Life Center, 2012)

Thomas, Baylis. *The Dark Side of Zionism: Israel's Quest for Security Through Dominance* (Plymouth, England: Lexington Books, May 2011)

Truman, Harry S. *1946–52: Years of Trial and Hope, Memoirs: Volume 2* (Doubleday & Co., 1956)

Viorst, Milton. *Zionism: The Birth and Transformation of an Ideal* (New York: St. Martin's Press, 2016)

Waxman, Dov. *The Pursuit of Peace and the Crisis of Israeli Identity* (New York: Palgrave MacMillan, 2006)

Zerubavel, Yael. *Recovered Roots: Collective Memory and the Making of Israeli National Tradition* (University of Chicago Press, 1995)

Zimbardo, Philip. *The Lucifer Effect: Understanding How Good People Turn Evil* (New York: Random House, 2008)

Endnotes

1   de Saint- Exupéry, 82.

Preface

2   Joe Keohane, "How facts backfire," *Boston Globe*, July 11, 2010.

3   Charles G. Lord, Lee Ross, and Mark R. Lepper, "Biased Assimilation and Attitude Polarization: The Effects of Prior Theories on Subsequently Considered Evidence," *Journal of Personality and Social Psychology 1979*, Vol. 37, No. 11, 2098-2109.

4   United States Environmental Protection Agency (EPA), epa.gov/asbestos/protect-your-family-asbestos-contaminated-vermiculite insulation.

5   Ibid.

6   Asbestos.com, "Libby," asbestos.com/jobsites/libby.

7   Madeksho Law Firm, "Biggest Asbestos Stories of 2019 so far," March 29, 2019, madeksholaw.com/asbestos-in-the-news.

8   US Department of Health and Human Services, Public Health Service, "Mortality in Libby, Montana (1979 - 1998)," August 8, 2002, atsdr.cdc.gov/HAC/pha/LibbyAsbestosSite/MT_LibbyHCMortalityrev8-8-2002_508.pdf, 1.

9   Jane Fritz, "Choking on lies in Libby", *Inlander*, March 1, 2001.

10   David McCumber, "As Libby asbestos cleanup gets done, the dying continues," *Montana Standard*, October 6, 2018.

11   Madeksho Law Firm.

12   Asbestos.com/jobsites/libby.

13   *Democracy Now*, "A Town Suffering for Generations: Decades of Asbestos Exposure by W.R. Grace Mine Leave Hundreds Dead, 1,200+ Sickened in Libby," April 22, 2009.

14   Margaret Heffernan, "The Dangers of Willful Blindness" ted.com/talks/margaret_heffernan_the_dangers_of_willful_blindness.

15   Ibid.

Chapter 1 — Willful Blindness is a Crime Against Humanity

16   Kierkegaard, cited by Ninna Gay, 141.
17   Finkelstein, *Beyond Chutzpah*, 2.

Chapter 2 — We Are All Palestinians and Israelis, Muslims, Christians and Jews

18   Jack, 70.
19   Sarah Tse, "Is Time Real?" *The Science Explorer*, October 15, 2015, thescienceexplorer.com/universe-real.

Chapter 4 — The Internal Logic of Oppression

20   Zimbardo, 432.
21   B'Tselem, "Human Shields," November 11, 2017, btselem.org/human_shields.
22   Ibid.
23   Human Rights Watch, *In a Dark Hour: the Use of Civilians during IDF Arrest Operations*, p. 2, Vol. 14, No. 2 (E), April 2002, hrw.org/reports/2002/israel2/israel0402.pdf.
24   United Nations Convention on the Rights of the Child, CRC/C/ISR/CO/2-4, 18, www2.ohchr.org/English/bodies/crc/docs/co/CRC-C-ISR-CO-2-4.pdf.

Chapter 5 — A Mitzvah to Kill

25   George Orwell, *1984* (Harcourt, Inc., 1949), 5.
26   Gidi Weitz, "Ben-Gurion in 1951: Only Death Penalty Will Deter Jews From Gratuitous Killing of Arabs," *Haaretz*, April 1, 2016.
27   Ibid.
28   Weitz, "Ben-Gurion in 1951."
29   Donkeys—David Ben-Gurion; Crocodiles—Menachem Begin; cockroaches—Rafael Eitan; snakes—Ayelet Shaked; psychopaths and serial killers—Benny Morris; animals—Eli Ben Dahan; shrapnel—Naftali Bennett; heads chopped off—Avigdor Lieberman; avengers—Rabbi Noam Perel (Secretary-General of World Bnei Akiva).
30   youtube.com/watch?v=6TG0vdzrmt4. Also, "Quote for the Day: The Daily Dish," *The Atlantic*, July 20, 2010, theatlantic.com/daily-dish/archive/2010/07/quote-for-the-day/184582.
31   Milgram, 34.

32   Zerubavel, 209.

33   Jaacov Reuel, "Sisco and the Masada Complex," *The Jerusalem Post*, August 3, 1971, cited by Ben-Yehuda, 245.

34   Mock, 232.

35   Ben-Yehuda, 244.

36   Waxman, 56.

37   Shilon.

38   Shlaim, *The Iron Wall*, 396.

39   Uri Avnery, "The Imperator," *Outlook*, January 7, 2014, outlookindia.com/website/story/the-imperator/289226.

40   Goldberg, 125.

41   Edward A. Gargan, "BASHIR GEMAYEL LIVED BY THE SWORD," *The New York Times*, September 15, 1982.

42   UNGA Resolution 37/123, December 16, 1982.

43   Seth Anziska, "A Preventable Massacre," *The New York Times*, September 16, 2012.

44   Ibid.

45   Ibid.

46   Ibid.

47   Ibid.

48   Khalidi, *Under Siege*, 171.

49   Anthony Lewis, "Israel's Bitter West Bank Harvest," *The New York Times*, July 22, 1984.

50   Segev, *The Seventh Million*, 399.

51   Israel Ministry of Foreign Affairs, "104 Report of the Commission of Inquiry into the events at the refugee camps in Beirut—8 February 1983," Volume 8: 1982-1984.

52   Ibid.

53   Gili Cohen, "British Files: Israel Sold Arms to Argentina During 1982 Falklands War," *Haaretz*, August 25, 2016.

54   "Jews targeted in Argentina's dirty war," *The Guardian*, March 24, 1999.

55   Uki Goñi, "The Long Shadow of Argentina's Dictatorship," *The New York Times*, March 21, 2016.

56   "Jews targeted in Argentina's dirty war," *The Guardian*.

57   Ibid.

58   Azriel Bermant, "Israel's Long History of Cooperation with Ruthless, anti-Semitic Dictators," *Haaretz*, July 4, 2018.

Chapter 6 — Ariel Sharon: The Deluding Power of Dualistic Thinking

59   Menuhin, 53.

60   BBC News, "Clashes Mar Mid-east Inquiry," March 25, 2001.

61   Jerusalem Domestic Television Service, Sept. 24, 1982. Reprinted in *The Beirut Massacre* (Claremont Research and Publications, New York, 1982), from the US Government Foreign Broadcast Information Services (FBIS), cited by Chomsky, *Fateful Triangle*, 31.

62   Chris McGreal, "We must rely on ourselves, says Sharon," *The Guardian*, January 26, 2005.

63   Morris, *Righteous Victims*, 270.

64   Ibid, 274.

65   Suarez, 307.

66   Avnery, "The Imperator."

67   Kimmerling, *Politicide*, 49.

68   E.H. Hutchison, 152-8, cited by Hirst, 308.

69   Kimmerling, *Politicide*, 49; Morris, *Righteous Victims*, 278.

70   "Orders, Operation Shoshana," Maj. Shmuel Meller in the name of Col. Meir Amit, General Staff Branch/Operations, to OC Central Command, OC Unit 101, etc., Oct. 13, 1953; and "Orders, Operation Shoshana," Maj. Alex Sharon, in the name of Central Command's operations officer, Lt. Col. David Elazar, to OC unit 101, etc., October 13, 1953, both in IDFA [Israeli Defense Forces Archive] 644/56//207, cited by Morris, *Righteous Victims*, p. 278.

71   Kimmerling, *Politicide*, 48–9.

72   Benzamin, 57, cited by Suarez, 307.

73   Ibid.

Chapter 7 — "True" Friends of Israel

74   Goldmann, 77.

75   *Democracy Now*, "Israel's First Lady of Human Rights: A Conversation with Shulamit Aloni," August 14, 2002, democracynow.org/2002/8/14/israels_first_lady_of_human_rights.

76   Gideon Levy, "Jeremy Corbin for U.K. Prime Minister," *Haaretz*, August 9, 2018.

77   Goldmann, 99, cited by Morris, *1948: The First Arab-Israeli War*, 393.

78   Anita Shapira, cited by Morris, *Righteous Victims,* 136.

79   Anthony Lewis, "Abroad at Home; The Logic of
        Peace," *The New York Times*, May 20, 1994.
80   Chomsky, *Fateful Triangle*, 15.
81   Sykes, 247, cited by Chomsky, *Fateful Triangle*, 16.
82   Suarez, 33.
83   Rabkin, 20.
84   Menuhin, 12.
85   Patai, 84.
86   Menuhin, 20.
87   Suarez, 33.
88   Theodore Herzl, Official Zionist newspaper,
        1897, cited by Dreyfus, 165–166.
89   "Israel Sides With anti-Semites," *Haaretz*, July 13, 2017.
90   Erna Paris, "Viktor Orban's war on George Soros and
        Hungary's Jews," *The Globe and Mail*, June 1, 2018.
91   Noga Tarnopolsky, "Netanyahu's Negotiating With
        Neo-Fascists for a 'Consensus View' of the Holocaust,"
        Daily Beast, December 12, 2018, goo.gl/Yh5fFy.
92   United States Holocaust Memorial Museum (USHMM), "Jewish
        Losses During the Holocaust: By Country," encyclopedia.ushmm.org/
        content/en/article/jewish-losses-during-the-holocaust-by-country.
93   Ilan Ben Zion, "Netanyahu greets Hungary's Orban
        as 'true friend of Israel,'" AP, July 19, 2018, apnews.
        com/938bb193c0894691bf42a6457d1fae4c.
94   Ibid.
95   Ibid.
96   Joshua Keating, "For Netanyahu and His American
        Friends, Criticizing Israel Is the Only Anti-Semitism
        That Matters," *Slate*, December 6, 2018.
97   *Israel Hayom* staff, "Joint Israeli-Polish statement on Holocaust
        law sparks outrage," *Israel Hayom*, July 6, 2018.
98   USHMM, op cit.
99   Yad Vashem, "Yad Vashem historians respond to the joint
        statement of the Governments of Poland and Israel concerning
        the revision of the 26 January 2018, amendment to Poland's
        Act on the Institute of National Remembrance," July 5, 2018,
        yadvashem.org/press-release/05-july-2018-07-34.html.
100   Ibid.

101 Mark Weiss, (in Jerusalem), "Joint statement from Israel and Poland PMs draws Holocaust centre ire," *The Irish Times*, July 6, 2018.

102 Ibid.

103 Glenn Greenwald, Andrew Fishman, "The Most Misogynistic, Hateful Elected Official in the Democratic World: Brazil's Jair Bolsonaro," *The Intercept*, December 11, 2014.

104 Alexander Reid Ross, "Hitler in Brasilia: The U.S, Evangelicals and Nazi Political Theory Behind Brazil's President-in-waiting," *Haaretz*, October 28, 2018.

105 Anthony Faiola and Marina Lopes, "Who is Jair Bolsonaro, the man likely to be Brazil's next president?" *The Washington Post*, October 28, 2018.

106 Alex Hochuli, "Brazil presidential election: Who is Jair Bolsonaro and why is he more dangerous than Trump?" October 28, 2018, nbcnews.com/think/opinion/brazil-presidential-election-who-jair-bolsonaro-popular-candidate-more-dangerous-ncna925011.

107 Fernando Enrique Cardoso, "How the unthinkable happened in Brazil," *The Washington Post*, October 29, 1018.

108 Jon Lee Anderson, "Southern Strategy," *The New Yorker*, April 1, 2019.

109 Guardian Staff, "Who is Jair Bolsonaro? Brazil's far-right president in his own words," *The Guardian*, October 29, 2018.

110 Bernie Sanders Tweet, @SenSanders, November 1, 2018.

111 Faiola and Lopes.

112 AP, "Bolsonaro: Holocaust crimes can be forgiven, not forgotten," April 12, 2019, apnews.com/6cf43132862f411 18f2f6affae6e4bdd?wpisrc=nl_todayworld&wpmm=1.

113 Hochuli, "Brazil presidential election: Who is Jair Bolsonaro and why is he more dangerous than Trump?"

114 JPOST.COM STAFF, REUTERS, "Brazilian President Bolsonaro Sworn In, Hugs Netanyahu," January 1, 2019, *The Jerusalem Post*.

115 Noa Landau, "Netanyahu Congratulates Bolsonaro for Brazil Election Win, Invites Him to Israel," *Haaretz*, October 29, 2018.

116 Ibid.

117 Jonathan Lis, "Israeli Right-wing Lawmaker to Meet Leader of Austrian Party With Nazi Roots," *Haaretz*, February 2, 2018.

Chapter 8 — The Territorial Answer to the Jewish Fear

118 Khalidi, *Palestinian Identity*, 102.

119   Morris, *Righteous Victims*, 657.
120   Suarez, 59. Also, see N. 103, 348-9.
121   Herzl, 75.
122   Rabkin, 20.
123   Herzl, 76.
124   Ben-Ami, xii.
125   Allan C. Brownfeld, "The Balfour Declaration at 100: Remembering Its Prophetic Jewish Critics," Spring-Summer 2017, *The Journal of the American Council for Judaism*.
126   Fromkin, 299.
127   Tom Segev, *One Palestine Complete*, 225.
128   Menuhin, N. 12, 259.
129   Ibid.
130   Segev, *One Palestine Complete*, 225.
131   Ibid.
132   *Statistical Abstract of the United States* (Washington, D.C. Government Printing Office, 1929), 100, historymatters.gmu.edu/d/5078.
133   Ernst, 176.
134   Ibid, 177.
135   Ibid, 176–177.
136   Cited by Suarez, 125.
137   Grodzinsky, 41, cited by Suarez, N. 234, 365.
138   Suarez, 119–120.
139   Morris, *Righteous Victims*, 162.
140   Shonfeld, 26.
141   Marchione, 285.
142   Suarez, 81-82.
143   Bo'az Evron, *Yediot Ahronot*, April 4, 1991, cited by Dr. Israel Shahak, "Internal Criticism of Racism Would Be Called 'Anti-Semitic' Outside Israel," *Washington Report on Middle East Affairs*, August/September 1991, 23.
144   Carter. 208-9.

Chapter 9 — A People Who Shall Dwell Alone

145   Cited by Waxman, 57.
146   "Word on the Street: Reason to Take Heart," JStreet.org, March 26, 2017.
147   Fathom Journal, "'There is no policy, we are on the edge

of a volcano,': An interview with Efraim Halevy," Winter 2015, fathomjournal.org/there-is-no-policy-we-are-on-the-edge-of-a-volcano-an-interview-with-efraim-halevy.

148 Gideon Levy: "Americans 'Are Supporting the First Signs of Fascism in Israel,'" Interview with Max Blumenthal, March 22, 2016, the Real News Network, therealnews.com/stories/thedges0318gideon.

149 BNC Statement, "Racism and Racial Discrimination are the Antithesis of Freedom, Justice & Equality," bdsmovement.net/news/"racism-and-racial-discrimination-are-antithesis-freedom-justice-equality."

150 Chemi Shalev, "Israel's Blacklisting of Quakers Is a Crime Against Jewish History," *Haaretz*, January 12, 2018.

151 "Principles for a Just and Lasting Peace Between Palestinians and Israelis," American Friends Service Committee, November 2011.

Chapter 10 — The Religion of Zionism

152 Israel Harel, "The Hypocrisy of Protesting the Nation-state Law," *Haaretz*, August 4, 2018.

153 Quoted in *Al-Hamishmar*, December 24, 1987, from an article in *Hehazit* (Summer 1943), cited by Ian S. Lustick, "Terrorism in the Arab-Israeli Conflict: Targets and Audiences," Crenshaw, 527.

154 For "avak adam" see Giladi, 17. For "human rubbish," see Jonathan Cook, "Israel's very own history of eugenics," September 25, 2014, jonathan-cook.net/blog/2014-09-26/israels-very-own-history-of-eugenics.

155 Einstein, 190.

156 "Commemorating 75 Years of Advancing Prophetic Judaism, Free of Nationalism and Politicization," by Allan C. Brownfeld, *The American Council for Judaism*, Winter 2017.

157 The Pittsburgh Platform, 1885, myjewishlearning.com/article/the-pittsburgh-platform-1885.

158 United Nations Trusteeship Library, cited by Torah Jews, "Rabbi Yosef Tzvi Dushinsky, Chief Rabbi of Jerusalem (1867-1948)," truetorahjews.org/dushinsky1.

159 "Letter to the UN Signed by Rabbi Uri Blau," Torah Jews, truetorahjews.org/uriblau.

160 Ibid.

161 Philip Weiss, "Trump's recognition of Jerusalem as

capital of 'Jewish people' is assault on my religion —
Queens rabbi," *Mondoweiss*, January 9, 2018.

162   YouTube, "No Jews," Published on September 9, 2016,
        Youtube.com/watch?v=G8CUFSHB114&t=7s.

163   Ibid.

164   Ibid.

165   Peter Beinart, "What a Liberal Think Tank Should
        Ask Bibi When He Visits Next Week."

Chapter 11 — Tribal Thinking

166   "IDF General in Bombshell Speech: Israel Today Shows Signs
        of 1930s Germany," *The Jerusalem Post*, May 4, 2016.

Chapter 12 — The Disinherited

167   Netanyahu's instruction to activists at a Likud conference
        in July 2001. Akiva Eldar, "Why Should Anyone Believe
        Netanyahu?" *Haaretz*, November 14, 2011.

168   Harriet Sherwood, "Israeli PM: illegal African immigrants threaten
        identity as Jewish state," *The Guardian*, May 20, 2012.

169   Anna Ahronheim, "ISRAEL COMPLETES HEIGHTENED
        EGYPT BORDER FENCE," *The Jerusalem Post*, January 18, 2017.

170   Jack Khoury and Barak Ravid, "Netanyahu's 'Wild Beast'
        Quote Was Apartheid-speak, Says Chief Palestinian
        Negotiator," *Haaretz*, February 10, 2016.

171   Human Rights Watch World Report 2018, "Eritrea: Events of 2017."

172   Amir Alon, "Standing with African migrants, former IDF
        fighters recall their 'hell,' *YnetNews.com*, March 27, 2018.

173   Amnesty International, "Israel: Deportation of
        African asylum-seekers is a cruel and misguided
        abandonment of responsibility," March 26, 2018.

174   Ibid.

175   Bradley Burston, "Blacklist: Top 13 Delegitimizers Who Should
        Be Denied Entry Into Israel," *Haaretz*, October 16, 2018.

176   Ruth Eglash and Loveday Morris, "Q&A with Israel's Interior
        Minister Aryeh Deri: Plan to deport thousands of Africans is
        not about race," *The Washington Post*, February 7, 2018.

177   Amnesty International, "Israel: Deportation of African asylum-
        seekers is a cruel and misguided abandonment of responsibility."

178   Marissa Newman, "Ahead of mass deportations, Knesset extends restrictions on immigrants," *The Times of Israel*, December 11, 2018.

179   Yarden Zur, "Israel Recruiting Inspectors to Deport Asylum Seekers by Force, Promising $9,000 Bonus," *Haaretz*, January 28, 2018.

180   Lee Yaron, "Israel to Deport LGBT Asylum Seekers to Rwanda, Uganda Despite Likely Persecution," *Haaretz*, March 4, 2018.

181   Beth McKernan, "Israel jails African asylum seekers refusing deportation," *Independent*, February 23, 2018. For $5,000 per deportee see Daniel Sokatch, "Netanyahu blamed me for his failure. I'm happy to take credit," *The Washington Post*, April 16, 2018.

182   Ilan Lior, "Asylum Seekers Deported from Israel to Rwanda Warn Those Remaining: 'Don't Come Here,'" *Haaretz*, February 2, 2018.

183   Uzi Dann, "Israel's Big Lie Revealed: Deported Asylum Seekers in Uganda Lament Broken Promises and a Grim Future," *Haaretz*, March 4, 2018.

184   Jesselyn Cook, "Israel Tells African Migrants, Asylum-Seekers to Leave or Go to Jail," *HuffPost*, January 5, 2018, huffpost.com/entry/israel-tells-african-migrants-asylum-seekers-to-leave-or-go-to-ja il_n_5a4fc2c6e4b003133ec79e39.

185   Lior, op. cit.

186   Ilan Lior, "20,000 Israelis Protest Deportation of African Asylum Seekers," *Haaretz*, February 24, 2018.

187   Anshel Pfeffer, "Netanyahu, Master Manipulator, Has Lost His Touch and Is Now at the Mercy of Facebook," *Haaretz*, April 3, 2018.

188   Toi Staff, "Netanyahu accuses EU, New Israel Fund of pressing Rwanda to nix migrants deal," *The Times of Israel*, April 3, 2018.

189   nif.org/about/faqs/.

190   Toi Staff, "PM pins deportation failure on New Israel Fund, demands Knesset probe," *The Times of Israel*, April 3, 2018.

191   Noa Landau and Lee Yaron, "Netanyahu Vows to Reopen Detention Facilities for Asylum Seekers After Israel Tells Court Deportation No Longer an Option, *Haaretz*, April 24, 2018.

Chapter 13 — Favoring One Side at the Expense of the Other

192   Chomsky, *Fateful Triangle*, xv.

193   Allan C. Brownfeld, "Making David Friedman ambassador to Israel is a boon for ISIS," *Mondoweiss*, December 22, 2016.

194   Hind Khoudary, Lubna Masarwa, Chloé Benoist, "'Burn them. shoot

them. kill them': Israelis cheer in Jerusalem as Palestinians shot in Gaza," *Middle East Eye*, May 14,,2018, middleeasteye.net/news/israelis-celebrate-jerusalem-palestinians-mourns-gaza-1200437883.

195 Chaim Levinson, "Netanyahu's Party Votes to Annex West Bank, Increase Settlements," *Haaretz*, January 1, 2018.

196 David M. Halbfinger, "Emboldened Israeli Right Presses Moves to Doom 2-State Solution," *The New York Times*, January 1, 2018.

197 IDF@IDF Spokesperson, cited by Ali Abunimah, "Israel admits, then deletes, responsibility for Gaza killings," *Electronic Intifada*, March 31, 2018.

198 Jack Khoury, Yaniv Kubovich and Almog Ben Zikri, "15 Killed, Dozens Wounded as Thousands Gather on Israel-Gaza Border," *Haaretz*, March 31, 2018.

199 Twitter.com/btselem/status/980042213718708224.

200 I24NEWS, "Spokesman for Netanyahu's Likud says all Gaza protesters 'legitimate targets,'" April 2, 2018, updated April 3, 2018.

201 Tovah Lazaroff, "There Are No Innocents In Gaza,' Says Israeli Defense Minister," *The Jerusalem Post*, April 8, 2018.

202 Statement by the High Commissioner for Human Rights, "Human Rights Council holds a special session on the deteriorating human rights situation in the occupied Palestinian territory," United Nations Human Rights Council, May 18, 2018.

203 Saree Makdisi, "Kill and Kill and Kill," *Counterpunch*, May 16, 2018.

204 Peter Beinart, "Is Israel's President an anti-Semite?," *Haaretz*, October 22, 2014.

205 WHO (World Health Organization), Health Cluster oPt, *Emergency Trauma Response to the Gaza Mass Demonstrations: A One-Year Review of Trauma Data and the Humanitarian Consequences*, May 2019, 14, reliefweb.int/sites/reliefweb.int/files/resources/WHO_Report_Web_Version_27-5-2019.pdf.

206 Berlin Wall Memorial, "Fatalities at the Berlin Wall, 1961-1989."

207 United Nations Human Rights Council, *The UN Independent Commission of Inquiry on the 2018 Gaza protests*, "No Justification for Israel to Shoot Protesters with Live Ammunition," February 28, 2019.

208 Amnesty International, "Israel/OPT: Use of excessive force in Gaza an abhorrent violation of international law," May 14, 2018.

209 Human Rights Watch, "Israel: Apparent War Crimes in Gaza," June 13, 2018, hrw.org/news/2018/06/13/israel-apparent-war-crimes-gaza.

210   United Nations Human Rights Council, "No Justification
       for Israel to Shoot Protesters with Live Ammunition."
211   Human Rights Council Fortieth session 25 February–22 March
       2019 Agenda item 7, Human rights situation in Palestine and
       other occupied Arab territories, "Report of the independent
       international commission of inquiry on the protests in the
       Occupied Palestinian Territory," 14, ohchr.org/Documents/
       HRBodies/HRCouncil/CoIOPT/A_HRC_40_74.pdf.
212   Ibid, 13.
213   Ibid, 18.
214   Medicins Sans Frontieres, "MSF teams in Gaza observe
       unusually severe and devastating gunshot injuries," April
       19, 2018, msf.org/palestine-msf-teams-gaza-observe-
       unusually-severe-and-devastating-gunshot-injuries.
215   United Nations, The Question of Palestine, "Humanitarian
       Coordinator Calls for Action to Prevent Further Loss of
       Life and Injury in the Gaza – Statement," un.org/unispal/
       document/humanitarian-coordinator-calls-for-action-to-prevent-
       further-loss-of-life-and injury-in-the-gaza-statement.
216   Reuters, "Health funding gap means 1,700 in Gaza may
       face amputations – U.N.," uk.news.yahoo.com/health-
       funding-gap-means-1-700-gaza-may-165542784.html.
217   Dan Williams, "Israeli joy, Palestinian fury over U.S.
       embassy launch in Jerusalem," *Reuters*, May 14, 2018.
218   Makdisi, "Kill and Kill and Kill."
219   Dana Milbank, "Nothing says 'Peace' Like 58 Dead
       Palestinians," *The Washington Post*, May 14, 2018.
220   Burston, "Blacklist: Top 13 Delegitimizers Who
       Should Be Denied Entry Into Israel."
221   Milbank.
222   Khoudary, Masarwa, Benoist, "'Burn them, shoot them, kill
       them': Israelis cheer in Jerusalem as Palestinians shot in Gaza."
223   Milbank.
224   Ibid. Also, David Israel, "Chief Rabbi Blesses Ivanka, Jared, Calls
       Trump 'King of Kindness,'" *JewishPress.com*, May 14,2018.
225   Connie Bruck, "The Brass Ring," *The New Yorker*, June 30, 2008.
226   TAC Staff, "In Sheldon Adelson, Far Right Israel Hits the
       Jackpot," *The American Conservative*, December 13, 2018.

227   youtube.com/watch?v=2EGgCdChPOw, July 2, 2010.

228   Milbank.

229   Daniel Burke, "Why evangelicals are 'ecstatic' about trump's Jerusalem move," December 6, 2017, cnn.com/2017/12/06/politics/american-evangelicals-jerusalem/index.html.

230   Milbank.

231   Eugene Scott, "A look at Robert Jeffress, the controversial figure giving the prayer at the U.S. Embassy in Jerusalem today," *The Washington Post*, May 14, 2018.

232   Mitt Romney Tweet, @MittRomney, May 13, 2018; cited by Matt Korade, Kevin Bohn and Daniel Burke, CNN, "Controversial US pastors take part in Jerusalem embassy opening," May 14, 2018.

233   Milbank.

234   Matt Korade, Kevin Bohn and Daniel Burke.

235   David D. Kirkpatrick, "For Evangelicals, Supporting Israel is 'God's Foreign Policy,'" *The New York Times*, November 14, 2006.

236   Korade, Bohn and Burke.

Chapter 14 — "Our Most Dependable Friends"

237   Mark D. Morelli and Elizabeth A. Morelli, 39.

238   Carter, 207.

239   Ibid, 17.

240   Morris, *Righteous Victims*, 668.

241   Transcript of Secret Talks between Egyptian National Security Adviser Hafez Ismail and US National Security Adviser Henry Kissinger (25–26 February 1973), CIE (Center for Israel Education).

242   Kissinger, cited by Shlaim, *The Iron Wall*, 315.

243   Merav Michaeli, "Israel's Leaders Sacrifice the People for Their Own Ego," *Haaretz*, April 13, 2011.

244   Ben-Ami, 166–7.

245   Milbank.

246   John Hagee sermon, talk2action.org/story/2008/5/15/141520/281. Also quoted by Sam Stein, "McCain Backer Hagee Said Hitler Was Fulfilling God's Will," *HuffPost*, May 29, 2008.

247   Sam Stein.

248   "Nationally Prominent Mega-Pastor Hagee Claims Hitler was a Half-Breed Jew" by Bruce Wilson, *The Huffington Post*, August 1, 2009. See *Jerusalem Countdown*, 185.

249   Hagee sermon. Also quoted by Sam Stein.

250   Nathan Thrall, "How the Battle Over Israel and Anti-Semitism Is Fracturing American Politics," *The New York Times*, March 28, 2019.

251   Hagee, 174, 56, cited by Bruce Wilson, "Greatest John Hagee Hits, Pt.1: Sourced Hagee Quotes at Your Fingertips," May 28, 2008, talk2action.org/story/2008/5/28/6363/30439.

252   Excerpt from John Hagee Sermon, "The Final Dictator," Sermon #2, March 16, 2003; cited by Bruce Wilson, talk2action.org/story/2008/6/1/163843/2726.

Chapter 15 — Inciting Anti-Semitism Cannot Cure Anti-Semitism

253   Coffin, 534.

254   Liz Essley Whyte, "Newest Arena for the Israel-Palestinian Conflict: Your State?" The Center for Public Integrity, May 1, 2019, publicintegrity.org/state-politics/copy-paste-legislate/newest-arena-for-the-israel-palestinian-conflict-your-state.

255   Office of the Texas Governor/Greg Abbott, "Anti-Israel Policies Are Anti-Texas Policies," May 2, 2017, gov.texas.gov/news/post/anti-israel-policies-are-anti-texas-policies.

256   "Title Four–Combating BDS Act of 2019," Sec. 402 (b).

257   J Street, T'ruah, July 30, 2019, jstreet.org/wp-content/uploads/2019/07/Truah-J-Street-Clergy-Letter-073019-name-city2.pdf.

258   Defense for Children International Palestine, "Military Detention," dci-palestine.org/issues_military_detention.

259   ACLU Statement on Senate introduction of 'Anti-Semitism Awareness Act,' May 23, 2018.

260   Harkabi, 220.

261   Anat Rosenberg, "Still Recovering from Harvey, Texas Hit With 'Hurricane Israel' Over anti-BDS Provision," *Haaretz*, October 21, 2017.

262   Ibid.

263   Joseph Gedeon, "The Most Evangelical States in America," September 22, 2017, 247wallst.com/special-report/2017/09/22/the-most-evangelical-states-in-america/9.

Chapter 16 — Ilhan Omar

264   Public Access America, "Ilhan Omar Addresses Council on

American-Islamic Relations," March 23, 2009, soundcloud.
com/publicaccessamerica/ilhan-omar-addresses-council.

265   Statement from Representative Ilhan Omar, Democrat of Minnesota,
int.nyt.com/data/documenthelper/594-statement-representative-omar-
antisemitism/68356c41b7f309ee2e0b/optimized/full.pdf#page=1.

266   bdsmovement.net/what-is-bds.

267   twitter.com/ilhanmn/status/100229514017
2664832?lang=en, May 31, 2018.

268   Ibid.

269   Emma Green, "Ilhan Omar Just Made It Harder to Have a
Nuanced Debate About Israel," *The Atlantic*, February 11, 2019.

270   Devan Cole, "House majority leader deletes tweet saying
Soros, Bloomberg, Steyer are trying to 'buy' election,"
October 28, 2018, CNN Politics, cnn.com/2018/10/28/
politics/tom-steyer-mccarthy-tweet/index.html.

271   Ibid.

272   Mike DeBonis and Rachael Bade, "Rep. Omar apologizes after
House Democratic leadership condemns her comments as 'anti-
Semitic tropes,'" *The Washington Post*, February 11, 2019.

273   C-Span video, February 12, 2019, c-span.org/video/?c4779771/
senator-schumer-representative-omar-apologize-reprehensible-tweets.

274   Ady Barkan, "What Ilhan Omar Said About AIPAC
Was Right," *The Nation*, February 12, 2019.

275   Sheryl Gay Stolberg, "Ilhan Omar Apologizes for Statements
Condemned as Anti-Semitic," *The New York Times*, February 11, 2019.

276   Cristina Marcos, "Rep. Omar apologizes for tweet about
Israel," *The Hill*, January 22, 2019, thehill.com/homenews/
house/426425-rep-omar-apologizes-for-tweet-about-israel.

277   Felicia Sonmez, "Trump says Rep. Ilhan Omar should
resign over her comments on Israel's U.S. allies,"
The Washington Post, February 12, 2019.

278   Kristen East, "Trump tweets image depicting Clinton, cash
and the Star of David," *Politico*, July 2, 2016, politico.com/
story/2016/07/donald-trump-hillary-clinton-star-david-225058.

279   twitter.com/vp/status/1095507111415607
296?lang=en, February 12, 2019.

280   Ilhan Omar speaking March 1, 2019 at 'Busboys and Poets'
Washington D.C., youtube.com/watch?v=HnRC6gFrUao.

281   Engel Statement on Representative Omar's Comments, March 1, 2019, foreignaffairs.house.gov/2019/3/engel-statement-on-representative-omar-s-comments.

282   twitter.com/aipac/status/11015966925483 33575?lang=en, March 1, 2019.

283   twitter.com/RepJuanVargas/status/1102636576524374016, March 4, 2019.

284   twitter.com/NitaLowey/status/1101903312394354688, March 2, 2019.

285   twitter.com/ilhanmn/status/1102296763292 139520?lang=en, March 3, 2019.

286   Eli Rosenberg, "President Trump targets Rep. Ilhan Omar with a video of Twin Towers burning," *The Washington Post*, April 12, 2019.

287   Manu Raju, "Why some Congressional Black Caucus members are upset about today's vote," CNN Politics, March 7, 2019, cnn.com/politics/live-news/anti-semitism-house-democrats/h_2600b62f2ca670e25d4c7d3c7af48cf9.

288   H. Res. 183, Congress.gov March 5, 2019, congress.gov/bill/116th-congress/house-resolution/183/text.

289   Eli Rosenberg, "Poster linking Rep. Ilhan Omar to 9/11 sparks outrage, injuries, in W. VA state capitol," *The Washington Post*, March 2, 2019.

290   Ibid.

291   soundcloud.com/publicaccessamerica/ilhan-omar-addresses-council.

292   Ibid.

293   Ibid.

294   Ibid.

295   Ibid.

296   Christina Goldbaum, "The New York Post Inspires Boycott with 9/11 Photo and Ilhan Omar Quote," *The New York Times*, April 14, 2019.

297   Ibid.

298   Ibid.

299   twitter.com/realDonaldTrump/status/1116817144006750209, April 12, 2019.

300   Colby Itkowitz, "'The president today made America smaller': Democratic candidates react to Trump's attack on Rep. Omar," *The Washington Post*, April 13, 2019.

301   Amanda Terkel, "Rep. Ilhan Omar Says Death Threats Have Increased Since Trump's Attack," *HuffPost*, April 14, 2019.

302 Nancy Pelosi, Speaker of the House, "Pelosi Statement on the Safety of Congresswoman Omar," April 14, 2019, speaker.gov/newsroom/41419.

303 Ibid.

304 Michael Brice-Saddler, "He easily found hundreds of death threats against Rep. Ilhan Omar. He wants Twitter to stop them," *The Washington Post*, April 16, 2019.

305 American Friends Service Committee, "Palestinian refugees and the right of return," afsc.org/resource/palestinian-refugees-and-right-return.

306 twitter.com/wsj/status/1096155883074211 840?lang=en, February 14, 2019.

307 Transcript: Sen. Chuck Schumer (D-NY), AIPAC Policy Conference March 5, 2018, policyconference. org/article/transcripts/2018/schumer.asp.

308 Philip Weiss, "Schumer says he opposed the Iran deal because of 'threat to Israel,'" *Mondoweiss*, March 19, 2018.

309 Louis Jacobson, "John Kerry says Iran nuclear agreement never sunsets. There's no sunset in this agreement," *Politifact*, September 3, 2015, politifact.com/truth-o-meter/statements/2015/sep/03/john-kerry/john-kerry-says-iran-nuclear-agreement-never-sunse.

310 Conor Friedersdorf, "A fascinating look at the political views of Muslim Americans," *The Atlantic*, August 3, 2011.

311 Ibid.

Chapter 17 — Clarifying One-Sided Arguments

312 "Ha-'Olam Kulo Negdenu" ["The whole world is against us"], lyrics by Yoram Taharlev, cited by Raz, 285.

313 Bradley Burston, "If You're Happy With This Israel, Clap Your Hands," *Haaretz*, July 24, 2018.

314 Peter Beinart, "What a Liberal Think Tank Should Ask Bibi When He Visits Next Week."

315 Fromkin, 517-18.

316 Ibid.

317 Jodi Rudoren, "Netanyahu Denounced for Saying Palestinian Inspired Holocaust," *The New York Times*, Oct. 21, 2015.

318 Ishaan Tharoor, "The real reason a Palestinian mufti allied with Hitler? It's not so shocking," *The Washington Post*, October 22, 2015.

319   William Booth, "Netanyahu says Palestinian gave Hitler idea
       for Holocaust," *The Washington Post*, October 21, 2015.
320   Ofer Aderet, "Yad Vashem's Chief Historian on Hitler and the
       Mufti: Netanyahu Had It All Wrong," *Haaretz*, October 22, 2015.
321   Michael A. Sells, "Fabricating Palestinian Responsibility
       for the Nazi Genocide," *Tablet Magazine*, November 4,
       2015, tabletmag.com/jewish-news-and-politics/194679/
       palestinian-responsibility-nazi-genocide.
322   Walid Khalidi, "Why Did the Palestinians Leave?" *Middle East
       Forum* (July 1959); Erskine Childers, "The Other Exodus," *Spectator*
       (12 May 1961), cited by Finkelstein, *Beyond Chutzpah*, 2-3.
323   Childers.
324   Morris, *The Birth of the Palestinian Refugee Problem Revisited*, 263.
325   Intelligence Service (Arab Section), "Migration of Eretz
       Yisrael Arabs between December 1, 1947 and June 1, 1948,"
       June 30, 1948, haaretz.co.il/st/inter/Heng/1948.pdf.
326   Ian Williams, "In Memoriam Erskine Childers 1929-1996,"
       Washington Report on Middle East Affairs, October 1996, 24.
327   Morris, *Righteous Victims*, 138.
328   D. Ben-Gurion to A. Ben-Gurion, October 5, 1937, Israel
       Defense Forces Archives, Ben-Gurion Correspondence,
       cited by Morris, *Righteous Victims*, 138.
329   Morris, *Righteous Victims*, 138.
330   Chomsky, *Fateful Triangle*, 161.
331   Patai, 88.
332   Suarez, 31.
333   On "Population Transfer Committee," see Joseph Massad, "The
       Future of the Nakba," May 13, 2018, *Electronic Intifada*. For
       Ben-Gurion quote, see Morris, *Righteous Victims*, 144.
334   Yosef Weitz, *Yomani Ve' igrotai Labanim* (My Diary and
       Letters to the Children), Vol. I, 181, cited by Morris,
       The Birth of the Palestinian Refugee Problem, 27.
335   Massad, "The Future of the Nakba."
336   Ben-Ami, 34.
337   Suarez, 273.
338   Ibid, 251.
339   Donald Neff, 65; cited by Suarez, 262.
340   Segev, *One Palestine Complete*, 401.

341 Ibid, 82.
342 Ben-Ami, 83.
343 Ibid.
344 Viorst, 256.
345 Ibid.
346 Carter, 108-9.
347 Ibid.
348 Begin, 335, cited by Chomsky, *Fateful Triangle*, 161.
349 Ibid.
350 Ilan Ben Zion, Associated Press, "Netanyahu: Israel to keep security control over West Bank," ABC News.Go.com, June 5, 2017.
351 Suarez, 241–2.
352 Tabarani, 66.
353 Benny Morris, *The Birth of the Palestinian Refugee Problem,* 179. Also see N. 99, 339.
354 unis.unvienna.org/unis/en/topics/un-general.html.
355 Edward Said, "The One-State Solution," *The New York Times Magazine*, January 10, 1999.
356 "The Iron Wall (We and the Arabs)," an essay by Vladimir Jabotinsky, first published in Russian on November 4, 1923.
357 Truman.

Chapter 18 — Ego Before God

358 Menuhin, 238.
359 Translations from Bible Gateway, Complete Jewish Bible (CJB).
360 Tamar Herman, Ella Heller, Nir Atmor, Yuval Lebel, *The Israeli Democracy Index: 2013*, The Israel Democracy Institute, 71, en.idi.org.il/media/3958/democracy-index-english-2013.pdf.
361 Ibid, 14.
362 Pew Research Center, "Israel's Religiously Divided Society," Section 1: "Comparisons between Jews in Israel and the U.S," March 8, 2016.
363 Michael Lipka, Pew Research Center, "More white evangelicals than American Jews say God gave Israel to the Jewish people," October 3, 2013.
364 Midrash Tanchuma, Naso, 16; see Tanya chapter 36. Cited by Yanki Tauber, *Beyond The Letter Of The Law* (Meaningful Life Center: 2012), 334.

365   Americans for Peace Now, peacenow.org/entry.
       php?id=2631#.W5eiNPYnaUk.

366   "The Great Gulf between Zionism and Judaism." Paper
       delivered by G. J. Neuberger, a member of Neturei Karta,
       at the Tripoli Conference on Zionism and Racism. The
       quotation is Neuberger's paraphrasing of Rashi's teaching.

Chapter 19 — Democracy or Ethno-Nationalism?

367   *Le Monde*, November 15, 1971.

368   Toi Staff, "TV host in hot water for saying control of West Bank
       turns troops into 'animals,'" *Times of Israel*, February 16, 2019.

369   jnf.org/site/PageServer?pagename=history.

370   Eitan Bronstein Aparicio, "Most JNF - KKL forests and sites are
       located on the ruins of Palestinian villages," Zochrot, April 2014.

371   Adalah.org, The Discriminatory Laws Database.

372   Ali Younes, "Knesset disqualifies bill seeking equal status
       for Jews and Arabs," *Al Jazeera*, June 5, 2018.

373   "Let the Knesset Decide," *Haaretz* Editorial, June 6, 2018.

374   AIPAC, Aipac.org/resources/us-and-israel/shared-values.

375   Marissa Newman, "Nearly half of Jewish Israelis want to expel
       Arabs, survey shows," *The Times of Israel*, March 8, 2016.

376   Chaim Levinson, "Nearly 100% of All Military Court Cases End
       in Conviction, Haaretz Learns," *Haaretz*, November 29, 2011.

377   Office of Palestinian Prime Minister Salam Fayyad, Reported
       by Mohammed Mar'i, "Israeli forces arrested 800,000
       Palestinians since 1967," *Saudi Gazette*, December 12, 2012.

378   Daniel Bernstein, "Knesset increases stone-throwers'
       sentences," *The Times of Israel*, July 21, 2015.

379   "The State of the World's Human Rights," Amnesty
       International Report 2017/2018, 209.

380   UNICEF, "Children in Israeli Military Detention:
       Observations and Recommendations," February 2013,
       reliefweb.int/sites/reliefweb.int/files/resources/UNICEF_
       oPt_Children_in_Israeli_Military_Detention_Observations_
       and_Recommendations_-_6_March_2013.pdf.

381   *The New Arab*, "Israel 'has arrested over 50,000 children since
       1967,'" March 16, 2019, alaraby.co.uk/english/news/2019/4/29/
       israel-has-arrested-over-50-000-children-since-1967.

382   Netta Ahituv, "'Endless Trip to Hell': Israel Jails
        Hundreds of Palestinian Boys a Year. These Are Their
        Testimonies," *Haaretz*, March 16, 2019.

383   US Department of State, "ISRAEL AND THE OCCUPIED
        TERRITORIES 2016 HUMAN RIGHTS REPORT," 76,
        state.gov/wp-content/uploads/2017/03/Israel-and-The-
        Occupied-Territories-The-Occupied-Territories.pdf.

384   Human Rights Watch, "Palestine: Israeli Police
        Abusing Detained Children," April 11, 2016.

385   Defense for Children International Palestine, "Military
        Detention," dci-palestine.org/issues_military_detention, op. cit.

386   "Broken Childhood, Palestinian minors in the fire line of
        Israeli repression," March 2016; Report submitted by Action of
        Christians against Torture, French–Palestine Solidarity Association,
        French Platform of NGOs for Palestine, French Human Rights
        League, and Yes Theatre, with the support of Defence for
        Children International–Palestine La Voix de l'enfant, 15.

387   Ibid.

388   Ibid.

389   Ibid, 18.

390   Ibid, 17.

391   Ahituv, "'Endless Trip to Hell.'

392   "The State of the World's Human Rights," Amnesty International, 209.

393   United Nations Human Rights Office of the High
        Commissioner, "Update on Settler Violence in the West
        Bank, including East Jerusalem," October 2013, 2.

394   "Children and Armed Conflict," Report of the Secretary-
        General, June 20, 2019, un.org/ga/search/view_doc.asp
        ?symbol=S/2019/509&Lang=E&Area=UNDOC.

Chapter 20 — Strategies of Dispossession

395   U.N., S1994/674, paragraph 130, undocs.org/S/1994/674.

396   Cited by Allan C. Brownfeld, "Anti-Zionism Is Not Anti-Semitism,
        And Never Was," AMEU (Americans for Middle East Understanding),
        ameu.org/Current-Issue/Current-Issue/2017-Volume-50/
        Anti-Zionism-Is-Not-Anti-Semitism,-And-Never-Was.aspx.

397   Finkelstein, *Beyond Chutzpah*, 222.

398   A Cry for Home, Mennonite Central Committee, mcc.

org/sites/mcc.org/files/media/common/documents/
acfh-factsheet-demolitions-us_2.pdf.

399   B'Tselem, "Through No Fault of Their Own: Israel's Punitive House Demolitions in the al-Aqsa Intifada," November 2004 Summary.

400   OCHA, "Under Threat: Demolition Orders in Area C of the West Bank," *In the Spotlight*, 3, September 2015, ochaopt.org/sites/default/files/demolition_orders_in_area_c_of_the_west_bank_en.pdf.

401   Almog Ben Zikri, "Israeli Court Orders Bedouin to Reimburse State for Cost of Demolishing Their Homes," *Haaretz*, August 22, 2017.

402   Wafa (Palestinian News and Info Agency), "Israel demolishes Naqab Bedouin village for 149th time," August 5, 2019, english.wafa.ps/page.aspx?id=c44yqua111168557412ac44yqu.

403   UNGA Res. 181, Part 1, Chapter 2/8.

404   Absentees' Property Law, March 14, 1950, paragraph 1(b)(1) –1(b)(1)(iii)(b).

405   Don Peretz, "The Arab Refugee Dilemma," *Foreign Affairs*, October 1954 Issue, cited by Qumsiyeh, Chapter 4.

406   Ibid.

407   Davis, 35.

408   Ibid.

409   Absentees' Property Law, paragraph 6.

410   Ibid, paragraphs 16 and 17.

411   Robinson, 47.

412   Khan al Ahmar, Rebuilding Alliance, rebuildingalliance.org/i-care-about-khan-al-ahmar.

413   Jacob Magid, "With demolition deadline passed, Bedouin village living on borrowed time," *The Times of Israel*, October 3, 2018.

414   U.N. Relief and Works Agency for Palestine refugees in the Near East, "Al Jabal: a study on the transfer of Bedouin Palestine refugees," May 8, 2013.

415   Amira Hass, "The Eviction of Khan al-Ahmar Stinks Up to High Heaven," *Haaretz*, September 4, 2018.

416   David M. Halbfinger and Rami Nazzal, "As Israel Pushes to Build, Bedouin Homes and School Face Eviction," *The New York Times*, June 24, 2019.

417   Feinstein.senate.gov/public/_cache/files/2/8/28fd589c-132e-4358-a085-86903290ca45/7B007E4C979E9D7AE0B3754C994DA8F9.2017.11.29-netanyahu-letter.pdf

418 schakowsky.house.gov/media/press-releases/schakowsky-and-colleagues-urge-pm-netanyahu-not-demolish-palestinian-village.

419 "Over 300 public figures from around the world: Forcible transfer of Khan al-Ahmar community a war crime," B'Tselem, June 11, 2018.

420 Noa Landau and Notam Berger, "European Countries Slam Impending Demolition of West Bank Bedouin Village: 'We'll Take Action,'" *Haaretz*, July 5, 2018.

421 Ibid.

422 Ibid.

423 Noa Landau and Notam Berger, "EU Countries File Protest Against Israel's Upcoming Demolition of Bedouin Village," *Haaretz*, July 5, 2018.

424 Ma'an News Agency, "Israel seals off Khan al-Ahmar with cement blocks," July 11, 2018 (updated July 12, 2018).

425 Amira Hass, "Israel Tells West Bank Bedouin: First Sign a Voluntary Eviction, Then We'll See if the New Location Stinks," *Haaretz*, September 1, 2018. Also, Yotam Berger, "Israel's Offer to Bedouin Community Facing Eviction: Evacuate Peacefully and Get a New Village," *Haaretz*, August 8, 2018.

426 Yotam Berger and Jack Khoury, "Israel's Top Court Okays Eviction of West Bank Bedouin Village of Khan al-Ahmar," *Haaretz*, September 5, 2018.

427 europarl.europa.eu/sides/getDoc.do?pubRef=-%2f%2fEP%2f%2fNONSGML%2bMOTION%2bP8-RC-2018-0384%2b0%2bDOC%2bPDF%2bV0%2f%2fEN.

428 Jacob Magid, "Bedouin village given till October 1 to evacuate or face demolition," *Times of Israel*, September 23, 2018.

429 *Telesur*, "Israel Declares Khan al-Ahmar Military Zone Ahead of Demolition," September 28, 2018, telesurtv.net/english/news/Israel-Declares-Khan-al-Ahmar-Military-Zone-Ahead-of-Demolition-20180928-0012.html.

430 "Khan Al-Ahmar flooded with waste water, again," Middle East Monitor (MEMO), October 15, 2014.

431 Noa Landau and Yotam Berger, "Why Israel Still hasn't evacuated the Bedouin Village That Sparked a Diplomatic Firestorm," December 2, 2018, *Haaretz*.

432 Tovah Lazaroff, "ISRAEL'S ATTORNEY-GENERAL

BEHIND KHAN AL-AHMAR DEMOLITION
DELAY," *The Jerusalem Post*, October 21, 2018.

433 Ibid.

434 Ibid.

435 Yaniv Kubovich, "U.S. Pressure Behind Israeli Delay in Evacuating Bedouin Village, Defense Official Says," June 18, 2019, *Haaretz*.

436 Jack Khoury, "Israel Revokes Citizenship of Hundreds of Negev Bedouin, Leaving Them Stateless," *Haaretz*, August 25, 2017.

437 Ibid.

438 Ibid.

439 Human Right Watch, "Israel: Jerusalem Palestinians Stripped of Status," August 8, 2017.

440 Nir Hasson, "Palestinians Now Make Up Some 40% of Jerusalem's Population," *Haaretz*, May 13, 2018.

441 Human Right Watch, "Israel: Jerusalem Palestinians Stripped of Status."

442 Ibid.

443 Dr. Mahdi Abdul Hadi, "Reviewing the Palestinian Political Scene 2015," The Palestinian Academic Society for the Study of International Affairs (PASSIA), Jerusalem, December 2015.

444 Human Right Watch, "Israel: Jerusalem Palestinians Stripped of Status."

445 Nir Hasson, "The Jerusalem Anomaly," Palestine-Israel Journal, Vol. 22 No. 4, 2017, pij.org/articles/1805/the-jerusalem-anomaly.

446 Jonathan Lis, "Israel Passes Law Allowing It to Revoke Permanent Residency of East Jerusalem Palestinians," *Haaretz*, March 7, 2018.

447 Jewish News Syndicate (JNS), "EU blasts Israel over Wadi al Hummus home demolitions," jns.org/eu-blasts-israel-over-wadi-hummus-home-demolitions.

448 *Israel Hayom* Staff, "EU attacks Israel over demolition of homes in capital," *Israel Hayom*, July 22, 2019.

449 Elad Benari, "US blocks attempt to condemn Israel at UN," *Arutz Sheva*, Israelnationalnews.com, July 25, 2019.

450 Tovah Lazaroff, Khaled Abu Toameh, "PA Threatens To Cut Ties With Israel Over Wadi Hummus Demolitions," *The Jerusalem Post*, July 23, 2019.

451 *Al Jazeera*, "How Israel is Judaizing East Jerusalem," December 6, 2017.

452 OCHA, "High numbers of Demolitions: the ongoing threats

of demolition for Palestinian residents of East Jerusalem," Ochaopt.org/content/high-numbers-demolitions-ongoing-threats-demolition-palestinian-residents-east-jerusalem.

453   Peace Now, peacenow.org.il/wp-content/uploads/2018/07/Peace-Now-Map-2018-East-Jerusalem-ENG.pdf.

454   Amira Hass, "Israel is Leading East Jerusalem Palestinian Down a Predestined Path," *Haaretz*, July 27, 2019.

Chapter 21 — Legalizing Discrimination

455   Toi Staff, "At 70, Israel's population is 8.842 million, 43% of world Jewry," *The Times of Israel*, April 16, 2018.

456   Chomsky, *Fateful Triangle*, 50.

457   Editorial, "A Ruling Rendered in Bad Faith," *Haaretz*, August 31, 2018.

458   Yotam Berger, "Israel's Top Court Ruling May Enable Mass Legalization of Settlement Homes in the West Bank," *Haaretz*, August 30, 2018.

459   Orly Noy, "Israel's Nation-State Law also discriminates against Mizrahi Jews," *+972*, January 2, 2019, 972mag.com/israels-nation-state-law-also-discriminates-against-mizrahi-jews/139541.

460   Allison Kaplan Summer and the Associated Press, "White Nationalist Richard Spencer Gives Israel as Example of Ethno-state He Wants in U.S.," *Haaretz*, October 19, 2017.

461   Ruth Eglash, "'Wonder Woman' takes on Netanyahu with anti-racism post on Instagram," *The Washington Post*, March 10, 2019

462   Ibid.

463   Ibid.

464   I24NEWS, "Opposition party petitions Israel's High Court against nation-state law," July 31, 2018.

465   Yossi Gurvitz, "Israeli Knesset rejects bill to 'maintain equal rights amongst all its citizens,'" Mondoweiss, December 12, 2018.

466   Allison Kaplan Sommer, "'Racist and Discriminatory': U.S. Jewish Leaders Warn against Passage of Nation-state Bill," *Haaretz*, July 14, 2018.

467   Ibid.

468   Ibid.

469   Ibid.

470   Gideon Levy, "The South African Model: Make Israel's Druze 'Honorary Jews,'" *Haaretz*, July 29, 2018.

Chapter 22 — Aliyah

471   Biemann, 290.

472   Armstrong, 21–22.

473   United Nations General Assembly, Second Session, Official Records, Ad Hoc Committee on the Palestinian Question, Summary Record of the Thirtieth Meeting, Lake Success, New York, November 24, 1947 (A/AC.14/SR.30). Cited in *Israel's Rights as a Nation-State in International Diplomacy* (Jerusalem Center for Public Affairs – World Jewish Congress, 2011), Ambassador Alan Baker [ed.], 54.

474   UN General Assembly, Second Session, Official Records, Verbatim Record of the Plenary Meeting, November 28, 1947, p.1391, cited in *Israel's Rights as a Nation-State in International Diplomacy*, 54.

475   Judy Malz, "In Bid to Counter Palestinian Efforts, Israeli Diplomats Told to Raise Issue of Jewish Refugees," *Haaretz*, September 11, 2012.

476   Yehouda Shenhav, "Hitching a Ride on the Magic Carpet," *Haaretz*, August 15, 2003.

477   Ibid.

478   Ibid.

479   Suarez, 279.

480   Ibid.

Chapter 23 — Intransigence

481   Transcript of Secret Talks between Egyptian National Security Adviser Hafez Ismail and US National Security Adviser Henry Kissinger (25–26 February 1973), CIE (Center for Israel Education).

482   Mordechai Sones, "AG drafts opinion: 'there is no Palestinian state,'" Arutz Sheva, November 26, 2018, israelnationalnews.com/News/News.aspx/255294

483   Thomas, xv.

484   Giladi, 71; see 65–74 for further discussion of Nasser's attempts to negotiate with Israel.

485   Michaeli, "Israel's Leaders Sacrifice the People for Their Own Ego."

486   JTA (Jewish Telegraphic Agency), "Hussein Offers 6-point Peace Plan, Hinged on Withdrawal; Says Nasser Approves," April 11, 1969.

487   Michael Rubner, Middle East Policy Council Reviews of Avi Shlaim, *Lion of Jordan: The Life of King Hussein in War and Peace* and Nigel Ashton, *King Hussein of Jordan: A Political Life*.

488   Raz.

489   Raz, cited by Noam Chomsky, "Palestine 2012 – Gaza
       and the UN resolution," December 1, 2012.

490   Raz.

491   Henry Siegman, "Imposing Middle East
       Peace," *The Nation*, January 7, 2010.

492   *Ha'olam Hazeh*, July 8, 1968, cited by Hirst, 348.

493   Shlaim, *The Iron Wall*, 291.

494   Golani, cited by Merav Michaeli, "Israel's Leaders
       Sacrifice the People for Their Own Ego."

495   Thomas L. Friedman, "Baker Cites Israel For
       Settlements," *The New York Times*, May 23, 1991.

496   Carter, 160.

497   Chris McGreal, "Sharon's deal for Palestine: no extra land,
       no army, no Arafat," *The Guardian*, December 6, 2002.

498   Swisher, 283.

499   Dennis Ross, xxiv (See text accompanying "Map
       Reflecting Actual Proposal at Camp David").

500   Swisher, 353.

501   Miller, 297.

502   *Democracy Now*, "Fmr. Israeli Foreign Minister: 'If I were a
       Palestinian, I Would Have Rejected Camp David," February 14, 2006,
       democracynow.org/2006/2/14/fmr_israeli_foreign_minister_if_i.

503   Swisher, 188.

504   Ibid, 145.

505   Carter, 150–152.

506   Ibid. 151.

507   Ibid, 150.

508   Swisher, 403.

509   Amira Howeidy, "PA relinquished right of
       return," *Aljazeera*, January 24, 2011.

510   *The Guardian*, Corrections and Clarifications, November
       26, 2013, theguardian.com/theguardian/2013/
       nov/26/corrections-and-clarifications.

511   Ibid.

512   Barak Ravid, David Landau, Aluf Benn and Shmuel
       Rosner, "Olmert to Haaretz: Two-state Solution, or
       Israel Is Done For," *Haaretz*, November 29, 2007.

513   Nathan Thrall, "What Future for Israel?" *The New York Review of Books*, August 15, 2013 Issue.

514   Josef Federman, "Abbas admits he rejected 2008 peace offer from Olmert," *The Times of Israel*, November 19, 2015.

515   Gershon Baskin, "A Declaration Of War On The Two-State Solution," *The Jerusalem Post*, September 11, 2019.

516   Peter Beinart, "Can Netanyahu be Trusted," *Haaretz*, March 21, 2015.

517   Jodi Rudoren, "Remarks by Former Official Fuel Israeli Discord on Iran," *The New York Times*, April 28, 2012.

518   youtube.com/watch?v=pK0QVgSUV6o.

519   Allan C. Brownfeld, "Examining Zionism – From Seeking a Refuge for Jews to Controlling Millions of Palestinians," *The American Council for Judaism*, Fall 2017.

520   Tovah Lazaroff, "Netanyahu: WE WILL NEVER ABANDON WEST BANK SETTLEMENTS TO RADICAL ISLAM," *The Jerusalem Post*, August 29, 2017.

521   Prime Minister Yitzhak Rabin: Ratification of the Israel-Palestinian Interim Agreement, The Knesset, October 5, 1995.

522   Ibid.

523   Ibid.

524   Alan Hart, "Is a peaceful resolution of the Israel-Palestine Conflict REALLY possible?" alanhart.net, November 5, 2014.

525   Ibid.

Chapter 24 — The Ongoing Theft of Land and Resources

526   Barak Ravid, "Quoting Medieval Talmudic Scholar, Deputy FM Tells Israeli Diplomats: This Is Our Land," *Haaretz*, May 21, 2015.

527   Ni'lin Media Group, Background Information and Reference Data, nilin.wordpress.com/nilin-village.

528   Ibid.

529   Meron Rapoport, "The Spirit of the Commander Prevails," *Haaretz*, May 27, 2007.

530   OCHA, *The Humanitarian Impact on Palestinians of Israeli Settlements and Other Infrastructure in the West Bank*, July 2007, 56, endnote 33.

531   Ibid.

532   William Booth and Sufian Taha, "A Palestinian's daily commute through an Israeli checkpoint," The *Washington Post*, May 25, 2017.

533 International Court of Justice – Ruling on Israeli Security
Wall – Justice El Araby's Concurring Opinion July 9, 2004.

534 Jaclyn Ashley, "Drowning in the waste of Israeli
settlers," *Al Jazeera*, September 18, 2017.

535 Alliance for Water Justice in Palestine, "Thirsty Farms,
Beleaguered Farmers," January 10, 2019.

536 UN Conference on Trade and Development, "The
Besieged Palestinian Agricultural Sector," 29, 2015.

537 David Butterfield, Jad Isaac, Atif Kubursi, Steven Spencer, "Impacts
of Water and Export Market Restrictions on Palestinian Agriculture,"
January 2000, socialsciences.mcmaster.ca/kubursi/ebooks/water.htm.

538 OCHA, "Demolitions in West Bank undermine
access to water," April 15, 2019, ochaopt.org/content/
demolitions-west-bank-undermine-access-water.

539 Camilla Corradin, "Israel: Water as a tool to dominate
Palestinians," *Al Jazeera*, June 23, 2016.

540 Palestinian Grassroots Anti-apartheid Wall Campaign, April 29,
2017, stopthewall.org/2017/04/29/join-our-march-right-water.

541 B'Tselem, "Acting the Landlord: Israel's Policy in
Area C, the West Bank," June 2013, 63.

542 UN-Water Decade Programme on Advocacy and
Communication and Water Supply and Sanitation
Collaborative Council, "The Human Right to Water and
Sanitation," Media Brief, 2, Un.org/waterforlifedecade/pdf/
human_right_to_water_and_sanitation_media_brief.pdf.

543 B'Tselem, "180,000 residents of Nablus suffering acute
water shortage since June," September 13, 2017.

544 Eloise Bollack, "Palestinian villages get 'two hours of water
a week,'" October 24, 2016, aljazeera.com/news/2016/10/
palestinian-villages-hours-water-week-161023105150024.html.

545 Dr. Elias Akleh, "Israel's Water genocide," May 19, 2014,
bibliotecapleyades.net/sociopolitica/sociopol_globalwater40.htm.

546 Mairav Zonszein, "Israeli troops shoot Palestinian activist in
head with 'less lethal' bullet," +*972 Magazine*, April 16, 2017.

547 Ma'an News Agency, "Israeli officer acquitted over fatal shooting of
Palestinian boy," October 31, 2012 (updated November 1, 2012).

548 "Palestinian protestors march to the apartheid wall to

confront Israeli occupation in Nil'in," International
Solidarity Movement, March 23, 2018.

549   B'Tselem, "Border police officer who shot a Palestinian boy
charged with negligent manslaughter," May 25, 2010.

550   Zonszein.

551   Daniel Bernstein, "Knesset increases stone-throwers' sentences."

Chapter 25 — Operation Cast Lead

552   Nehemia Shtrasler, "Operation Peace for
Election," *Haaretz.*, November 20, 2012,

553   Gilad Sharon, "A Decisive Conclusion is Necessary,"
November 18, 2012, *The Jerusalem Post.*

554   Human Rights Watch, "Indiscriminate Fire: Palestinian
Rocket Attacks on Israel and Israel Artillery Shelling in the
Gaza Strip," July 2007, Vol. 19, No. 1(E), 117, 33, 6, 51,
hrw.org/sites/default/files/reports/iopt0707web.pdf.

555   Ibid, 51.

556   "Summary of Rocket Fire and Mortar Shelling in 2008," Intelligence
and Terrorism Information Center at the Israel Intelligence
Heritage & Commemoration Center (IICC), 5–6, 2009.

557   Human Rights Watch, "Israel: Gaza Beach Investigation
Ignores Evidence," June 19, 2006, hrw.org/news/2006/06/19/
Israel-gaza-beach-investigation-ignores-evidence.

558   IICC, "The Six Months of the Lull Arrangement," 2, December
2, 2008. Also, see Sderot Media Center, "The Six Months of the
Lull Arrangement," terrorism-info.org.il/en/article/18366.

559   Ibid, 3.

560   Ibid, 2.

561   "Israel Rejected Hamas Ceasefire Offer in December,"
Huffington Post, January 9, 2009.

562   Reuters, "Israel Kills Scores in Gaza Airstrikes," December 27, 2008.

563   Reuven Pedatzur, "The Mistakes of Cast Lead,"
Haaretz, January 8, 2009, cited by Norman Finkelstein,
Gaza: An Inquest into Its Martyrdom, 23.

564   Noam Chomsky, interviewed by Christiana Voniati, "Chomsky on
Gaza," February 16, 2009; countercurrents.org/voniati160209.htm.

565   Chris McGreal, "Israel incursion into Gaza replays well-
worn blueprint," *The Guardian*, January 4, 2009.

566   "What Hamas Wants," *Mideast Mirror* (22 December 2008), cited
       by Norman Finkelstein, *Gaza: An Inquest into its Martyrdom*, 32.

567   Jeffrey White, "Examining the Conduct of IDF Operations
       in Gaza," March 27, 2009, The Washington Institute.

568   Amnesty International, "Israel/Gaza: Operation 'Cast Lead':
       22 days of Death and Destruction," July 22, 2009.

569   B'Tselem, "B'Tselem publishes complete fatality figures
       from Operation Cast Lead," September 9, 2009.

570   U.N. General Assembly, Human Rights Council, A/HRC/10/
       NGO/2, February 23, 2009, unispal.un.org/DPA/DPR/
       unispal.nsf/0/D11A4B71DA415D52852575740060C8D2.

571   United Nations General Assembly, HUMAN RIGHTS
       IN PALESTINE AND OTHER OCCUPIED ARAB
       COUNTRIES, "Report of the United Nations Fact-
       Finding Mission on the Gaza Conflict, Conclusions and
       Recommendations," September 24, 2009, paragraph 1893.

572   pinterest.com/pin/697213586039843906. Also cited by
       multiple sources including Yasmin Alibhai-Brown, "The war
       between Israel and Hamas has its roots in Britain's shameful
       betrayal of the Palestinians," *Independent*, November 18,
       2012, and Noam Chomsky, "Palestine 2012 – Gaza and the
       UN resolution," Chomsky.info, December 1, 2012.

Chapter 26 — Do You Sleep With Your Shoes On?

573   Cited by Maimonides Caring Committee, Temple Beth
       Rishon, bethrishon.org/maimonides-caring-committee.

574   David Rose, "The Gaza Bombshell," *Vanity Fair Magazine*, April 2008.

575   Ibid.

576   McGeough, 377, cited by Finkelstein, *Gaza: An
       Inquest into its Martyrdom*, N. 38, 13.

577   Sara Roy, "Where's our Humanity for Gaza,"
       Boston Globe, November 23, 2012.

578   Ibid.

579   World Health Organization, "Occupied Palestinian Territory: WHO
       steps up emergency response in the Gaza Strip," June 2017.

580   Ibid.

581   2018 Humanitarian Needs Overview, "Occupied Palestinian
       Territory," November 2017, 31, bit.ly/2BLdM29.

582   "Gaza Ten Years Later," United Nations Country Team
       in the occupied Palestinian territory, 2, July 2017.
583   Al Mezan Center for Human Rights, "Israeli Naval Forces Open Fire at
       Fishermen, Detaining Two and Seizing Their Boats," August 26, 2018.
584   B'Tselem, "Israel destroying Gaza's fishing sector," January 29, 2017.
585   Fares Akram and Jodi Rudoren, "Raw Sewage and
       Anger Flood Gaza's Streets as Electricity Runs Low,"
       The New York Times, November 20, 2013.
586   "Gaza Ten Years Later," 20. This report gives volume in cubic
       meters. 120,000 cubic meters = 4.2 million cubic feet.
587   Middle East Monitor (MEMO), "Beaches of the Gaza
       Sea are almost fully contaminated," June 26, 2014.
588   Medical Aid for Palestinians (MAP), "Gaza experiencing
       'humanitarian emergency' warn[s] MAP," August 24, 2017.
589   Amira Hass, "Palestinian Protesters in Gaza: Don't
       Wound Us – Kill Us," *Haaretz*, August 15, 2018.
590   Medical Aid for Palestinians.
591   "Gaza Ten Years Later," 20.
592   Ibid, 2.
593   Zafrir Rinat, "Ninety-seven Percent of Gaza
       Drinking Water Contaminated by Sewage, Salt,
       Expert Warns," *Haaretz*, January 21, 2018.
594   Fanack Water, "How Does the Water Crisis Impact
       Life in Gaza?" July 9, 2018, water.fanack.com/specials/
       gaza-water-crisis/water-crisis-and-life-in-gaza/#_ftn2.
595   Physicians for Human Rights – Israel, "Safeguarding
       Gazan Social Determinants of Health," April 2016.
596   Sandy Tolan, "Gaza's drinking water spurs blue baby
       syndrome, serious illnesses," Al Jazeera, October 2, 2018.
597   OCHA, "Study warns water sanitation crisis in Gaza may
       cause disease and possible epidemic," November 16, 2018,
       ochaopt.org/content/study-warns-water-sanitation-crisis-
       gaza-may-cause-disease-outbreak-and-possible-epidemic.
598   Rinat.
599   Norwegian Refugee Council (NRC) and OXFAM and PREMIERE
       URGENCE INTERNATIONALE, "Israel Tightens Gaza
       Blockade Civilians Bear the Brunt," July 2018, oxfamilibrary.

openrepository.com/bitstream/handle/10546/620527/
mb-gaza-israel-blockade-civilians-270818-en.pdf.

600   NoCamels: Israeli Innovation News, nocamels.com/2017/05/
desalination-israel-drought-water-shortage.

601   Ibid.

602   Rowan Jacobson, Ensia, "Israel Proves the Desalination Era Is
Here," *Scientific American*, July 29, 2016, scientificamerican.
com/article/israel-proves-the-desalination-era-is-here/.

603   "'Malnutrition Common for Gaza Kids,'"
The Jerusalem Post, April 11, 2007.

604   Physicians for Human Rights–Israel, "Safeguarding
Gazan Social Determinants of Health."

605   Charlie Hoyle, "Mental health in Palestine among
world's worst," *The New Arab*, May 12, 2017.

606   Ibid.

607   Muhammad Shehada, "How Turkey Has Become the
Palestinian Promised Land," *Haaretz*, July 10, 2018.

608   Lawrence Wright, Letter from Gaza, "CAPTIVES:
What really happened during the Israeli attacks,"
The New Yorker, November 9, 2009 Issue.

609   Ibid.

610   .Amira Hass, "The Missing Reports on Herbicides in Gaza," *Haaretz*,
July 9, 2018; Michael Schaeffer Omer-Man, "IDF admits spraying
herbicides inside the Gaza Strip," *+972*, December 28, 2015.

611   Hass, "The Missing Reports on Herbicides in Gaza."

612   Ibid.

613   Michael Schaeffer Omer-Man, "Gaza farmers demand IDF
compensation for herbicide spraying," *+972*, July 11, 2016.

614   Tina Bellon, "Groundskeeper in Bayer in U.S. weed-killer case
accepts reduced reward," Reuters, October 31, 2018, reuters.com/
article/us-bayer-glyphosate-lawsuit/groundskeeper-in-bayer-in-u-
s-weed-killer-case-accepts-reduced-award-idUSKCN1N638T.

615   M. Huovinen, J. Loikkanen, J. Naarala, K. Vahakangas, "Toxicity
of Diuron in Human Cancer Cells," US National Library of
Medicine National Institutes of Health, Epub June 15, 2015.

616   Ashrita Rau, "Malnutrition in Palestine,"
Borgen Magazine, May 20, 2015.

617   Human Rights Watch, "Israel: Record-Low in Gaza
       Medical Permits," February 13, 2018.

618   Amira Hass, "For Some Gazans in Need of Medical Treatment, the
       Wait for an Exit Permit Ends in Death," *Haaretz*, December 4, 2017.

619   Amira Hass, "Israel Delays Half of Gazans Seeking to Leave Strip
       for Medical Care, WHO Says," *Haaretz*, August 14, 2017.

620   Maram Humaid, "Gaza halts treatment for cancer patients
       as siege worsens," *Aljazeera*, August 14, 2018.

621   Ibid.

622   "Letter from President Bush to Prime Minister Sharon," Office of
       the Press Secretary, The White House, April 14, 2004, georgewbush-
       whitehouse.archives.gov/news/releases/2004/04/20040414-3.html.

623   Avi Shlaim, "Withdrawal is a Prelude to
       Annexation," *The Guardian*, June 21, 2005.

624   Ari Shavit, "The Big Freeze," *Haaretz*, October 8, 2004.

625   Ibid.

626   Nicholas Watt and Harriet Sherwood, "David
       Cameron: Israeli blockade has turned Gaza Strip into
       a 'prison camp,'" *The Guardian*, July 27, 2010.

627   Index Mundi, Gaza Strip Demographics Profile 2018.

628   Suarez, 31.

629   Ofer Aderet, "Israeli Prime Minister After Six-Day
       War: 'We'll Deprive Gaza of Water, and the Arabs
       Will Leave,'" *Haaretz*, November 17, 2017.

Chapter 27 — Yetzer Hara: The Evil Inclination

630   "Israel troops admit Gaza abuses," BBC News, March 19, 2009.

631   Pappe, 78.

632   *Ben-Gurion's Diary*, January 1, 1948, cited by Pappe, 69.

633   Cypel, 42.

634   Ibid, 68.

635   Yaakov Katz, "'IDF THE MOST MORAL ARMY IN
       THE WORLD,'" *The Jerusalem Post*, June 11, 2006.

636   Amir Oren and Amos Harel, "Haaretz Defense Editor
       Ze'ev Schiff Dies at 74," *Haaretz*, June 20, 2007.

637   Ibid.

638   Noam Chomsky, "'Exterminate all the Brutes': Gaza 2009,"

Based on a talk at the Center for International Studies MIT, Jan. 19, 2009, chomsky.info/20090119.

639 Jonathan Cook, "Breaking the Silence about Israel's occupation of Hebron," October 8, 2018, jonathancook.net/2018-10-08/breaking-the-silence-about-israels-occupation-of-hebron.

640 "Olmert says settlers' attacks on Palestinians are 'Pogroms,'" France 24, December 7, 2008, france24.com/en/20081207-olmert-says-settlers-attacks-palestinians-are-pogroms-.

641 *The Jerusalem Post*, "IDF SOLDIER WHO SHOT SUBDUED PALESTINIAN DRIVEN BY 'TWISTED IDEOLOGY,'" April 29, 2016.

642 "An Enemy image is a vital munition of war. 1) A shooting in Hebron shakes the Israeli society," Crazy Country, September 8, 2017, adam-keller2.blogspot.com/2017/09/an-enemy-image-is-vital-munition-of-war.html.

643 Ronen Bergman, "The Frightening Truth About Israeli Society," *The New York Times*, January 6, 2017.

644 Bradley Burston, "This Is Netanyahu's Dying Israel. Where the Doctor Is the Disease," *Haaretz*, November 21, 2017.

645 *Al Jazeera*, "Israel Cuts Elor Azaria's Sentence by Four Months," September 27, 2017.

646 Burston, "This Is Netanyahu's Dying Israel. Where the Doctor Is the Disease."

647 Jonathan Ofir, "Elor Azarya returns home to a hero's welcome after 9-month prison term for killing Palestinian," *Mondoweiss*, May 11, 2018, mondoweiss.net/2018/05/returns-welcome-palestinian.

648 Ibid.

649 Ibid.

650 Ibid.

651 Yotam Berger, "Elor Azaria Receives Hero's Welcome at Scene of Hebron Shooting, *Haaretz*, July 3, 2018.

652 Naama Lanski, "'I have no remorse for killing terrorist,' Hebron shooter says," *Israel Hayom*, August 29, 2018, modified May 12, 2019.

653 Charlotte Silver, "Two Israelis charged in firebombing that killed Palestinian family," *The Electronic Intifada*, January 4, 2016.

654 Rebecca Stead, "Remembering the arson attack that orphaned Ahmed Duwabshe," MEMO (Middle East Monitor), July 31, 2018.

655 Ibid.

656 Chaim Levinson, "Video Shows Jewish Radicals Celebrating Wedding by Stabbing Photo of Dawabsheh Baby," *Haaretz*, December 24, 2015.

657 Celisa Calacal, "Senior Israeli Rabbi Calls for the Mass Execution of Palestinians," AlterNet, June 21, 2017.

658 The Forward and Daniel Estrin, "The King's Torah: A Rabbinic Text or a Call to Terror?" *Haaretz*, January 22, 2010.

659 Shapira and Elitzur, *207*.

660 The Forward and Daniel Estrin.

661 Yotam Berger, "Right-wing Extremists Protest West Bank Arson Murder Trial: 'Your Grandson's on the Grill,'" *Haaretz*, June 22, 2018. And, "Settler youth taunt Dawabsheh grandfather outside court," *Ynet News*, June 20, 2018.

662 Yotam Berger, "Israeli Court Opens Trial of West Bank Arson Murder to Public," *Haaretz*, September 6, 2018.

663 *Haaretz*, "Israeli Minor Indicted in Palestinian Family Murder Gets Plea Deal," May 12, 2019.

664 *Al Jazeera*, "Palestinian family slams Israeli plea deal in 2015 arson attack," May 14, 2019.

665 Toi Staff, "Jewish extremist Meir Ettinger to be freed from prison," *The Times of Israel*, May 17, 2016.

666 APN (Americans for Peace Now), "Hard Questions, Tough Answers" with Yossi Alpher, February 25, 2019; peacenow.org/entry.php?id=30394#.XHQ41-hKiUk.

667 Jacob Magid, "Justice minister meet with parents of Jewish murder suspects, drawing flak," *The Times of Israel*, January 7, 2019.

668 Ibid.

Chapter 28 — The Insanity of War

669 Shulman, 284.

670 Partners for Progressive Israel, "Israel Killed its Hamas Interlocutor," November 16, 2012.

671 Dr. Mustafa Barghouti, "It's Time to Stop the Ferocious Israeli Attacks on the Civilians of Gaza," Palestine Monitor, November 19, 2012, palestinemonitor.org/details.php?id=6h80qoa982yi4ljhrnf5.

672 Report of the United Nations High Commissioner for Human Rights on the implementation of Human Rights Council resolutions S-9/1 and S-12/1, 4.

673   "Israel/Gaza: Israeli Airstrike on Home Unlawful," December 7, 2012, hrw.org/news/2012/12/07/israel/gaza-israeli-airstrike-home-unlawful#.

674   Nancy Kanwisher, Johannes Haushofer, & Anat Biletzki, "Reigniting Violence: How Do Ceasefires End?" *Huffington Post*, January 6, 2009.

675   Al-Haq/Law in the Service of Man, *Punishing a Nation: Human Rights Violations during the Palestinian Uprising, December 1987–December 1988* (Boston: South End Press, 1990), 4, cited by King, *A Quiet Revolution, 9.*

676   Amira Hass, "Broken Bones and Broken Hopes," *Haaretz*, November 4, 2005.

677   Stanley Cohen, "Criminology and the Uprising," *Tikkun Magazine*, September–October 1988, 60, cited by King, N. 36, 361.

678   "Schmuck, Schnorrer, Schlock, Shmate, Shiksa, Shyster, Shnook, Shlemiel…Shmuel (Rosner)," NormanFinkelstein.com, June 1, 2018.

679   *Report of the detailed findings of the Commission of Inquiry on the 2014 Gaza Conflict*, ohchr.org (United Nations A/HRC/29/CRP.4), 22 June 2015, 78, paragraph 293.

680   Report of the Independent Commission of Inquiry on the 2014 Gaza Conflict – A/HRC/29/52, June 24, 2015, paragraph 20. Available for download at ohchr.org/EN/HRBodies/HRC/CoIGazaConflict/Pages/ReportCoIGaza.aspx#report.

681   Ibid.

682   Ibid, paragraph 21.

683   Ibid, paragraph 23.

684   UNICEF, State of Palestine Humanitarian Situation Report, August 4, 2014, 2, unicef.org/appeals/files/UNICEF_State_of_Palestine_SitRep_4Aug2014.pdf.

685   Human Rights Watch, "Israel: In-Depth Look at Gaza School Attacks," September 11, 2014.

686   "Families Under the Rubble: Israeli attacks on inhabited homes," (Amnesty International Ltd: London, 2014), 5, amnesty.org/download/Documents/MDE150322014ENGLISH.PDF.

687   Breaking the Silence, "Press Release: This is How We Fought in Gaza 2014," May 3, 2015.

688   Ibid.

689   Al-Hamishmar, May 10, 1978, cited by Hirst, 568.

690   Cypel, N. 11, p. 496.

691   Jonathan Cook, "Israeli general mounts challenge to Netanyahu

by flaunting Gaza carnage," *Redress Information and Analysis*, January 28, 2019, redressonline.com/2019/01/israeli-general-mounts-challenge-to-netanyahu-by-flaunting-gaza-carnage/.

692   Personal e-mail to Richard Forer.

Chapter 29 — Is Dialogue Between the Israel and Palestinian Sides Effective?

693   Leo Tolstoy, *The Kingdom of God is Within You*, Translated from the Russian of Count Leo Tolstoy by Constance Garnett, New York, 1894, gutenberg.org/cache/epub/4602/pg4602-images.html.

Afterword

694   Ami Ayalon, "The occupation is tearing Israel apart. We need the United States' help to end it," *The Washington Post*, November 22, 2019.

695   Vaclav Havel, *Disturbing the Peace*, 181-182, cited by Vaclav Havel Library Foundation, vhlf.org/havel-quotes/disturbing-the-peace.

696   Haaretz Services and Agencies, "Ex-Shin Bet Heads Warn of 'Catastrophe' Without Peace Deal," *Haaretz*, November 14, 2003.

697   J Street National Conference - Opening Session, October 26, 2019, Youtube.com/watch?v=rvXsugfPE54.

698   Ibid.

Index

Symbols

Judah, Kingdom of 73

A

G

H

J

T